The Complete Garmin G1000

A Pilot's Handbook

By: Michael G. Gaffney

9th Edition

Printed in the United States of America
ISBN 979-8-9886709-9-5

Table of Contents

Forward

"The Complete Garmin G1000: A Pilot's Handbook"

Thank you for choosing this handbook as your introduction to flying a Garmin G1000 equipped aircraft, one of the most sophisticated, yet powerful aircraft avionic systems ever devised. This handbook has been designed to take a very practical, no-nonsense approach to teaching pilots how to operate this powerful system that has become standard delivery equipment in most general aviation aircraft.

This handbook is built on fourteen chapters that will be extremely useful to learn about the G1000 aircraft. We present many new concepts including ones that the Federal Aviation Administration is now recommending helping pilots and flight instructors cope with the integrated avionics suite without sacrificing situational awareness while they operate the aircraft.

This handbook is based on the "Technically Advanced Aircraft (TAA) Featuring the Garmin G1000 Course" originally developed by the author as a 14 CFR 141 approved syllabus for students at a flight school with G1000 aircraft when no such curriculum existed. It is based on a Scenario-based pilot ground school training course delivery methodology concepts but incorporates scenario-based learning. The original program was developed under a program the FAA called FAA/Industry Training Standard (FITS) and has been progressively updated 8 times since then including this the 9th edition. The FAA does not formally have a FITS program anymore but has taken its tenets and incorporated them into the Airmen Certification Standards (ACS) in the form of Scenario-based training.

This manual utilizes the building block theory of learning, which recognizes that each area of knowledge or skill must be presented based on previously learned knowledge or skills. Each chapter is based upon training scenario objectives where the pilot takes an active part in the briefings and debriefings with the chapter lessons. They do this by partaking in the learning using preplanned scenarios. After all chapters of this handbook are complete, there is a self-evaluation to record the level of learning that has been achieved. The pilot should only continue to the next chapter when they achieve the desired level of proficiency as defined in the chapter completion standards.

FAA Scenario-based training compliance

The chapter lesson plans in this program were designed to be compliant with scenario-based instruction guidelines recognized by the FAA as the most effective way to teach complex avionics. All the chapters were designed to follow a real world, scenario-based learning situation that will help the Pilot in Training (PT), more quickly and more permanently benefit from the value of the chapter material and incorporate those lessons into everyday flying procedures. This is important for the Pilot in Training (PT), so that these chapters can reinforce the situational awareness and concepts of Single Pilot Resources Management (SPRM), aeronautical decision making, and overall aviation safety.

We sincerely hope every pilot who flies the G1000 benefits from the material in this handbook.

Note: Our special thanks go out to the following organizations for their direct and indirect assistance in providing information, pictures, answers, and in general patience during the production of this handbook over the past nine editions. Their help indicates their commitment to general aviation and aviation safety.

- **ASA Publications**
- **Garmin Corporation**
- **Textron Aviation**
- **Cirrus Aircraft Corporation**
- **The Federal Aviation Administration**
- **Diamond Aircraft**
- **Cessna Aircraft**
- **Piper Corporation**

Garmin PC Trainer

If new to the G1000, we highly recommend that you purchase the G1000 PC training software from Garmin that can operate on your PC while you are studying this handbook. You can order that training software at the following [link](#) or enter the following address into your browser: https://www.garmin.com/en-US/p/702391

Warning: Because there are differences between manufacturers and even among models by model year, pilots are cautioned to always use the aircraft operating handbook and checklists provided with their aircraft. The information contained in this program is general and advisory in nature and is designed to provide the pilot with important technique information but cannot be relied upon as the sole source of information for the model aircraft they are flying.

Chapter One: Technically Advanced Aircraft (TAA)

Chapter Objectives:

The objective of this chapter is for the pilot to demonstrate understanding regarding the definition of scenario-based instruction and technically advanced aircraft (TAA) and how they relate to the safe operation of aircraft equipped with the G1000 glass cockpit. In addition, the pilot will be able to distinguish between the scan flow of a traditional aircraft and a TAA aircraft. The pilot will understand why the distractions of the TAA aircraft can pose an increased burden on flight safety if a smooth and consistent scan flow is not maintained.

Completion Standards:

The pilot will be able to understand the definition of scenario-based training and TAA and how they interrelate as to the safe operation of aircraft equipped with the G1000 glass cockpit. In addition, the pilot will be able to distinguish between the scan flow of a traditional aircraft and a TAA aircraft and understand why the distractions of the TAA aircraft can pose an increased burden on flight safety if a smooth scan flow is not maintained. These completion standards will be verified by successful completion of the chapter quiz at the end of this section with correct answers to all questions. When the pilot has correctly answered all the chapter quiz questions, then they may proceed to the next chapter.

Introduction to Technically Advanced Aircraft (TAA)

The Garmin G1000 equipped aircraft falls into a class of aircraft configurations referred to by the Federal Aviation Administration (FAA) as technically advanced aircraft or TAA. TAA aircraft all follow a variety of aircraft categories based on system complexity, but for the most part, one can define TAA aircraft as:

Definition: <u>TAA Aircraft</u> (Figure 1.1) *An aircraft which has a Primary Flight Display (PFD), a Multi-function Flight Display (MFD), a Flight Management System (FMS) which provides a way for the pilot to enter and retrieve information from a database, and an autopilot which can couple to the guidance system, usually supplemented by computer software. Glass cockpit aircraft are generally considered synonymous with TAA.*

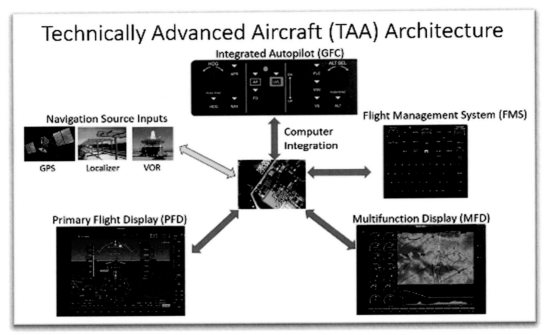

Figure 1.1 – Chief components of a TAA aircraft

Looking at this definition of TAA aircraft, we can see that there are at least three requirements for an aircraft to be classified as TAA. Notice that the definition says nothing about being a glass cockpit aircraft, just that it has a Primary Flight Display (among other things) rather than round dial instruments. It just so happens that as technology has caught up with cockpit design, so has the FAA's acceptance of using glass cockpit displays to replace traditional flight instrumentation in the panel.

Look at the following pictures to see the evolution of cockpits leading up to TAA designation.

Figure 1.2 – Traditional aircraft panel (1969 Citabria 7ECA)

Figure 1.3 – Traditional aircraft panel (2002 Cessna Skyhawk SP)

Figure 1.4 – Traditional aircraft (1998 Diamond Da20-C1)

Figure 1.5 – Technically Advanced Aircraft (TAA) panel (Piper Archer)

Figure 1.6 – TAA Garmin Perspective Plus Cirrus SR20

Figure 1.7 – TAA G1000 Equipped King Air 300/350))

TAA aircraft are significantly more complex than traditional aircraft because the systems that make these functions operate and integrate are controlled by a computer. They are subject to additional amounts of training on the part of the pilot and maintenance personnel. Not only is this training required in order for the pilot to properly operate the system, but it is required in order to interpret system malfunctions that may or may not constitute a real emergency. The FAA believes that the scenario-based training model is the most effective model for pilots to learn about TAA aircraft. It is important to ensure the safe operation of such an aircraft because of the distractions that having so many rich features can present to the basic tasks of piloting an aircraft.

Scan Flow

One of the biggest challenges that pilots have when transitioning to a glass cockpit aircraft such as the G1000, is to use an orderly instrument and automation management strategy without losing concentration on the basic tasks of flying the aircraft. We call this "Scan Flow."

Definition: <u>Scan Flow</u> *The order used by the pilot or crew of an aircraft when monitoring the various components of the flight deck, the systems, the electronics and radios, while at the same time maintaining situational awareness outside of the aircraft.*

Scan Flow for Traditional (non-TAA) Aircraft

When we were first taught to fly an aircraft in visual flight rules (VFR), many pilots had a relatively simple aircraft and cockpit with basic flight and engine instruments required by 14 CFR Part 91.205. The following diagram (figure 1.8) represents the basic flow of a traditional aircraft. The boxes represent what the pilot does with their eyes and their attention as they scan the cockpit and their surroundings outside the aircraft.

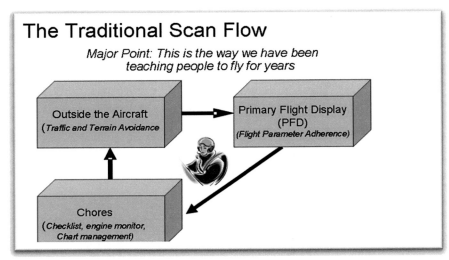

Figure 1.8 – Scan Flow of traditional aircraft

Scan Flow for TAA Aircraft

With the increasing complexity of TAA aircraft, we must modify our scan flow to balance out the time we spend monitoring our systems in a way which does not materially impact the attention we are spending on the fundamentals of flight and situational awareness. The biggest distraction for us is the addition of the Multi-function Flight Display (MFD). As we will see in the following chapters, the MFD contains many important functions which help enhance the pilot's "electronic" situational awareness, but also represents a significant distraction due to its vibrant colors and robust menu functions which tends to command the pilot's attention. We like to say that *"People will watch the MFD of a TAA aircraft like a kid watching cartoons on a Saturday morning"*. Don't get caught in this trap. Learn the scan flow and keep it going at all times. It is not uncommon for a pilot to become focused on a cockpit task for long periods of time. The scan flow diagrams help the pilot remember to keep their eyes moving, even if the task they are working on is not complete.

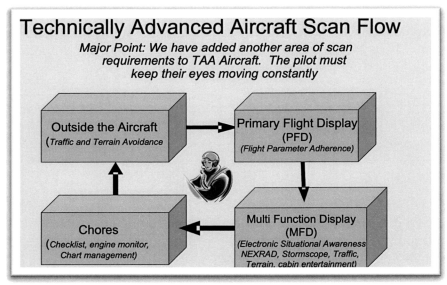

Figure 1.9 – Scan Flow for TAA Aircraft

How to Use the Scan Flow in a TAA aircraft

If we look at the tasks that the pilot is being asked to monitor and look at the time available for each task, we see that each area could be allocated only 15 seconds per minute of flight. In other words, the pilot should divide their attention evenly even when they are focusing on a complex task that may demand more time from that minute. For example, the pilot is flying along on a trip between their home airport and another local airport that is not tower controlled. The pilot receives an aural traffic advisory from the G1000. Which is more important to the pilot: to look out the window to spot the traffic or to look on the Multi-function Flight Display to identify where the traffic alert came from? The answer in this scenario is both! In this case, the pilot must rapidly look between the two areas in their scan while not losing altitude or letting their heading drift off.

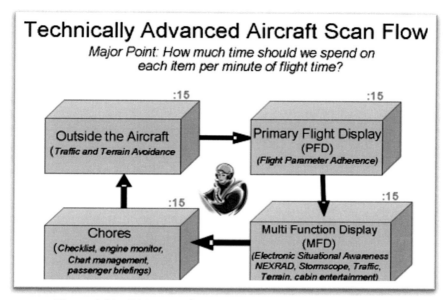

Figure 1.10 –TAA aircraft Scan Flow and dividing our attention

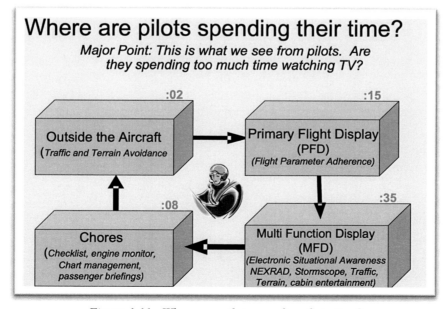

Figure 1.11 –Where are pilots spending their time?

Single Pilot Resource Management

Definition: Single Pilot Resource Management (SPRM) *A methodical process used in the cockpit piloted by a single crew member to ensure that all procedures are adhered to, vigilance is maintained, aeronautical decision making is optimized, and safety is enhanced.*

Definition: Crew Resource Management (CRM) *A methodical process used in the cockpit piloted by coordinated actions of multiple crew members to ensure that all procedures are adhered to, vigilance is maintained, aeronautical decision making is optimized, and safety is enhanced.*

The advent of technically advanced aircraft has brought about the need to review the procedures used in the cockpit of these aircraft to prevent a spike in preventable accidents. The airlines and pilots of crewed aircraft have used Crew Resources Management (CRM) for years to avoid preventable accidents from occurring; and it has worked. Single Pilot Resources Management (SRM) was created from the lessons learned from CRM procedures developed originally by scheduled air carriers because of accidents and incidents where pilots were distracted. SPRM is a mindset, an approach to professionally managing the cockpit and the systems of more complex aircraft. It combines all the major safety disciplines such as using aeronautical decision making and employing a good, consistent scan flow and planning ahead of the path of the aircraft to avoid stressful situations that can lead to good pilots making poor or uninformed decisions.

Use of Aircraft Checklists

According to the experts, one of the most important things that the pilot can do to properly manage the pilot's aircraft and avoid otherwise preventable occurrences is to use the pilot's checklist in a timely manner. The manufacturer provides a checklist for every aircraft when it is delivered based upon the equipment that is most commonly installed in that aircraft. The G1000 system is an example of a system which has an extensive checklist associated with it. This will allow the pilot to use the system to help them make sure that they have remembered everything. It is acceptable for pilots to create a more complete checklist by amending the manufacturer's checklist items with ones of the pilot's own, but never eliminate any items from the manufacturer's basic list. An example of this is an aircraft that has radar installed. The checklist may not remind the pilot to turn the radar off for ground operations or to turn it on once airborne. By adding items that the pilot learns from this course or from the pilot's flight instructor, the pilot will be enhancing the safety of every operation that they conduct. If the pilot is using a handheld checklist, add or highlight important items. The important part is to use the checklist every time that a flight is conducted and to incorporate the onscreen checklist as a part of safe operations.

Figure 1.12 – Onscreen electronic checklist

Introduction to Scenario-based instruction

The Federal Aviation Administration (FAA) is tasked by the US Congress with overseeing and regulating aviation. Part of this task involves promoting aviation safety and creating regulations which pilots, mechanics, aircraft manufacturers, aircraft operators, and flight training professionals follow to ensure that safety of flight is maintained for the flying and the non-flying public. As cockpit automation has evolved from jet cockpits to finally reaching general aviation in the last several years, it became clear that traditional teaching methodologies could no longer ensure that pilots could stay ahead of that technology safely, especially as aircraft design provided for faster aircraft speeds. To address this, the FAA, working with experts throughout general aviation developed a training methodology called FITS. Over time, FITS has evolved into scenario-based instruction methodology embedded within the Airmen Certification Standards (ACS).

Definition: <u>FAA/Industry Training Standard (FITS)</u> (Figure 1.13) *A training methodology and accompanying set of training standards which uses a student-centric, scenario-based approach to teach complex procedures to reduce the total number of general aviation accidents by integrating risk management, aeronautical decision making, situational awareness, and single pilot resource management into every flight operation.*

Figure 1.13 – Original FAA FITS program components

This handbook employs scenario-based training techniques to help the pilot most effectively learn about the G1000 and its safe operation while enhancing their aeronautical decision making. Each chapter has been carefully constructed to promote the pilot's thorough understanding of the area covered in that chapter. As the pilot progresses through this handbook, pay close attention to the chapter description and its stated goals for learning comprehension. At the end of each chapter is a chapter quiz which portrays a flight scenario for which the quiz questions are based.

In ground or software-based training for pilots, we can classify the level of FITS learning accomplishment into three main areas: Perceive, Understand, and Correlate.

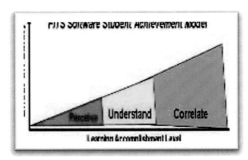

Figure 1.14 – FITS Student Achievement Model

- **Perceive** –at the completion of the chapter, the pilot will be able to *describe* the scenario activity and understand some underlying concepts, principles, and procedures that comprise the topic, but may not yet understand how this fit in the grand scheme.

  Note: Progression to the next scenario should not be attempted until the pilot can function at the Understand level.

- **Understand**– at the completion of the chapter the pilot will be able to *show proficiency* with the scenario topic in terms of definitions, basic usage, and applicability, and can start to demonstrate those topics in lab sessions or in a chapter exam.

  Note: This is the minimum grading level that the pilot can be considered at in order to complete the chapter and move on to the next chapter.

- **Correlate** – at the completion of the chapter, the pilot is <u>thoroughly proficient </u>with the topic without referring back to the appropriate reference area in the chapter or the Garmin Cockpit Guide that comes with the aircraft and can correlate this topic with other topics and can properly integrate those topics with risk management, aeronautical decision making, situational awareness, and single pilot resource management into the pilot's flight operations.

  Note: This grading level would be considered above average for the pilot to complete the chapter and move on to the next area.

The pilot's learning goal is to "perceive", then "understand" the material presented and by the end of the program, the pilot can correlate the material that the pilot has covered with all the other aviation experiences. This will guarantee the most thorough level of knowledge transfer and result in the most enjoyable experience with using the G1000 glass cockpit system.

Conclusion

The pilot must maintain vigilance in the cockpit and avoid the automation distractions that tend to steer them away from flying the aircraft and performing basic cockpit management duties. This premise is the same regardless of whether the pilot is flying any aircraft with a plethora of technology and certainly applies to aircraft equipped with a G1000 glass cockpit system. Let us go to the chapter quiz and see if the pilot is ready to move into the G1000 system overview in chapter two.

Remember

- ❑ TAA aircraft are ones with a Primary and Multi-function Display (PFD) and (MFD), an integrated autopilot, and some kind of flight management system to control them.
- ❑ Scenario-based training is the recommended training methodology for TAA aircraft by the FAA and many insurance companies because student centered training and scenarios produce longer lasting training results that are believed to have a positive effect on operational safety.
- ❑ The biggest distraction to pilots flying TAA aircraft is distractions of the Multi-function Flight Displays (MFD) including trying to remember how to perform functions that may be buried in submenus.

Chapter Debriefing

The pilot has now covered the area of the scenario-based training methodology in a TAA aircraft and why it is so crucial to properly learn to fly the G1000.

- ❑ Understanding the concept of scenario-based training will help the pilot understand that in ground or flight training, it is important that the lessons be based upon scenarios to help the pilot learn more effectively. It is this scenario, and the pilot's participation in constructing it and learning from it that will result in the most effective learning experience for the pilot as well!
- ❑ Understanding why technically advanced aircraft are different from traditionally equipped aircraft will help the pilot realize that it is because the complexity of the cockpit and the requirement to maintain a constant vigilance over it and management of it requires a more disciplined scan flow looking at four major areas rather than three.
- ❑ Understanding that Single Pilot Resources Management (SPRM) is a skill and discipline that is important to enhance safety while operating the G1000 aircraft. The pilot will realize that planning ahead of the path of the aircraft and not getting caught flying an aircraft with systems the pilot doesn't fully understand or cannot remember the exact procedures for can be hazardous to safety.

Understanding these areas and correlating them into your everyday flying skills and application of them to the operation of a G1000 equipped aircraft will enhance situational awareness and increase overall piloting safety. It's time to take the quiz and then to move to chapter two!

The Chapter Quiz Scenario

This Chapter Quiz Scenario (CQS) is designed to take a real-world flight situation and utilize it in the flow of the G1000 cockpit system so that the pilot can participate in the decisions about how to safely operate their aircraft. The pilot can then determine whether they "understand" and can even "correlate" the material covered with their existing aeronautical knowledge and are prepared to use this information in a way which will enhance their operational safety while using the G1000 equipped aircraft.

In this session, the pilot will be asked to evaluate the differences between a conventional aircraft and a TAA aircraft. The pilot in training should imagine a flight scenario where they are flying a G1000 equipped aircraft between Spirit of St. Louis Airport (KSUS) and Kansas City Downtown airport (KMKC), both tower-controlled airports. Consider the following questions about this scenario:

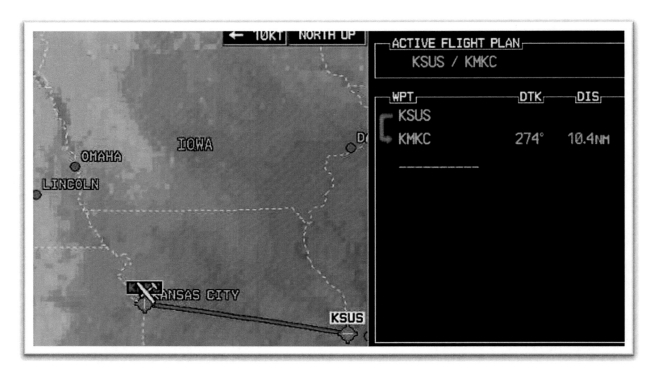

Figure 1.7 – Chapter One Scenario

Question 1: How does the pilot distinguish that they are flying a TAA aircraft?

    a) The aircraft has a GPS with a color map and weather.

    b) The aircraft has a PFD, MFD, an autopilot, and a flight management system (FMS) to control them.

    c) The aircraft has an autopilot with altitude hold.

Question 2: Why is the scan flow different for TAA aircraft than for traditional aircraft?

     a) The pilot must look inside the aircraft more.

     b) The pilot has an extra item in the scan, usually an MFD.

     c) There is no difference in the scan flow.

Question 3: What are some of the hazards associated with the TAA scan flow as the pilot approaches the destination airport in this scenario?

     a) Fixation on one area of the scan flow.

     b) Too many items to scan.

     c) The system is too complicated to use and should be turned off.

Question 4: What is the correct statement regarding scenario-based training (SBT) and its relationship to the training in the G1000?

     a) SBT is designed to help pilots better at practicing stalls and slow flight.

     b) SBT is only useful when learning glass cockpit aircraft systems.

     c) The pilot should be able to understand or correlate the material they study to operate in the most safety conscious manner.

Question 5: What statement is true regarding the use of an aircraft checklist in the TAA cockpit for this flight?

     a) The checklist is not as important on such a short flight.

     b) The on-screen checklist will eliminate the need for a handheld checklist.

     c) The on-screen checklist once activated will help reduce cockpit workload but may not include all items of importance to the pilot.

Grading Criteria:

The pilot will know when they have completed this chapter when they get all of the answers correct. When the pilot completes the exam, grade the answers with the answer key in the back of this handbook. Incorrect answers should be researched by going back to the appropriate reference area in the chapter or the Garmin Cockpit Guide that comes with the aircraft. Once the pilot has achieved all the correct answers, they may proceed on to the next chapter. Come back to items in this chapter at any time.

Chapter Two: Garmin G1000 System Overview

Chapter Objectives:

The objective of this chapter is for the pilot to learn and demonstrate understanding and proficiency regarding the basic G1000 system components and the interoperability of the line replaceable units (LRU) by reviewing the content of this chapter and then taking the chapter quiz at the end which will check their knowledge about the material covered.

Completion Standards:

When this chapter is complete, the pilot will be able to understand the features of the basic G1000 system components and the interoperability of the line replaceable units (LRU) that make the system work. The pilot will know when they have met the completion standards of the chapter when they have correctly answered all the quiz questions at the end of this section. If any questions are scored as incorrect, go back to the appropriate reference area in the chapter or the Garmin Cockpit Guide that comes with the aircraft. When the pilot has correctly answered all the chapter quiz questions, then they may proceed to the next chapter.

G1000 System Overview

Figure 2.1 – The Cessna G1000 and Cirrus Perspective Plus panels visible to the pilot

The G1000 glass cockpit automation system was introduced to general aviation aircraft in November 2003 and quickly evolved to be one of the most prominent systems installed in new aircraft manufactured today. Garmin, based in Olathe, Kansas has become synonymous with dependable aircraft and marine based GPS receivers and appliances. Cessna, Diamond, Piper, and Cirrus have all standardized their cockpits using the Garmin G1000 glass cockpit system for their general aviation aircraft manufactured in 2004 and later. The most significant advance in the design of a system like the G1000 is that it is a software driven computer that depends upon very specific software version control that may vary from model to model and even year to year. The same G1000 installed in a Cessna may look and act differently from the same system installed in a Cirrus even though it is fundamentally the same system using the same mechanical components. This is very significant for general aviation because it is the first time that the FAA has allowed for the certification of small aircraft that used largely generic parts and components between the aircraft manufacturers that only were differentiated by software programs that were installed after manufacture and updated periodically to provide for revisions to the systems without removing the components from the aircraft.

> **Definition: <u>G1000 Equipped Aircraft</u>** *An aircraft which has an integrated glass cockpit model G1000 (or variant) manufactured by Garmin Corporation of Olathe, Kansas installed in place of the traditional aircraft instruments and radios.*

The diagram above (figure 2.1) portrays the portion of the system that is visible in the cockpit for both Cessna and Cirrus general aviation aircraft. This array of components is actually three different components installed in close proximity to each other giving the appearance of a common installation. These three components are a small part of the overall system. The components are referred to as line replaceable units (LRU). The left screen is called the Primary Flight Display (PFD) and contains the flight instruments and other aspects of the system of most interest to the pilot in maintaining flight parameter adherence. The right screen is called the Multi-Function Flight Display (MFD) and contains the information of interest to the pilot in maintaining electronic situational awareness. The middle section of the Cessna is called the Audio Panel and is the main navigation, communication, intercom, and overall audio control input device signal routing. Cirrus places all these functions in a control panel below or near the PFD. We will learn about each of these in the next several chapters.

Standby Instruments

Figure 2.2 – Left image is using Garmin G5 and right is using traditional standby instruments

Most general aviation manufacturers have chosen to outfit G1000 equipped aircraft with a set of standby instruments either powered by traditional power sources or with a Garmin G5 integrated standby unit to use in the event of a G1000 system malfunction. As the pilot starts to learn the G1000 system, they will find they can quickly adapt to using the electronic flight instruments contained in the system. Most pilots are glad that the standby instruments are there, just in case. Keep these in your scan flow to help you keep the big picture of what your aircraft is doing. As you get more time in the G1000, you will find less need to look at them, but the pilot should still crosscheck them periodically as a matter of good operating practice.

Line Replaceable Units (LRU)

The G1000 system is a solid-state, electrically powered integrated cockpit automation system that does not require any gyroscopes to operate but instead uses accelerometers and other leveling technologies to determine orientation in conjunction with external navigation sources and internal geographic databases. In contrast to desktop computers and other self-contained electronic devices, it was designed using a modular component concept called line replaceable units (LRUs).

> **Definition: Line Replaceable Unit (LRU)** *A decentralized equipment design started in the late 1970s which separates parts of a common system or components of a system into a discreet aircraft location such as an equipment box, tray, or circuit board, facilitating ease of aircraft or system maintenance and troubleshooting. This design philosophy is common in military and large transport aircraft.*

This LRU design philosophy is advantageous to the pilot because it provides for subsystem redundancy and system modularity keeping system maintenance upkeep and software and database updating easy. Notice in the following diagram (figure 2.3) that the PFD, the MFD, and the Audio Panel are the pilot interface point to the rest of the LRUs of the system. Once the pilot understands how to use the controls of these visible components, they have mastered the entire system. The other hidden components of the system may generate messages to the pilot, but the pilot does not need to interface with them or operate them. They move data and messages back and forth between components to facilitate the overall operability of the system. The diagram below shows the many LRUs to the G1000 system. The gray blocks represent Garmin components each with their own part number and the green blocks represent other external components or data interface units.

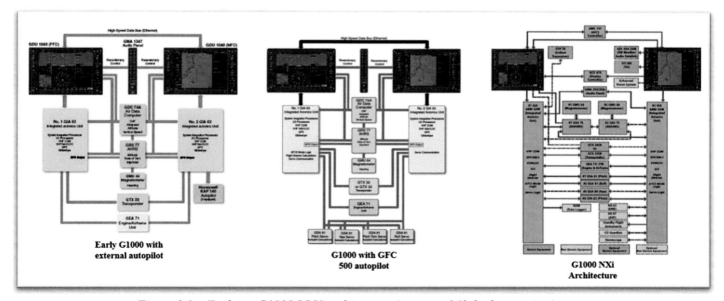

Figure 2.3 – Evolving G1000 LRU architecture (see page 263 for larger view)

This LRU design philosophy is advantageous to the mechanic because it provides for ease of subsystem maintenance. If a component of the system fails, the system generates "codes" which can be interpreted by the mechanic and then only that affected LRU need to be replaced. Like an automobile, once the mechanic understands how to check the status of the components by reading and interpreting the codes, they have mastered the management and maintenance of the entire system.

The system is comprised of twelve or more different LRUs depending upon the manufacturer, each is responsible for one or more functions that comprise the entire system. A system such as the G1000 allows for replacing the individual component that failed instead of replacing large parts of the system. This makes for quick changeovers and less time in the maintenance shop. Another beneficial feature of the G1000 system is that all parts are interchangeable between the different make and models of aircraft since the content of the system is software driven. In this section, we will provide a system overview and all the components. With all Garmin products, product nomenclature follows a very specific naming standard. The first letter is always a "G" to designate Garmin. The second two letters generally will be an abbreviation for the major function of the component. The numbers typically have no real meaning to the end user but simply represent a series number of the Garmin engineering department's final release of the product. For instance, the GDU 1040 is a "Garmin Display Unit" that is 10.40 inches measured diagonally. A larger version of that display unit used larger aircraft could be 12 inches or 15 inches diagonally and might be named accordingly.

System Cooling

Figure 2.4 – The LRU cooling fan installed under the instrument panel

One of the biggest enemies of electronic systems is the buildup of heat. Garmin has designed its G1000 system with several system cooling fans to move heat away from the LRUs as soon and as efficiently as possible. There are vents built into the aircraft in several strategic locations that need to be familiar to the pilot. One is on top of the instrument panel glare shield. Pilots should be careful not to place charts or checklists on the glare shield that might hinder avionics cooling. Another critical cooling area is in the avionic rack installed in the rear of the aircraft. This is designed so it can't be covered by the pilot, but the pilot can be vigilant to the sound of the cooling fans, or the lack of them at system power up. Operating with an inoperative cooling fan will generate a message on the crew alerting system. Sometimes tripping, then resetting a circuit breaker can resolve the problem and extinguish the alert but not all aircraft have circuit breakers dedicated to avionic cooling fans.

On the checklist of many TAA aircraft is the requirement for the pilot to check for the operation of the avionics cooling fan during the preflight. The pilot can do this by simply listening to the sound of the fan when the avionics master switch is activated. If the pilot does not hear any fan noise during preflight, they should not continue the flight until it is investigated by maintenance. If the pilot observes a caution or a warning in the alerts area of the PFD during flight, they should try to troubleshoot and report it to maintenance after the flight. The appearance of a cooling fan failure does not constitute an emergency and the pilot can continue the flight to the destination if all other aspects of the system are normal. The pilot should not initiate another flight in the aircraft until it is inspected by a qualified shop. Continued flight with failed cooling fans can degrade the longevity of the equipment from heat related stress and damage but seldom will result in immediate avionics failure.

Garmin Display Unit (GDU)

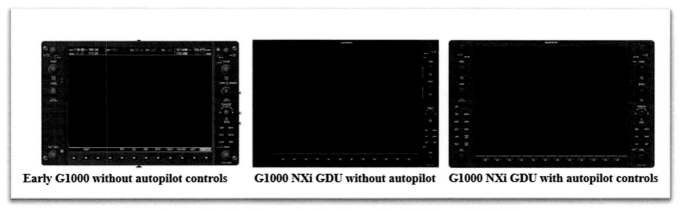

Early G1000 without autopilot controls   G1000 NXi GDU without autopilot   G1000 NXi GDU with autopilot controls

Figure 2.5 – The Garmin Display Unit in the G1000 and G1000 NXi

The display unit is the most visible part of the G1000 system because it is installed in front of the pilot. The GDU-1040, 1042, and 1044 are display units for various aircraft models and can serve as the PFD and/or the MFD. Except for aircraft with the Garmin autopilot installed, such as the Cirrus aircraft products, the part number may be the same for the two units. On those aircraft with the non-Garmin autopilot installed, the displays are identical and can serve as either the PFD or the MFD if the software is updated so the system knows which display to send the information to. The display units communicate with each other and the GIA 63/64W through a high-speed data bus. These screens are only an inch thick and only weigh about 10 pounds each. That is because they do not have large system processors located in them other than to facilitate display and pilot input functions. Care of the screen should be accomplished by following Garmin instructions as found in the aircraft POH, but in general, using a soft cloth and a non-ammonia-based glass cleaner such as eyeglass cleaning solutions are the best for removing smudges and fingerprints. Keep pointed objects away from the screens to avoid scratching them.

Control knob function – "Bump-Scroll- and Twist"

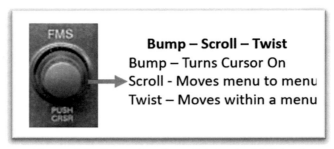

Figure 2.6 –Bump, Scroll, and Twist the FMS knob

The bezel around the display units contains many keys and knobs; many of which have multiple functions. They may be identical, or they may have different shapes to help the pilot identify them. These knobs and keys covered more thoroughly in chapter three, are the main interfaces of the system for the pilot. Some knobs control single functions and others contain multiple functions. A knob may have a bump and twist, and multifunctional knobs like the FMS know may have three functions consisting of an inner, an outer, and a push function. To help the pilot understand functional differences of these knobs, we will refer to this as "bump, scroll, and twist" motions.

Garmin Integrated Avionics Units (GIA)

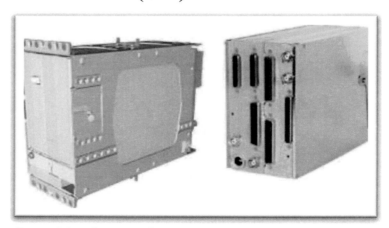

Figure 2.7 – The GIA 63/ GIA 63W Integrated Avionics control unit

There are typically two of these units installed in the aircraft, but some jet and turboprop model aircraft may have three. Each one contains a navigation receiver, a communications transceiver, a glideslope receiver, and a GPS receiver. The GIA-63/63W also serves as the main microprocessor hub for almost all functions and data for the entire system. Units with a W in the model number indicate that unit is WAAS capable and certified under FAA TSO 146. Ones without the W designation are older units and were certified under FAA TSO 129A. The GIA serves as the main communication hub for the entire system by linking all of the system LRUs with both the PFD and MFD displays. The GIA units are installed in the rear avionics bay of most aircraft installations. It is cooled by an avionics fan to prevent premature electronic component failures caused by heat buildup. Most of the system's functions are only visible to the pilot through the display screens. The pilot will see screens and crew advisories that refer to GIA number 1 and GIA number 2. In general, GIA number 1 provides information to the PFD and NAV 1 and COM 1 and GIA number 2 provides data to the MFD and NAV 2 and COM 2, but this is largely transparent to the pilot unless one of them fails or is moved offline by a circuit breaker. The GIA units have a data bus between them that moves data between the two units in a process called "cross-filing"; so, they act as one integrated system. When the system is fully functional, all of the navigation and data functions are available to the pilot and data can be entered into the system from either the PFD or the MFD keys and knobs through the cross-filling process. When either one of the GIA units malfunctions, the pilot may not have access to some of the communication or navigation functions. These GIA units have proved to be very reliable but as we will see in later chapters, the pilot must be able to operate the system after a component failure.

> **Definition: <u>Automation Cross-filling</u>** *A process where data entered on one display unit is simultaneously updated on the other unit to avoid conflicting data that could lead to errors in the system. An example might be entering a Com frequency on one display would be placed on the other display immediately after the entire frequency is completed.*

Garmin Reference System (GRS)

Figure 2.8 – The Garmin Attitude Heading Reference System (AHRS)

In some versions of the G1000, Garmin placed a separate LRU for the Air Data Computer (ADC) and the Attitude Heading Reference system (AHRS). In stand-alone installations, such as in single engine Cessna models, the attitude heading reference system, also known as AHRS, provides the attitude, heading, rate of turn, and yaw information to the GDU displays via the GIA computers. The unit contains advanced tilt sensors, accelerometers and rate sensors and is fully contained in the sealed box shown in the diagram. The GRS also interfaces with two other LRUs called the Air Data Computer (GDC) and the magnetometer (GMU) in order to provide the pilot with a complete picture of the aircraft's position relative to the horizon. This unit also uses GPS signals sent from the GIA computers. The actual attitude and heading information is sent to the GDU displays and to the GIA computers in a asynchronous data bus that is constantly being updated as the aircraft moves along the earth's surface and changes its attitude in reference to the horizon. The AHRS unit requires very little initialization time and is accomplished while the aircraft is moving, and bank angles of up to 20 degrees. The AHRS will operate in the absence of the other reference inputs like the GPS, ADC, or magnetometer. When power is activated and the AHRS starts to initialize, the pilot will first see red Xs covering several of the instruments on their Primary Flight Display. This is normal. As soon as the unit is ready, it will automatically remove the red Xs from the screen letting the pilot know that the system is ready.

> *Note: Never attempt a takeoff with an instrument displaying a red X.*

Garmin Magnetic Unit (GMU)

Figure 2.9 – The Garmin Magnetic Unit (GMU)

The Garmin Magnetic Unit (GMU) is a solid-state device which senses magnetic field vectors from the earth and converts them to magnetic course and heading information for forwarding to the GRS AHRS LRU. This device is located at a remote point on the aircraft such as out on the middle of the wing free from magnetic inference caused by electronic systems of the aircraft. It should be handled with care by maintenance personnel. No magnetic tools should be used in its vicinity in order to maintain its functional integrity. It is possible for this unit to fail, and the GRS AHRS unit could continue to function, but magnetic heading information would be removed from the Horizontal Situation Indicator (HSI) on the PFD.

Garmin Data Computer (GDC)

Figure 2.10 – The GDC 74A Data Computer

The Garmin Data Computer (GDC) is like a Pitot Static system with an E6B flight computer built in. This LRU is responsible for deriving, airspeed, altitude, rate of climb and receives outside air temperature information from the Garmin Temperature Probe (GTP) to compute true airspeed, density altitude, pressure altitude, and other elements important to the G1000 system for performing its multitude of tasks. Notice from diagram 2.10 that it has two hose connection nipples for connection to the pitot line and the static line. If this unit were to be removed from the aircraft or either of the pitot or static lines removed by maintenance, the IFR pitot static check required by 14 CFR 91.411 would be invalidated and must be conducted before further IFR flight to ensure system integrity.

The Garmin Flight Reference Computer Garmin Sensor Unit (GSU) or (ADAHRS)

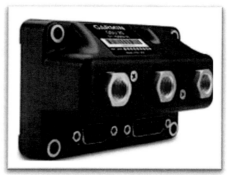

Figure 2.11 – Various models of the Garmin Sensor Unit (GSU) or ADAHARS

In advanced G1000 systems such as the Garmin G1000 NXi systems installed in Cirrus, Pilatus, and King Air 300/350 aircraft, an ADAHARS unit is installed which combines the functionality of the AHRS and the Air Data Computer (ADC). In these aircraft, the Magnetometer still provides heading reference data to the system via the remote GMU. Many installations have dual ADAHRS units for system redundancy. When dual units are installed, the GIA computers constantly monitor data for inconsistencies between the units and the computers query the pilot to reconcile differences between the two ADAHRS units. The tolerance for variance is tight; typically, a few knots of speed or other variables before the pilot is alerted. If the system queries the pilot, the pilot can select which unit they want to follow or they can ignore the warning if the data difference is small. If the aircraft is equipped with a single or multiple ADAHRS units, it will not need an Air Data Computer since the functions are accomplished in the more advanced functionality of the ADAHRS and simplifies connections to other LRUs. Notice the data connectors on the units. These connectors can contain 9, 15, or even more pins all which have specific functionality to carry data either synchronously or asynchronously between LRUs.

Garmin Engine/Airframe Interface Unit (GEA)

Figure 2.12 – Various Garmin Engine/Airframe interface units (GEA)

The Garmin Engine/Airframe Interface Unit (GEA) is the processing unit for all the engine and airframe instrumentation sensors including fuel levels, manifold pressure, engine RPM, oil temperature/pressure, cylinder head temperature, electrical system integrity, exhaust gas temperature, fuel flow, and vacuum pressure (if installed). If the engine is turbine powered, it will also receive information regarding turbine inlet temperature, Turbine speeds, bleed air pressures and temperatures and pressurization variables. The system can also provide airframe information like door or canopy latch integrity, landing gear position, flap position, angle of attack sensor information and other data but this will vary by aircraft manufacturer and engineering design. The GEA unit is largely invisible to the pilot as only the information is shown on the engine and airframe monitoring display or the crew advisory and alerting system. Notice the D-sub electrical connectors. Each of the pins in these connectors have specific functionality to carry data either synchronously or asynchronously between the data sources and the other LRUs. Since many engine, temperature, and pressure sensors produce "analog" data and the computer needs information in digital format to facilitate computer processing, the GEA unit serves as the "Analog to Digital Converter" or "A to D" converter for short. We will see later that the G1000 has built in logic testing that tests the derived data for validity. If data coming off these airframe or engine sensors is converted into "nonsense" numbers considered out of reasonable boundaries, the unit will alert the pilot that the variable is suspect or even red X the data from the pilot's view. This self-testing data validation of the G1000 is very powerful in preventing the pilot from making decisions or being distracted by faulty data that is clearly out of normal operational bounds.

It is important for the pilot to note that an engine parameter that develops a red X may not indicate an imminent failure or emergency. Every situation requires the pilot to look at the system methodically and wholistically. For instance, a red X on engine oil temperature while oil pressures and head temperatures remain normal indicate a failed sensor or connecting wiring. If the oil temperature was showing red line with oil temperature below the green arc or above the green arc, this would indicate imminent engine failure. Aeronautical decision making would dictate aborting a takeoff with any engine instrument indicating a red X, but imminent shut down of an engine would be indicated if the indication were in the red band on either indicator.

Garmin Audio Manager (GMA)

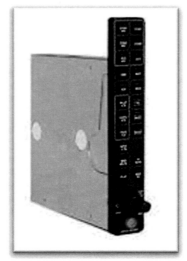

Figure 2.13 – The Garmin GMA 1347D Audio panel

The Garmin Manager (GMA) is the main audio and communication hub of the G1000 system. It serves a function like a traditional aircraft audio panel, but like other LRUs in the G1000 system, it performs other functions as well. The GMA unit is made of solid-state components but contains all the pilot controls for selecting audio input and output like its analog predecessors found on traditional paneled aircraft. It integrates navigation, communication, marker beacon, music mixing as well as intercom audio control. The unit also contains an audio recorder which records transmissions on the selected communication radios and allows the pilot to retrieve them in order from most recent to oldest. The unit operates similar to many other audio panels. Contained in the audio panel are the controls for the intercom and the reversionary mode backup key. This device and its options are covered in more detail in chapter eight.

Garmin Transponder (GTX)

Figure 2.14 – The GTX 345R Mode S Transponder control box with ADS-B In/out

The Garmin GTX Transponder is a "Mode S" and ADS-B compliant radar transponder which fully supports the FAA ATC system mode A, C, and S radar transponder standards. In addition to receiving and decoding the standard transponder signals, it also fully supports the Mode S digital functions which include ground mode, data from ATC data interrogations and ADS-B in and out. The GTX is remote installed in an avionics rack and not visible to the pilot and all functions are controlled either on the Primary Flight Display (PFD) and on models equipped with a central control console, additional controls can be found on the Garmin Control Unit (GCU). These are covered in detail in chapter seven.

Garmin Temperature Probe (GTP)

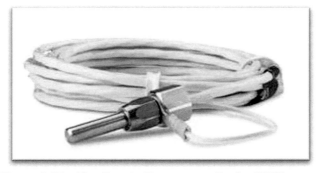

Figure 2.15 – The Garmin Temperature Probe (GTP) sensor

The Garmin Air Temperature Probe (GTP) is used to transmit the outside air temperature to the Garmin Air Data Computer or ADAHRS unit via the Garmin Engine Airframe (GEA) interface unit for processing. The pilot should physically check the condition of this unit prior to flight to make sure that the probe mast and the moisture seal at the bottom of the probe are not damaged. It is installed on top of aircraft such as Cessnas and on the bottom of other aircraft such as Diamond and Cirrus Aircraft. Other manufacturers' locations will vary. The pilot has no visible controls for this device. If it is functioning, ambient temperatures will appear on the Primary Flight Display (PFD) and in planning menu screens on the Multi-function Flight Display (MFD) . It also produces data inputs used for the calculation of density altitude, True Airspeed (TAS) and other integral calculations related to aircraft performance depending upon the aircraft model. If the temperature or True Airspeed (TAS) displays contain a red X, it is a sign to the pilot that the GTP probe is broken, or its data is corrupt.

Garmin Data Link (GDL)

Figure 2.16 – The Garmin Data Link (GDL) control unit

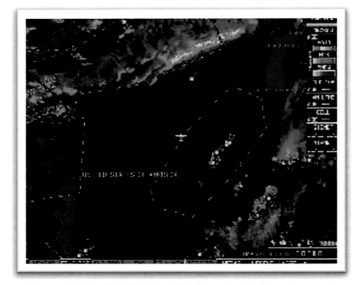

Figure 2.17 – The XM Satellite Receiver in Weather mode

The Garmin Data Link control unit (GDL) is the external data link hub that connects the G1000 to bring both weather and entertainment to the aircraft. The unit has mainly incorporated incoming data capabilities using the Sirius/XM satellite network, but new capabilities are being developed which will allow asynchronous data transmissions both to and from the aircraft. The advantage of the Sirius/XM network is that it is broadcast in the S-band frequency so that uplink is possible at any altitude in North America. The Sirius/XM subscription offerings are organized and charged in service tiers with increasing levels of weather and entertainment containing a wide variety of information including NEXRAD RADAR depiction (Figure 2.17), XM lightning data, cloud tops, echo tops, METAR and TAF information, TFRs, SIGMETS and AIRMETS, and even hurricane track information. The G1000 equipped aircraft are being either delivered or retrofitted with the Garmin Data Link (GDL) products so that they can take advantage of this enabling technology. You will see more information about this in the Multi-Function Display (MFD) chapter ten.

Garmin Flight Control (GFC) Autopilot system

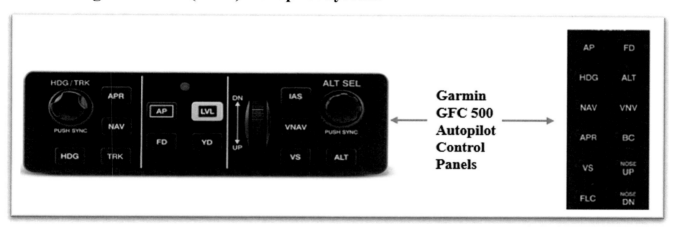

Figure 2.18 – The Garmin Flight control (GFC) panels

As we learned earlier, a technically advanced aircraft (TAA) must include an autopilot. Shown in Figure 2.18 are two of the Garmin autopilot control panels that the pilot will use to set flight parameters. Typically, the autopilot uses aircraft navigation signals, attitude information and other aircraft performance factors to control the aircraft using electromechanical servos connected to aircraft control cables. The autopilot can precisely control the aircraft to maintain various parameters set by the pilot such as altitude, airspeeds and vertical speeds in climbs and descents. It can also link to navigation signals, routes, flight plans, instrument procedures and climb and descent profiles. The autopilot functions and interfaces to the system will be further detailed in chapter twelve.

Conclusion

The G1000 system is made up of separate but integrated control devices known as line replaceable units (LRU) that interact with each other to produce an avionics production in the cockpit which appears seamless. The separation of the LRUs allows the system to function autonomously and provides for ease of operation, troubleshooting, and maintenance. The locations of the LRUs are specifically selected by the aircraft manufacturer to provide distribution of weight across the aircraft to keep within the airframe original certification weight and balance envelope. Most of the LRUs have no controls other than what the pilot sees in the cockpit. The system is operated using software that resides within one or more units and that software defines behaviors of the system even if the LRUs are identical to that installed in another manufacturer's airframe. This provides for part interchangeability and prevents maintenance personnel from having to understand discrete repair procedures like they have had to do on previous generations of aircraft cockpit designs.

Remember

- ❑ The LRUs provide for redundant data flow within the system.
- ❑ Each LRU is operated by system software which enables or disables functions of the system as determined by the airframe manufacturer.
- ❑ Adequate cooling is essential to ensure LRU longevity but does not constitute an inflight emergency.
- ❑ Systems annunciations are provided to the cockpit display units to report LRU integrity and to provide the pilot with adequate time to make decisions upon any system degradation. They will typically use the three letter LRU abbreviation as shown in this chapter.

Chapter Debriefing

We have now covered the area of the G1000 system modules and the concept of line replaceable units (LRU) and the pilot should now see that a technically advanced aircraft (TAA) such as the G1000 is constructed and operated differently than traditional aircraft.

- ❑ Now that the pilot understands that the G1000 uses LRUs to create redundancy for its systems and that this redundancy is what makes these systems so dependable, then they should also be able to distinguish basic cause and effect of LRU system properties and their failures.
- ❑ Now that the pilot understands why knowing the functions of these LRUs and their basic interdependencies will help them to troubleshoot the aircraft properly when necessary and to aid in the proper decision making when error codes arise, then they also should realize that these systems can dramatically improve their situational awareness by providing them with information they never before had at their fingertips.
- ❑ Now that the pilot understands that this system is a digital system featuring many systems which are driven by software and computers, then the pilot will realize the importance of keeping the software and the databases which drive it current and up to date.

If the pilot not only understands these three areas, but also can correlate these three major points into their everyday flying skills and apply these skills to the operation of the G1000 aircraft, then they are ready to take the quiz and then to move to chapter three!

Chapter Two Quiz: System Overview and Line Replaceable Units

The Chapter Quiz Scenario

This Chapter Quiz Scenario (CQS) is designed to suggest a real-world flight situation and use the pilot's new knowledge of the G1000 to answer some situational questions about how to safely operate their aircraft. They can then determine whether they "understand" and can even "correlate" the material covered with their existing aeronautical knowledge and are prepared to use this information in a way which will enhance their operational safety while using the G1000 equipped aircraft.

In this chapter quiz, the pilot will be asked to demonstrate their understanding of the G1000 system block diagram, the interrelationship of the system components, and how each component provides flight reference, navigation, communication, and aircraft system information to them when flying the G1000 equipped aircraft.

The pilot should imagine a flight scenario where they are flying a G1000 equipped aircraft. between Kansas City Downtown airport (KMKC) and Lexington, Missouri (KLXT), a non-tower-controlled airport. Consider the following questions about this scenario:

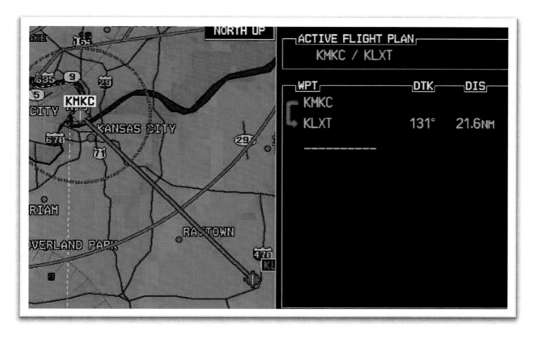

Figure 2.19 – Chapter two quiz scenario

Question 1: The pilot is flying on this flight to the destination airport and their magnetometer fails. What information will they lose?

    a) **Altitude information.**

    b) **GPS and course guidance information.**

    c) **Heading information as reported on the PFD HSI.**

Question 2: What does an AHRS control for the G1000 system?

    a) Reference information such as Attitude, Heading, and turn rate.

    b) Engine temperature information.

    c) Altitude and Airspeed information.

Question 3: What does the ADAHRS control for the Garmin Perspective Plus system?

    a) Reference information such as Altitude, Airspeed, Attitude, Heading, and turn rate.

    b) Engine temperature and pressure information.

    c) Altitude and Airspeed information.

Question 4: Flying on this scenario to the destination, the pilot receives a system annunciation "GIA Cooling Fan failure". What should they do?

    a) Consider the flight circumstances and using aeronautical decision making, proceed to their destination unless other cautions or warnings appear.

    b) Land as soon as possible to avoid avionics failure.

    c) Press CLR to see if the fault resets itself using the GEA control key.

Question 5: Preparing for takeoff, a red X appears on the oil pressure gauge. What should be done?

    a) Abort the takeoff and return to have the Garmin Reference System (GRS) LRU replaced.

    b) Abort the takeoff and cross check other indicators looking for other abnormalities to determine if shut down is required.

    c) Abort the takeoff and immediately shut off the engine to avoid damage.

Question 6: Flying this scenario, the true airspeed box has a red X on it, but the flight instruments on the PFD appear normal. What happened to the system?

    a) The PFD has a wiring problem.

    b) The aircraft has a plugged or iced over pitot tube.

    c) The GTP OAT temperature probe has developed a problem.

Grading Criteria:

The pilot will know when they have completed this chapter when they get all of the answers correct. When the pilot completes the exam, grade the answers with the answer key in the back of this handbook. Incorrect answers should be researched by going back to the appropriate reference area in the chapter or the Garmin Cockpit Guide that comes with the aircraft. Once the pilot has achieved all the correct answers, they may proceed on to the next chapter. Come back to items in this chapter at any time.

Chapter Three: Knob, Key and Control Functions

Chapter Objectives:

The objective of this chapter is for the pilot to learn and demonstrate understanding and proficiency regarding the G1000 knob, key, and control functions by reviewing the content of this chapter. They will then take the chapter quiz at the end which will check their knowledge about the material covered.

Completion Standards:

When this chapter is complete, the pilot will be able to understand the features of the G1000 knob, key, and control functions. The pilot will know when they have met the completion standards of the chapter when they have correctly answered all the quiz questions at the end of this section. If any questions are scored as incorrect, go back to the appropriate reference area in the chapter or the Garmin Cockpit Guide that comes with the aircraft. When the pilot has correctly answered all the chapter quiz questions, then they may proceed to the next chapter.

Introduction to information and controls contained in the G1000

Figure 3.1 – Cirrus SR20 Garmin Perspective cockpit layout

The G1000 is an integrated avionics and flight data display system. This system is installed in many different aircraft models, but in general the G1000 knobs, keys, and controls all perform the same functions. This flexibility allows pilots an unprecedented transportability to operate across multiple aircraft platforms with familiarity of one system and transition training to others. The G1000 system allows the user to display and/or modify the following areas and information:

1. Flight instrumentation – The flight instrumentation is contained on the PFD situated in front of the pilot. It contains the same kind of information one would expect on a conventional aircraft cockpit but some of the information is represented in a more efficient vertical tape format. The pilot will learn much more about this in the PFD chapter five.

2. Navigation instrumentation – The navigation instrumentation is represented by a course deviation indicator (CDI) needle that is located on top of the electronic representation of the heading indicator. When these two pieces of information are combined, we call this a horizontal situation indicator (HSI). The HSI can show GPS, NAV 1 or NAV 2 information by pressing the CDI softkey. The pilot will learn more about this in the PFD chapter five.

3. GPS/Moving Map Database - the heart of the G1000 system is two independently operating highly accurate GPS receivers and their software driven interface with the Jeppesen map database containing information about terrain, obstacles, and information about known aeronautical waypoints and facilities. These units interact with the portions of the G1000 which tracks information about spatial orientation location data, and together produce a truly integrated avionic suite, and highly dependable glass cockpit system.

4. Communication radios – The G1000 uses its computers to operate two integral digital VHF COM transceivers.

5. Navigation/VOR radios - The G1000 uses its computers to operate two integral digital VHF NAV receivers to provide reliable information for the tracking of VORs, Localizers, and ILS transmitters.

6. Aeronautical Database – The Jeppesen databases are updated via a Secure Digital (SD) style disk similar to those used by digital cameras but also can be loaded across a Wi-Fi network if a CONNEXT interface is installed. Once the information is loaded into the system, it is used by the various parts of the G1000 until that data expires. The system keeps track of the expiration date and alerts the pilot when it is time to update the database.

7. Engine instrumentation – The G1000 has an interface system with the engine and the airframe systems which provide real time information monitoring. When there is an abnormality in the engine or airframe systems, this information is shown to the pilot on both the engine indicators and the Crew Alerting System.

8. Flight planning functions – One of the powerful elements of the G1000 is in the area of integrated flight planning. Once the pilot masters the procedure of creating and reusing flight plans instead of using the **D->** navigation key, they will find that their cockpit workload has been greatly reduced. We will cover flight planning in chapter eleven later in this handbook.

Navigating Around the G1000

Knobs, Keys, and Controls

Figure 3.2 – The Garmin Display Unit (GDU) display screen

The G1000 (GDU) display screen has several general parts that the pilot must become familiar with. The knobs, controls, and keys are similar between the PFD and the MFD because the units are identical (except in aircraft utilizing the Garmin Autopilot. In these aircraft, the PDF will have added controls to control the autopilot functions.) It is the system software that makes the PFD and the MFD different. Let us first look at the functions of all the knobs and controls.

GDU Display Softkeys

Figure 3.3 – GDU display "softkeys"

The softkeys that underlie both the PFD and the MFD are used to change the options shown on the screen and to make common menu selections in particular modes of PFD and MFD operation. These options will be discussed more in detail in other chapters.

RANGE Selector knob

Figure 3.4 – Range selector knob

Pilots consider the RANGE selector knob (Figure 3.4) somewhat confusing because it has multiple functions and modes. In addition to having range control authority of the MFD Map and the PFD INSET Map, it also controls joystick functions for moving the mouse pointer around the map. Twisting the knob controls the zoom function of the MFD map or PFD inset. It can zoom out as far as 2000 miles and can zoom in as close as 500 feet. If the menus are set up with auto-zoom (recommended) the map sometimes may be set to a resolution that does not suit the pilot's needs and the pilot can use the RANGE knob to adjust this. Pressing in (Bumping) on the knob activates the "Pan" pointer function and a box appears on the top of the MFD map to show relative position to the point where the joystick is currently focused. These options will be discussed more in detail in the MFD and the PFD chapters.

HDG or HEADING Selection Knob

Figure 3.5 – HDG Heading selection knob

The HDG or Heading selection knob (Figure 3.5, 3.6, 3.7, and 3.8) is the control knob where the desired heading is set on the HSI. The Heading bug that it controls on the HSI is what the autopilot follows when it is engaged in HDG track mode. When the autopilot is not engaged, it simply serves as a heading reference for the pilot.

Figure 3.6 – Depiction of HDG bug and CRS selection pop-up boxes on HSI

Figure 3.7 – HDG knob is "Bumped" to sync HDG bug to current heading

Figure 3.8 – HDG bug centered to lubber line" after "Bumping" HDG knob

"Twisting" the knob changes the heading left and right and "Bumping" the knob takes the heading bug and synchs it to the top of the indicator or as we call it, the "lubber line." This is very useful when using the autopilot in HDG mode. It is recommended that the pilot does this when tracking VOR and LOC courses once they determine a heading that will hold the wind track angle constant.

ALT or ALTITUDE Selection Knob

Figure 3.9 – ALT knob moves the Altitude bug reference pointer

Figure 3.10 – ALT bug set to 3000 feet

The ALT or Altitude selection knob sets the desired reference altitude on the Altimeter vertical tape. The ALTITUDE bug that it controls can be used as a manual reference by the pilot without autopilot usage and can also be used by the Autopilot to determine level-off altitudes in climb or descent autopilot modes. It can also be used to initiate autopilot "stay here" mode when engaging the Autopilot when already level.

The ALT bug will be used by the integrated autopilot found on G1000 installations with the integrated GFC/GMC 500 and GFC/GMC 700 autopilot systems. The outside knob controls thousands of feet and the inside knob controls hundreds of feet.

> *Note: External autopilots such as the KAP 140 and STEC 50 found on older Cessna, Diamond, and Kodiak aircraft, may not use the altitude bug for autopilot altitude input, and require the pilot to set altitude modes on those autopilot controls independent of the G1000. More information can be found in chapter twelve.*

CRS/BARO Selection Knob

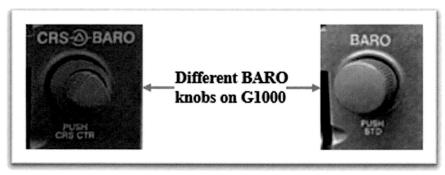

Figure 3.11 – BARO knob sets the altimeter setting into the G1000

Figure 3.12 – Altimeter setting read under Altimeter vertical tape

The CRS/BARO or Course and Barometric pressure selection knob controls two different functions. One, it allows the altimeter setting to be entered into the G1000 for processing. Second, it functions to adjust the OBS needle when operating in NAV 1 or NAV 2, or GPS OBS navigation mode. Notice the different shapes of the inner and outer knobs. Garmin did this to allow the pilot the tactile feel for ease of correct key identification. Bumping the inner knob set the altimeter setting to 29.92. A common error that pilots make is to accidentally twist the inner knob when they intended to scroll the outer knob resulting in inaccurate altimeter settings. The pilot will see more about the CRS and OBS functions later in the PFD chapter five.

> *Note: Pilots are encouraged to learn to operate controls by tactile feel to maintain situational awareness in other areas of their scan flow. They should always verify that their input is correct and the intended knob was actuated to avoid automation confusion.*

Flight Management System (FMS)

Figure 3.13 – Flight Management System (FMS) controls on different versions of the G1000

The FMS control knob is where modes and menus are activated resulting in information being entered into the G1000 system. Some versions of the G1000 such as the Cirrus and Pilatus NXi systems have a keyboard to do these functions (GCU), but Cessna, Diamond, and Piper versions of the system use the same style of inner and outer knob function as found on the Garmin GNS panel mounted navigator transceivers such as the GNS 650. Each of these keys has a similar function on the PFD and the MFD but the behaviors and the appearance of the menus that the controls produce may be different due to the size or "real estate" of the screen that is dedicated to the resulting menu.

Flight Management System (FMS) Control Knob

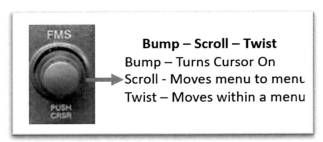

Figure 3.14 – FMS knob uses the "bump, scroll and twist" to activate menus

The FMS control knob has three main controls associated with it. The outer knob, the inner knob and then the "push for cursor," which we refer to as "bump, scroll, and twist." Turning or scrolling the outer knob navigates in a tab function between different items in a menu or between different menus. The inner knob acts like a selection knob which brings up choices within a question such as "yes" or "no," "accept" or "cancel," and others and we call this "twist." The "press for cursor" or "bump" knob toggles between cursor on and cursor off. When the cursor is on, a blinking cursor will appear on the screen. When the cursor is blinking, it is not possible to navigate away from that menu or page using the inner or the outer knob.

Note: When cursor is blinking, the scroll and twist functions of the outer and inner knob cannot navigate away from the current page or menu. To navigate to a different page, the pilot must bump the cursor again to turn it off.

ENT or Enter Key

Figure 3.15 – ENTER key

The ENTER key is used to accept menu options or commit selections of the G1000 into or out of the database or into any menu option. The pilot will find this key very important as the G1000 always seeks confirmation of an entry before committing or executing the input command.

CLR or CLEAR Key

Figure 3.16 – The CLEAR key

The CLEAR key is used to empty or clear a selection from an input field. It also serves to back up to the last menu or selection just as the "back" key works in a computer browser. If the pilot ever makes a mistake in inputting information in a menu or selection, press the CLEAR key. The CLR key will also be used later to delete waypoints from a flight plan. On the MFD, pressing and holding the CLR or CLEAR key is the simplest and quickest way back to the top-level chapter and page or the MAP page 1. We call this going to "Home."

> *Note: The pilot should not attempt to use the CLR key remove waypoints from loaded procedures such as Instrument approaches, Departures, or Arrivals. There are other ways to achieve the desired results and they will be discussed in later chapters.*

D-> or "Direct to" Key

Figure 3.17 – Direct to key

The **D->** key is used to direct the aircraft toward a particular waypoint from the G1000 waypoint database. It is also used to direct the aircraft towards a particular point within a flight plan. Flight plans with multiple airports can be confusing to the pilot as the flight plan points the aircraft along the route towards the ultimate destination. In these cases, the **D->** key can make an interim waypoint of that flight plan the temporary destination so that the system offers procedures such as instrument approaches and airport data for that waypoint without removing the rest of the information from the flight plan. The **D->** key is also useful for redirecting the aircraft to a waypoint when it has drifted off a straight-line course or has been vectored away from the course by ATC. Many pilots misuse this key when they should be creating a flight plan instead. We will discuss this in greater detail in chapter eleven.

*Note: When in Autopilot NAV mode, the NAV function will not ARM until the HSI CDI DBAR is within one course dot from centered. Using the **D->** key is a quick way to force the autopilot to ARM from its current location. This would not be appropriate if ATC directed the pilot to fly along an airway or specific NAV radial. More on this in chapter eleven.*

MENU Key

Figure 3.18 – Menu key

The menu key is used to bring up context sensitive menu selections for a particular screen or mode. On the PFD, the MENU key brings up a menu box which controls the PFD and the MFD brightness. The menu key also allows the pilot to switch in and out of full screen mode on the MFD. This is useful during instrument approach operations allowing the pilot to have an instrument chart on the left and the map or flight plan on the right side of the MFD. The Menu key brings up limited options on the Primary Flight Display, but brings up a host of other menu options on the MFD. These will be addressed in more detail in the respective PFD and MFD chapters five and ten.

PROC or PROCEDURE Key

Figure 3.19 – PROC control key

The PROC or procedure key calls up the menu to select instrument procedures such as instrument approaches, instrument departures (SID) and instrument arrivals (STAR). Both the PFD and the MFD can call up this option, but the menu that this key calls up is slightly different on the PFD and the MFD. The MFD menu box is far more detailed. These will be addressed in more detail in the respective PFD and MFD chapters five and ten and in Instrument Procedures chapter thirteen.

FPL or FLIGHT PLAN Key

*Figure 3.20 – **FPL** flight plan control key*

The **FPL** or FLIGHT PLAN key calls up the menu to select information for creating, editing, or monitoring a flight plan. Both the PFD and the MFD can call up this option, but the menu that this key calls up is much different on the PFD and the MFD. The MFD menu box is far more detailed. These will be addressed in more detail in the respective PFD and MFD chapters five and ten and in flight planning chapter eleven.

Flight Management System - The Garmin Control Unit (GCU) Panel

Figure 3.21 – Garmin GCU Panel used on Cirrus Perspective Plus equipped aircraft

Many advanced single engine and light jets equipped with the G1000 provide another cockpit LRU called a Garmin Control Unit (GCU). Many of the same controls, including the FMS knob and the RANGE knob are installed on this remote panel. Specific details will be covered later.

Navigation radio controls (NAV)

Figure 3.22 – NAV Radio controls

The NAV controls section is for selecting VHF radio frequencies such as VOR and Localizer frequencies. The outer knob ring selects the MHz portion of the frequency in the inner portion of the knob ring selects the KHz portion of the frequency. For instance, to select the NAV frequency 117.4, the pilot would use the outer knob to select the <u>117</u> and the inner knob to select the <u>.40.</u>

Figure 3.23 – NAV radio frequency display

The blue box always represents the target of all control movements including volume and represents the standby position where new frequencies are added. The top line is NAV 1, and the bottom line is NAV 2 the signals for which originate in the respective GIA1 or GIA2 computer LRU. Wherever this blue box is highlighted is where all control inputs, including volume, are directed.

Figure 3.24 – NAV Radio controls

To select between entering information into NAV radio 1 and NAV radio 2, press in or "bump" the inner portion of the NAV knob. The blue box moves up and down between the NAV 1 and NAV 2.

Figure 3.25 – NAV frequency toggle key

Once the pilot enters the new desired NAV frequency into the blue box, use the NAV frequency toggle key or "flip-flop" key to move it from the standby position to the active position. They are now free to enter a new frequency into the standby position using the knob or they can select a frequency from the WPT or NRST dropdown menus and press ENT to copy that frequency into the blue box.

Figure 3.26 – NAV frequency auto identification feature

The G1000 has an automatic station identification feature that shows the station identifier next to the station frequency. This is accepted by the FAA as a valid station identification for the purposes of an FAA check ride, but the applicant on a check ride is expected to confirm the station identifier.

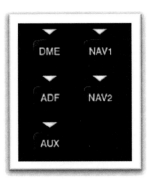

Figure 3.27 – NAV audio selection on the GMA Audio Panel

To listen to the Morse code identifier or to listen to any FSS transmission over that NAV frequency, the pilot must press the NAV 1 or NAV 2 keys on the GMA Audio Panel in order to direct that audio source to the headsets or the speakers. The default mode is that NAV radio audio is off.

Figure 3.28 – NAV volume ID knob

To select volume of the selected NAV station, use the Volume/ID knob. It will only adjust the volume of the radio currently selected by the blue box around its frequency. To audibly identify that station, press the volume knob in momentarily to activate the ID portion of the NAV radio and press the NAV 1 or NAV 2 key to turn on audio. The Morse code identifier coming through the audio panel will be accentuated and become clearer. The use of this key can also aid the automatic identifier that comes up next to the station frequency for distant stations.

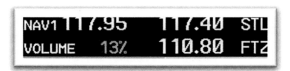

Figure 3.29 – NAV volume percent display

As the volume is adjusted, the pilot will see a % symbol appear in the window to let them know where the volume is currently set. The volume knob only affects the volume of the radio with the blue highlighting box around its frequency.

NAV Radio Control Summary

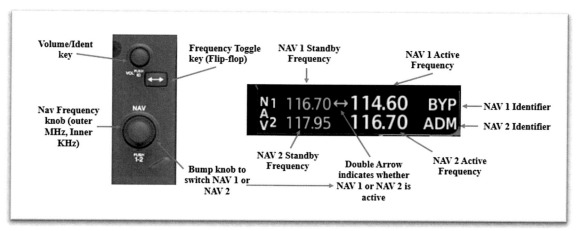

Figure 3.30 – NAV frequency controls

❏ The NAV 1 and NAV 2 controls are located on the upper left-hand corner of the screen. NAV 1 is located and the top row and NAV 2 on the bottom. The active NAV frequencies will be on the right (closest to screen) and standby on the left (farthest from the screen).

❏ To change the frequency, the blue box must be around the frequency they wish to change. To move the box from NAV 1 to NAV 2, push the NAV frequency selector knob in.

❏ The NAV frequency selector is located on the left-hand side of the Garmin Display Unit (GDU), the outer knob ring controls MHz and the inner knob ring controls kHz.

❏ To audibly identify a VOR or LOC, make sure the appropriate NAV 1 or NAV 2 is selected on the audio panel. Then press the NAV volume control "in" on the upper left-hand side of the GDU. "ID" will appear in between the standby and active frequency position and the Morse code identifier will be heard.

❏ The VOR or LOC identifier will also be displayed to the right of the active NAV frequency. For example "STL" will appear if St. Louis VOR is in the active frequency.

❏ The color of the active NAV frequency depends on what is selected as the current CDI needle on the heading indicator. If VOR or LOC 1 is selected, then the active frequency in NAV 1 will be green. And if VOR or LOC 2 is selected as the CDI, the active NAV 2 will be green.

COMMUNICATION Radio Controls (COM)

Figure 3.31 – COM frequency control group

The COM controls section is for selecting VHF radio communication frequencies such as tower and ground control frequencies. The operation of the COM radios is very similar to that just discussed for the NAV radios. The outer knob ring selects the MHz portion of the frequency in the inner portion of the knob ring selects the KHz portion of the frequency. For instance, to select the COM frequency 136.975, use the outer knob ring to select the <u>136</u> and the inner knob ring portion to select the <u>.975.</u>

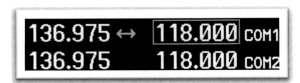

Figure 3.32 – COM frequency display box

Figure 3.33 – COM frequency control knob

To select between entering information into COM radio 1 and COM radio 2, the pilot would press in or "bump" the inner portion of the COM knob. The blue box moves up and down between COM 1 and COM 2.

Figure 3.34 – COM frequency toggle key

Figure 3.35 – COM frequency toggle selected box after flip-flop

Once the pilot puts the new desired COM frequency into the blue box, they use the COM toggle select key or "flip-flop" key to move it from the standby position to the active position. They are now free to enter a new frequency into the standby position using the knob or they can select a frequency from the WPT or NRST dropdown menus and press ENT to copy that frequency into the blue box. Some G1000 installations provide a popup window that allow the pilot to specify whether they want the frequency to be sent to COM 1 or COM 2 and whether the pilot wants the new frequency to go to the active or standby position.

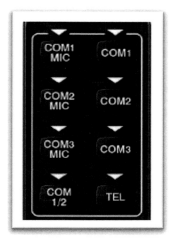

Figure 3.36 – COM frequency selection on the GMA Audio Panel

To listen to the radio selected, the pilot must press the MIC1 or MIC2 key on the GMA Audio Panel in order to direct that radio audio to the speaker or the headsets. Notice that Garmin has provided for a third radio on the GMA audio panel. There will be more on this in the Audio Panel chapter eight.

Figure 3.37 – COM volume/SQ select knob

To adjust the volume of the selected COM station, use the Volume/Squelch knob. It will only adjust the volume of the radio currently selected by the blue box around its frequency. To check for the level of the volume or to listen to distant stations, press the VOLUME/SQUELCH knob to turn off the automatic squelch feature of the radio. When the radio is receiving a transmission, the display will show an RX next to the active frequency. If the pilot does not hear any transmission but sees the RX, it is an indication that either the volume is set too low or the COM is set to the other radio. When the pilot transmits, a TX will appear next to the active frequency. This is a way the pilot can verify if there is a doubt about the operation of the radios and can help the pilot troubleshoot potential communication disruptions.

Figure 3.38 – COM frequency volume percent display

As the volume is adjusted, the pilot will see a % symbol appear in the window to let them know where the volume is currently set. This avoids turning down a radio by accident because they did not realize that the blue box was set on another COM radio.

Note: Volume is always directed at the COM radio highlighted by the blue box.

Note: It is always recommended that the pilot checks the volume of a radio by pressing the volume knob prior to transmitting on a new frequency to avoid "stepping" on the frequency with insufficient volume.

Com Radio Control Summary

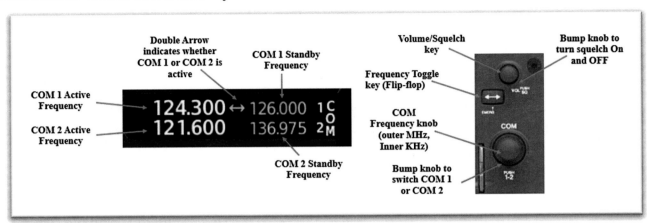

Figure 3.39 – COM radio control group

- ❑ Both COM 1 and COM 2 are located on the upper right-hand corner of the GDU.
- ❑ To change the frequency, turn the COM knobs on the right-hand side of the GDU above the BARO and CRS selector. Use the outer knob ring to change MHz and the inner knob ring to change kHz.
- ❑ The top row will display the active and standby frequencies for COM 1. The bottom row will display the active and standby frequency for COM 2.
- ❑ The standby frequency is located on the right and can be changed by pushing in the COM frequency selector knob and moving the blue box over standby frequency on either COM 1 or COM 2.
- ❑ Once the pilot has changed the frequency and would like to make it the active frequency, press the "frequency toggle or flip-flop" key just below the volume control.
- ❑ The active frequency that the pilot is transmitting and receiving on will be green. All inactive frequencies will be white.
- ❑ To adjust the volume for COM 1, the blue box must be on the standby frequency in COM 1. Then turn the volume control knob on the very top right of the GDU to adjust the volume. A percentage of volume level will appear between the active and standby frequencies.
- ❑ To adjust the volume for COM 2, the pilot must press in the frequency selector knob to move the blue box down to the standby frequency on COM 2. Then use the volume control just like with COM 1.
- ❑ Push the volume control knob in to hear the squelched static of the frequency and thus weaker signals.
- ❑ Pressing and holding the frequency toggle (flip-flop) key will set that emergency frequency 121.5 in the active radio indicated by the blue box
- ❑ RX and TX will appear next to the active frequency of COM 1 or COM 2 to indicate transmissions being sent or received on that radio.

Using the Knobs, Keys, and Controls with the Right-hand

Figure 3.40 – Using right-hand to access G1000 controls on different versions of the G1000

Now that we have explored the function of all the controls of the GDU display units, we can explore the best way for the pilot to utilize all these controls. Because the PFD and the MFD are installed next to each other with the GMA audio panel in the middle or right below it on a GCU, we can see that every control of the system can be accessed using the pilot's right hand freeing them to fly the aircraft with their left hand. This will free the pilot's attention to maintain an effective scan-flow while avoiding costly distractions. Since traditional NAV-COM radios had the COM on the left and the NAV on the right, Garmin put the NAV on the left side of the display screen and the COM on the right side so that when combined, the pilot found the COM and NAV controls in a familiar orientation.

Conclusion

In this chapter, we looked at all the knobs, keys, and controls of the GDU display units and looked at how to operate them. We demonstrated that most of the knobs have multiple functions and move in several different motion planes depending upon what the pilot needs to do with the control. It will take a little getting used to, but once the pilot practices the operation of these controls, they will find that operating the G1000 integrated cockpit system is logical and well laid out.

Remember

❑ The controls have different functions depending upon whether they are scrolled, bumped, or twisted.

❑ The same knob on the PFD and the MFD may produce a different view of the same menu function due to screen "real estate" space availability.

❑ The system is laid out to be fully functional with the pilot's right-hand freeing their left-hand to control the aircraft.

❑ A thorough knowledge of the controls and what they do will free the pilot's attention to maintain an effective scan-flow while avoiding costly distractions.

Chapter Debriefing

We have now covered G1000 knobs, keys, and controls and the pilot should now have a good understanding about how to operate the functions of the system using them so the sequence of keystrokes and functions are correct.

- ❑ Now that the pilot understands that the G1000 knobs, keys, and controls are generally the same between the PFD and the MFD, then they should understand that using a combination of the two with the right-hand frees up the left-hand to do the flying!
- ❑ Now that the pilot understands that the NAV and COM controls on the G1000 require some planning so that the sequence of keystrokes are correct, then the pilot will also understand that this NAV and COM arrangement gives them more flexibility over NAV and COM operation than in traditional aircraft.
- ❑ Now that the pilot understands that this system offers a host of features for general aircraft that offer unprecedented situational awareness, then they will understand that practicing keystroke knowledge of the knobs, keys, and controls will make the job of operating this system much easier and more satisfying.

If the pilot not only understands these three areas, and also can correlate these three major points into their everyday flying skills and apply these skills to the operation of the G1000 aircraft, then they are ready to take the quiz and then to move to chapter four!

Chapter Three Quiz: Knob and Control Functions

The Chapter Quiz Scenario

This Chapter Quiz Scenario (CQS) is designed to suggest a real-world flight situation and use the pilot's new knowledge of the G1000 to answer some situational questions about how to input the information they need to safely operate a G1000 equipped aircraft. The pilot can then determine whether they "understand" and can even "correlate" the material covered with their existing aeronautical knowledge and are prepared to use this information in a way which will enhance their operational safety while using the G1000 equipped aircraft.

In this chapter quiz, the pilot will be asked to demonstrate their understanding of the G1000 knobs, keys, and controls to ensure that they are ready to proceed to the next chapter.

For this quiz scenario, imagine that the pilot now has several hours of experience in the G1000 equipped aircraft. Consider a flight scenario of flying a G1000 equipped aircraft between Kansas City Downtown airport (KMKC) and Columbia, Missouri (KCOU), a tower-controlled airport. Answer the following questions about this scenario:

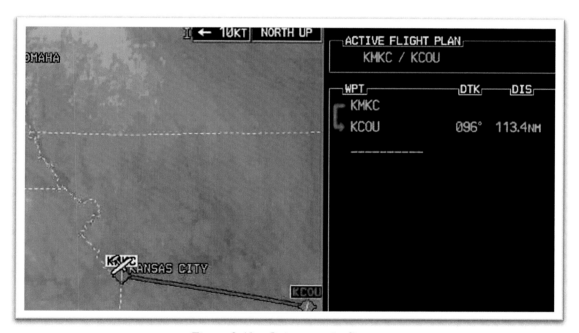

Figure 3.41 – Quiz scenario diagram

Question 1: The pilot is preparing to depart and is getting their weather from the local AWOS at Kansas City Downtown airport. Where do they put the altimeter information into the G1000 equipped aircraft?

    a) **Through the Autopilot BARO key and this sets the entire aircraft.**

    b) **Enter it into the G1000 using the Baro knob and into the standby altimeter using the altimeter Kollsman knob.**

     c)   **Enter it into the GPS database using the ALT knob on the GDU.**

Question 2: The pilot has completed their departure, and wants to place the KCOU arrival CTAF frequency into the number 2 COM. How is this done and made active?

     a)   **Key in the frequency with the PFD keypad and press enter.**

     b)   **Use the inner and outer knobs of the FMS knob to select the frequency and then press the frequency toggle** key.

     c)   **Use the inner and outer knobs of the COM knob to select the frequency and then press the toggle frequency** key **to make it active.**

Question 3: The pilot is now airborne and wants to center the heading bug and the Altitude bug on their current heading and altitude. How do they do this?

     a)   **Press the D-> key and then select HDG and ALT.**

     b)   **Turn the ALT and the HDG knob counterclockwise until they are centered.**

     c)   **Press in ("bump") on the HDG and ALT knobs to center these settings.**

Question 4: The pilot is trying to tune in ATIS on COM 2 to get the weather at the KCOU airport and finds that they hear nothing in their headset. What can they do with the G1000 radios to help?

     a)   **Turn the volume up on the GMA Audio Panel.**

     b)   **Make sure the blue box is around the active frequency and then turn up the volume control using the VOL/SQ knob.**

     c)   **Pressing the VOL/SQ** key **will turn off the squelch and allow them to hear the station at an increased distance.**

Question 5: If the pilot were flying this scenario and was halfway to their destination, and wanted to hear the NAV radio identifier for an upcoming VOR, and did not see the station identifier show up next to the frequency, how could they increase the sensitivity of the NAV radio that they were listening to?

     a)   **Turn the volume up more using the NAV VOL/ID knob.**

     b)   **Make sure the blue box is around the active frequency and then turn up the VOL/ID volume control knob.**

     c)   **Press the NAV** key **and pressing (bump) the NAV VOL/ID knob in to amplify the Morse code of the identifier.**

Question 6: How can the FMS selection knob be used to retrieve information from menus within the G1000?

    a) **Twist the knobs to select automatic search and then press ENT to make a final selection.**

    b) **Turn the inner knob and outer knobs to alphabetically spell station names and then press ENT for Entering the selection.**

    c) **Bump the inner knob to activate cursor, scroll with the outer knob to move to the correct field and twist the inner knob to select the final choice in the drop-down box followed by pressing ENT.**

Question 7: How does the pilot use the GCU FMS knob to navigate menus within the Garmin Perspective Plus MFD?

    a) **Twist the knobs to select automatic search and then press ENT to select the desired choice in the drop-down menu.**

    b) **Turn the inner knob and outer knobs to alphabetically spell station names and then press ENT to make the final menu selection.**

    c) **With the cursor off, scroll the outer knob to move to the correct menu and twist the inner knob to select the final choice in the drop-down box.**

Grading Criteria:

The pilot will know when they have completed this chapter when they get all the answers correct. When the exam is completed, grade the answers with the answer key in the back of this handbook. Incorrect answers should be researched by going back to the appropriate reference area in the chapter or the Garmin Cockpit Guide that comes with the aircraft. Once the pilot has achieved all the correct answers, then proceed on to the next chapter. Come back to items in this chapter at any time.

Chapter Four: Powering Up the G1000

Chapter Objectives:

The objective of this chapter is for the pilot to demonstrate understanding regarding the power-up sequence of the G1000 by reviewing the content of this chapter. The pilot will then take the chapter quiz at the end which will check their knowledge about the material covered.

Completion Standards:

When this chapter is complete, the pilot will be able to understand the power-up sequence of the G1000. The pilot will know when they have met the completion standards of the chapter when they have correctly answered all the quiz questions at the end of this section. If any questions are scored incorrect, go back to the appropriate reference area in the chapter or the Garmin Cockpit Guide that comes with the aircraft. When the pilot has correctly answered all the chapter quiz questions, then they may proceed to the next chapter.

Getting Ready to Power-up the G1000

Where the G1000 gets its Power

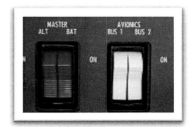

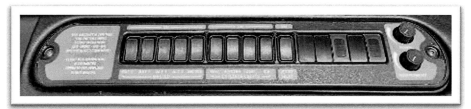

Figure 4.1a – Cessna Master and Avionics   *Figure 4.1b – Cirrus Master, Alternator, and Avionics switches*

The G1000 system is a fully integrated system and is tied into the aircraft electrical system by the aircraft manufacturer. Traditionally, when we started an aircraft, we would turn on the Master Switch, start the engine, and then we would turn on the avionics master switch to avoid voltage spikes from damaging our radios during the power fluctuations of starting the engine.

The G1000 has been designed to operate on a very wide range of voltages so the possibility of avionics damage from voltage spikes during engine start no longer have to be of concern for system longevity. So, when we turn the master switch on, the essential portions of the G1000 powers up at that time. The non-essential parts of the system are powered up with the Avionics switch after engine start.

Another thing that we have learned with the advent of digital power management systems featured in the G1000 is that there is a measurable difference in electrical current consumption between turning on the master switch with the "battery only" side of the switch and turning it on with both sides of the switch which engages the alternator portion of the circuitry. Engaging the alternator is essential after the engine is running but for preflight and starting sequences, the battery may be weakened from the process of elongated periods of flight plan programming and other pre-engine start duties. It is especially hard on a battery during cold temperatures. So, in times of prolonged or extended battery use, it is permissible to use the battery side of the master switch to do many preflight engine start duties.

Figure 4.3 – Cessna G1000 electrical bus

Once the engine starts, then actuate the "alternator" side of the master switch and watch the battery voltage quickly rise up to 28 volts and the ammeter show a positive charge. The pilot will also see the Low Voltage caution on the crew alerting system go out. Using this procedure allows the pilot to check the status of the charging system after the engine starts and to preserve battery power for operation.

Caution: Use of this procedure is recommended only when it is amended to the checklist to prevent the possibility that the pilot could forget to turn on the alternator after engine start.

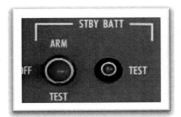 

Figure 4.4a – Cessna Standby battery switch   *Figure 4.4b – Cessna Standby battery*

Many aircraft manufacturers have designed their G1000 aircraft with a standby battery and a standby battery circuit breaker bus for controlling or operating the system only from that battery in the event of an emergency. This picture above is the standby battery and its controlling switch from a Cessna aircraft. It has a test position that pilots are required to check prior to starting the aircraft. Making sure that this self-test switch illuminates the test light for 20 seconds will ensure that the standby battery has sufficient power to power the system in the event of an electrical power problem or alternator failure.

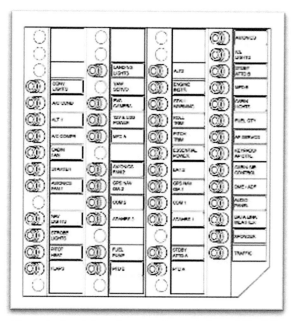

Figure 4.5 – Cirrus Aircraft circuit breaker panel consisting of 13 different electrical busses

Start-up Flow

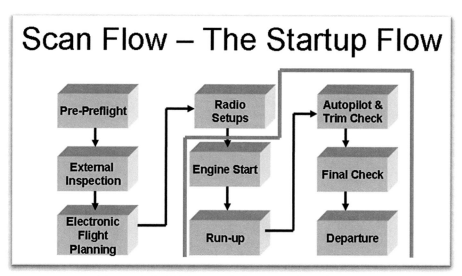

Figure 4.6 – TAA aircraft departure flow diagram

The pilot must be aware that the TAA aircraft utilizes a different "flow" with regards to engine startup and preparation for departure. Because of the many distractions in the cockpit, the pilot is advised to always use a checklist and to make sure that they never attempt any system setup or flight plan programming tasks while the aircraft is taxiing. It is better to request a delay from ATC in copying the clearance and wait to a stopping point during the taxi to make their adjustment than it is to risk accidentally running off the taxiway.

Power ON

Figure 4.7 – Cessna and Cirrus G1000 system startup screens

When the G1000 first powers up, it displays the screen shown above to show the pilot the status of the system software and the database expiration dates. Expired databases are shown in yellow. It is very important that the pilot read and understand the messages that appear on this screen. By pressing the right-most softkey, it indicates to the system that the pilot has accepted the status of database expirations and system software.

Note: Never attempt IFR flight when this screen indicates missing or out of date databases.

System Databases

Figure 4.8 – System database version display page

There are several databases that the G1000 uses to perform its functions. The onscreen checklist is available on many models. The pilot is not able to change the factory provided checklist for their aircraft model, but the onscreen checklists support check and click style checklist updating as they progress along the checklist items. For additional checklist items the pilot wishes to execute, they may need a supplemental handheld checklist.

System software – System software should be thought of as the operating system of the G1000 and the version that Garmin uses to program the functions for that particular aircraft model. All features are worked out with the manufacturer before such a software release is approved. Only an authorized person or avionics shop can install these updates and the appropriate aircraft logbook entries must be made including software versions installed and whether the aircraft was flight checked. The aircraft owner or operator will typically get a service bulletin from the aircraft manufacturer letting them know what features of the G1000 behaviors this software will modify. This should be followed up with a revision to the Pilots Operating Handbook manual supplements concerning the G1000. Always keep the supplements in the aircraft up to date so that there is a ready reference if assistance is needed during a flight or during an emergency. When the aircraft was delivered, the manufacturer provided a system base version CD or SD card for that model aircraft. This original version should be kept with the aircraft POH and a copy should be made to keep with the aircraft logbooks so that anytime updates are made, a copy of the base software is available for the system to use as reference. Each time major software releases are made to the system, Garmin provides a new system software base CD or SD card, if they want the old one replaced. When this happens, this becomes the new base software CD. Mark the old original version with a sharpie marker that it is "superseded" and put it aside for safekeeping. Garmin has been migrating to downloadable software updates and these are intended to only be installed by authorized Garmin service centers.

Base Map Region – This is the government provided geodetic databases that the G1000 uses to aid in the construction of maps and basic geography shown on the screen. There are a number of datum selections available in the Aux system setup screen. Garmin recommends using the WGS84 datum for most North American applications.

Aviation Database – This is the government provided database that is updated every 28 days by internet subscription. Without this update, the aircraft is not properly prepared for IFR flight because the system is not updated with important airport, instrument approach, and other safety critical information that is released by the NOAA and the FAA on a cycle similar to that of Instrument Approach Chart and Chart Supplement directories.

Terrain Database – This database contains important information about the global database of terrain elevation; In other words, dirt and rocks. No manmade obstacles are contained in this database. This is updated semi-annually or as prescribed by Garmin and Jeppesen.

Obstacle Database – This database contains important information about the local database of obstacle elevations; In other words, towers and smokestacks. No earth based obstacles are contained in this database. This is updated semi-annually or as prescribed by Garmin and Jeppesen.

Figure 4.9 – Secure Digital (SD) software update card

Figure 4.10 – SD card reader for updating databases

Updating Databases – Databases are updated using a Secure Digital card similar to those used in a digital camera. Typically, you can use any data loader or the one provided with the G1000 aircraft to download the update from the internet onto the SD card using the card reader that came with the G1000. It is recommended to use a card that is 16GB or larger. To update the database, first log into the Garmin database updater software and download the specific subscription database that matches your aircraft tail number. Then insert the SD card into the top SD card slot on the face of the GDU for the PFD with the power off. Turn the aircraft power on. Once the PFD starts to power up, it will detect the card and ask for permission to update the aviation database. Press Enter for yes. The database will be uploaded into the system. Turn the power off. Repeat the process for the MFD. The system will not allow the database to load a version that is older than what is already installed in the aircraft. The system also will not startup if the database version is not identical in the PFD and the MFD.

Profiles

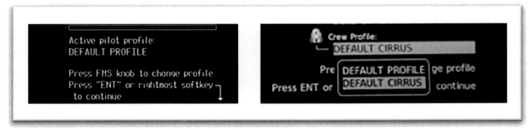

Figure 4.11 – Profiles selection for various G1000 aircraft

Many manufacturers support a concept called Profiles. A Profile is a preconfigured set of standard system defaults that can vary from pilot to pilot. For instance, let's say that three pilots own an aircraft together. One pilot is from the US and likes their map in North-up mode, the second pilot is from Canada and likes the metric system; and the third pilot likes everything like the first pilot, but they like the screen in Track-up mode. The Profiles section allows up to 25 different configurations to be saved and recalled at G1000 startup. Each pilot can save their profile and assign it a name from the AUX SETUP menu, which we will cover later in the MFD chapter ten.

Initial Power on-screen

Figure 4.12 – Initial Power on-screen

Because the G1000 has engine instruments integrated into the display unit screens, the instrumentation must appear on the screen to monitor engine conditions during start. The pilot must look at factors such as Oil Pressure and Fuel Flow to assure an efficient and productive engine start sequence. This is the same screen that the pilot would see in the reversionary mode by pressing the RED key on the bottom of the GMA audio panel. This screen is normal until the avionics master switch is engaged. As each of the LRUs power up, the red Xs will be replaced with the proper indication for that instrument.

Note: If any of the areas of the screen remain with a red X after start, first confirm that the avionics master switch is on. Then if the red Xs persist, then the pilot must investigate before continuing the flight.

Conclusion

In this chapter, we looked at the startup sequence for initializing the G1000 system. The pilot probably noticed that some of the procedures discussed here are different from anything they have done before in other traditional paneled aircraft. The system provides information to the pilot by covering up inaccurate information provided by system or airframe sensors whose data sources are missing or have become compromised. Once the system properly initializes each instrument and passes self-tests, the red Xs are removed, and data is displayed properly.

Remember to closely monitor the engine gauges during the engine start sequence and make sure that each gauge rises within a reasonable amount of time into a yellow or green operating range as prescribed by the aircraft and engine manufacturer.

Different aircraft manufacturers have different procedures, so use this as a general guide and by all means, follow the checklist provided by the manufacturer for the aircraft flown.

Remember

- ❑ A TAA aircraft uses a different startup flow sequence than traditional aircraft.
- ❑ System and database updates should be kept current prior to attempting flight.
- ❑ Red Xs cover instruments during initialization sequence until the G1000 deems the data as reliable.
- ❑ The pilot with "reasonable training and knowledge" may update the aviation database but a logbook entry must be made to record that action.
- ❑ Only authorized personnel should attempt system software updates.
- ❑ Never attempt database updates while the aircraft is in flight.
- ❑ Never attempt system adjustments or programming tasks while the aircraft is being taxied.

Chapter Debriefing

We have now covered the area of the G1000 startup procedure and the pilot should now understand why it is crucial to properly operating technically advanced aircraft (TAA) equipped with the G1000.

- ❑ If the pilot understands the concept of how to properly startup the G1000, then they should also understand how to recognize when all of the systems have initialized correctly.
- ❑ If the pilot understands the concept of which systems initialize with the master switch and which initialize with the avionics master switch, then they should also recognize the basics of the electrical system and how it feeds power to the G1000 and its systems.
- ❑ If the pilot understands about the various system software and databases and how they feed the G1000 its information to function, then they should also understand the importance of maintaining current database information as provided by Garmin and Jeppesen and avoiding operation of the system with out-of-date information.

The pilot should not only understand these three areas, but also correlate these into their everyday flying skills, and apply these skills to the operation of their G1000 aircraft. They should now be ready to take the quiz and then to move to chapter five!

Chapter Four Quiz: Powering Up the G1000

The Chapter Quiz Scenario

This Chapter Quiz Scenario (CQS) is designed to offer a real-world flight situation and use the pilot's new knowledge of the G1000 to answer some situational questions about how to safely operate their aircraft.

In this chapter quiz, the pilot is asked to demonstrate their understanding of the power-up sequence of the G1000 to determine whether they "understand" and can "correlate" the material covered with their existing aeronautical decision making knowledge and are prepared to use this information in a way which will enhance their operational safety while using the G1000 equipped aircraft.

During this quiz scenario, imagine that it has been some time since the pilot was at the airport. They have just climbed into the cockpit and are preparing to take this flight between Kansas City Downtown airport (KMKC) and Columbia, Missouri (KCOU), back to Whiteman AFB, and then back to KMKC. Consider the following questions about this scenario:

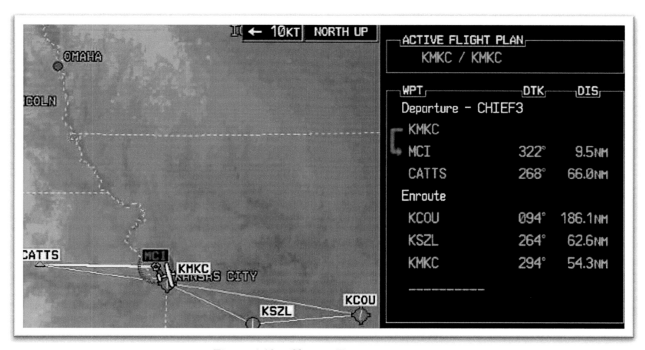

Figure 4.13 – Chapter Four quiz scenario

Question 1: How would the pilot check the level of fuel in their fuel gauges in the G1000 equipped aircraft prior to starting the preflight?

    a) Turn on the master switch and the avionics master and turn on the fuel gauges by pressing enter.

    b) Turn on the G1000 initiation-screen using the master switch or the standby battery switch, if so equipped and wait for the red Xs to disappear.

    c) The fuel gauges will turn on when the engine is started.

Question 2: Before the flight today, what is the best way to make sure that the databases are current for IFR Flight?

    a) Pull out the SD Card from the MFD and read the expiration date off the label of the SD card.

    b) Start the G1000 PFD using the master switch and read the expiration date on the flight planning screen.

    c) Start the G1000 MFD using the master switch and avionics switch if necessary and read the expiration dates on the initiation (Splash)-screen.

Question 3: The pilot received a service bulletin with a new system base software update announcement from the aircraft manufacturer requiring the aircraft get its system software updated ASAP. Which of the following is true regarding this software update?

    a) The pilot can follow the instructions and update the software using their laptop computer.

    b) The pilot will have to get an authorized person to install the software update and receive a logbook entry.

    c) The pilot can ignore the software update because the G1000 downloads all of its updates automatically from satellites.

Question 4: The pilot has just completed the startup sequence for their flight in the G1000 aircraft and notice their COM 2 and NAV 2 frequency boxes still have a red X through them. What should they do?

    a) Check to see that the avionics master switch is on and that no circuit breakers are popped.

    b) Shut the system down right away because it has developed a malfunction.

    c) Reach over and press the COM and NAV keys to turn on the radio with the blue box pointer.

Question 5: The pilot is taxiing to their departure runway to do the pre-departure checks and autopilot and trim system checks, and they receive a call from ground control amending their departure clearance. What should they do?

      a) Start looking at charts while taxiing and input route and clearance changes while taxiing to meet departure times.

      b) Reach over and twist in the changes to the flight plan as it is only a small change.

      c) Acknowledge the change and wait until the aircraft is safely stopped at the run-up area to input the change into the G1000 to avoid a taxi distraction incident.

Grading Criteria:

The pilot will know when they have completed this chapter when they get all the answers correct and demonstrate a solid understanding of the material. When the exam is completed, grade the answers with the answer key in the back of this handbook. Incorrect answers should be researched by going back to the appropriate reference area in the chapter or the Garmin Cockpit Guide that comes with the aircraft. Return to this chapter anytime to review material or questions. Now it is time to proceed on to chapter five.

Chapter Five: Primary Flight Display (PFD)

Chapter Objectives:

The objective of this chapter is for the pilot to demonstrate understanding regarding the Primary Flight Display (PFD) of the G1000 by reviewing the content of this chapter. The pilot will then take the chapter quiz at the end which will check their knowledge about the material covered.

Completion Standards:

When this chapter is complete, the pilot will be able to describe and explain functions and modes of the G1000 Primary Flight Display (PFD). The pilot will know when they have met the completion standards of the chapter when they have correctly answered all the quiz questions at the end of this section. If any questions are scored as incorrect, go back to the appropriate reference area in the chapter or the Garmin Cockpit Guide that comes with the aircraft. When the pilot has correctly answered all the chapter quiz questions, then they may proceed to the next chapter.

The Primary Flight Display

Figure 5.1 – Primary Flight Display (PFD)

The Primary Flight Display (PFD) is always situated in front of the pilot, so therefore on most aircraft, it is on the left side of the cockpit. It has most of the same features as the conventional cockpit except that the instruments are situated on a display screen and use a computer to optimize their display characteristics for the pilot. Let us compare the two types of cockpit arrangements to help the pilot see how the different instruments have been placed and how they should be interpreted.

PFD Display features compared to Traditional Instruments

Figure 5.2 – Traditional aircraft panel instruments

When the pilot first looks at the G1000 panel, they see several instruments that jump out and look familiar. But as they spend more time, they find certain trusted instruments appear to be missing from the electronic display screen. Don't worry! All the instruments and their functions are there and have just been transformed to a more logical location to take advantage of time-tested pilot scan techniques to group information together.

Airspeed Indicator

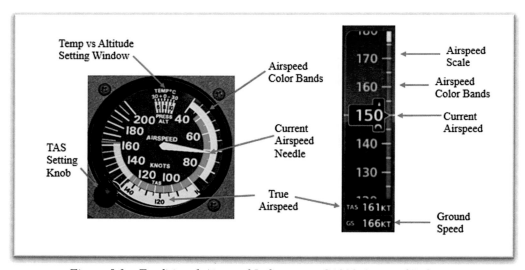

Figure 5.3 – Traditional Airspeed Indicator vs G1000 Airspeed Indicator

Notice the differences between the traditional instrument and the G1000 representation?

❑ The traditional indicator was driven by a net difference between pitot and static pressure and drove a needle through the movement of a calibrated steel coil spring.

❑ The G1000 indicator on the G1000 is in a vertical tape format more closely aligned with what jets use on their cockpit systems.

❑ All of the colored arcs are true to form, and the pilot will feel more at home because they can read the instrument easier with a digital and graphical tape readout.

❑ The G1000 shows the numerical indicated airspeed value in the box while tape with color arc bands move up and down.

❑ Airspeed value on a "tape" scale shown by pointer next to the digital readout.

❑ Rate of change "trend indicator" on right side of tape shows what airspeed will be in 6 seconds allowing pilot to monitor airspeed trends. Trend indicators are shown in magenta.

❑ True airspeed readout on the bottom of tape as opposed to using knob on traditional indicator.

❑ Airspeed "bugs" for Vr, Vx, Vg, and Vy slide up and down with the tape allow the pilot to monitor critical airspeeds.

❑ Groundspeed readout is shown below the airspeed tape on the PFD.

Attitude Indicator

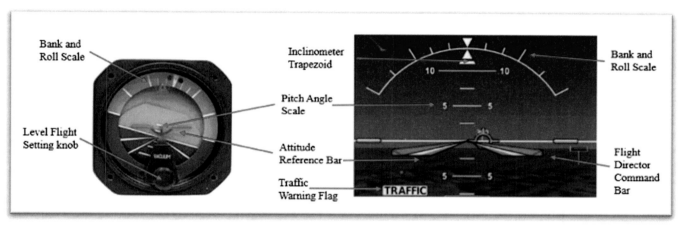

Figure 5.4 – Traditional Attitude Indicator vs G1000 Attitude Indicator

Notice the differences between the traditional instrument and the G1000 representation?

❑ The traditional indicator was powered by a spinning gyro driven by vacuum pressure drawn through the case of the instrument by the vacuum pump or in some cases by an electric motor.

❑ The pilot needed to set the orange wing reference on the traditional indicator by using a knob.

❑ The G1000 indicator on the G1000 is a very similar ground versus sky format but much larger with other information integrated onto its face.

❑ G1000 shows traffic alert symbol on the screen to catch the pilot's attention during a traffic intrusion.

❑ There is no gyro in the G1000, so the pilot need not worry about tumbling gyro or precession errors.

❑ G1000 display much larger, translucent representation shows horizon in blue and ground in brown.

❑ Autopilot portrays flight director command bars clearly on display.

❑ Shows pitch and bank scales more clearly.

❑ Red "chevrons" show at both 30deg. pitch up and down showing the pilot the way to level flight.

❑ Skid/slip indicator is indicated by the "trapezoid" at the top of the roll scale, right below the bank pointer.
❑ The coordination trapezoid below the triangle moves to indicate the direction of rudder required.

Altimeter

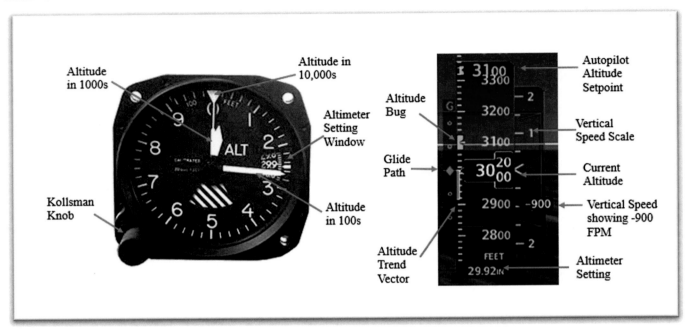

Figure 5.5 – Traditional Altimeter vs G1000 Altimeter

Notice the differences between the traditional instrument and the G1000 representation?

❑ The traditional altimeter was driven by static pressure interacting with an aneroid bellows chamber which expanded and contracted with changes in pressure as altitude changed.
❑ The altimeter indication on the G1000 is in a vertical tape format more closely aligned with what jets use on their cockpit systems.
❑ Numerical readout of altitude bug setting shown on top is controlled by ALT knob and can be centered to current altitude by pressing ALT set knob.
❑ Numerical altitude value shown in the pointer box.
❑ Current altitude value on a "tape" scale shown by pointer.
❑ Altimeter setting shown on bottom of scale set with BARO set knob.
❑ Rate of change "trend indicator" on left side of altitude tape tells where altitude will be in 6 seconds alerting pilot to altitude change trends.
❑ Remember that the altitude bug does not transfer information to an external (King KAP 140) autopilot and cannot be used to set or hold altitude on those older systems.
❑ G1000 NXi systems with the integrated autopilot are fully linked to the altitude bug settings.

Altitude Select Knob

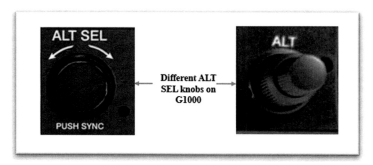

Figure 5.6 – Altitude bug select knob on different versions of the G1000

As discussed in chapter three, the altitude select knob is used to set the altitude reference bug. Turning the same knob on the MFD also moves the bug pointer on the PFD.

- o   The altitude select knob is located on the lower left side of the GDU on some G1000 models and on others, the altitude set knob is on the GFC/GMC 500 or GFC/GMC 700 autopilot control panel.
- o   The numerical value of the altitude selected is shown above the altitude tape on PFD.
- o   A blue altitude bug will be shown on the altimeter when the selected altitude is in view.
- o   Turning the outer knob will change the bug in 1000ft. increments while turning the inner knob will change the altitude by 100ft. increments.

BARO Selector for Entering in Altimeter Setting

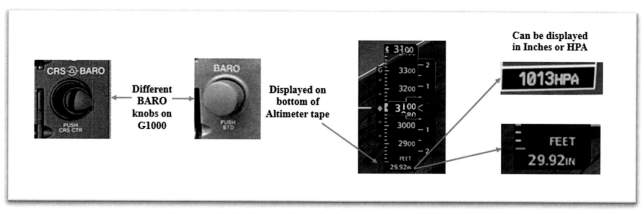

Figure 5.7 – BARO knob on different versions of the G1000

As discussed in chapter three, the CRS or COURSE and BARO or barometric pressure selection knob is used to set the altimeter setting into the G1000 system. The CRS knob is the inner knob and has a different function. Turning the same knob on the MFD also moves the BARO and CRS displays on the PFD.

- o   The BARO knob is on the right-hand side of the GDU and is the outer knob ring of the CRS selector.
- o   Turning the BARO Selector right will increase the altimeter setting shown in the window below the Altitude tape. Turning it to the left will decrease it.

> *Note: Adjusting the barometric pressure using the BARO knob is only one of either two or three places in the aircraft where altimeter setting must be entered depending upon whether the aircraft is equipped with the Garmin autopilot.*

Heading indicator (Horizontal Situation Indicator (HSI))

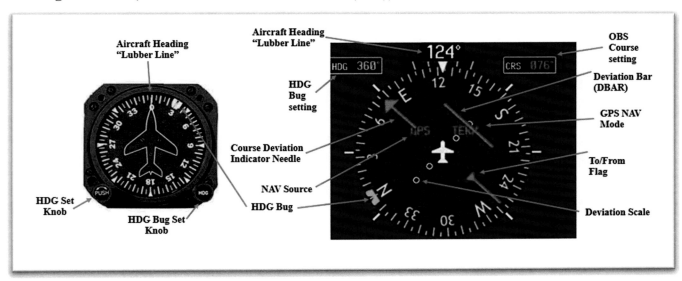

Figure 5.8 – Traditional Heading Indicator versus the G1000 HSI

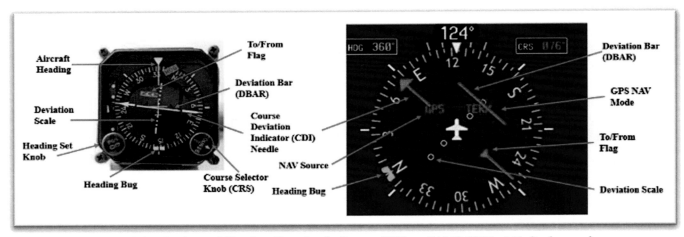

Figure 5.9 – Traditional Heading Situation Indicator (HSI) vs G1000 HSI in 360 display mode

Notice the differences between the traditional heading indicator and the new G1000 representation?

- ❏ Traditional indicator was a gyroscope driven instrument, typically powered by vacuum or electric and was prone to precession errors. Although some installations used a flux gate to slave the compass, the setting knob was required to be set on other installations prior to and during flight to keep the instrument calibrated with the magnetic compass.
- ❏ The G1000 HSI is an all-electronic instrument with no gyros that is powered by the GMU Magnetometer rendering precise heading information at all times.
- ❏ Value shown is always magnetic course.

❑ Numerical value of heading shown in box at top of display.
❑ Blue heading bug controlled by the HDG knob and can be centered by pressing HDG in (bump).
❑ Magnetometer automatically sets compass so there is no knob to set and there is no precession like a traditional instrument.
❑ Can be shown in 360-degree or Arc view mode using the PFD softkey.
❑ The blue box to the left of the top of the indicator represents what the heading bug is set to, and this is what autopilot follows when set in HDG mode.

HSI in Arc Display mode

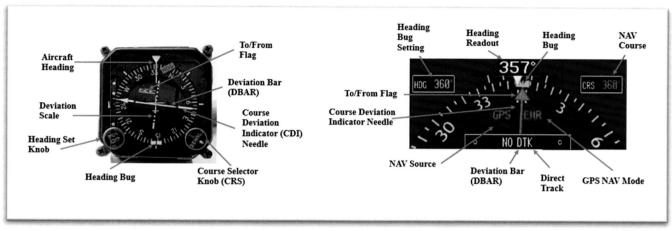

Figure 5.10 – HSI display in ARC display mode

For G1000 systems with Synthetic Vision (SynVis) installed, the PFD display screen can have map, terrain, and obstacle elements superimposed on the Attitude Indicator portion of the PFD. In this case, the pilot may wish to view more of those details while flying along their flight planned route. This is a perfect scenario for the Arc display mode. What this mode does is to display only the top portion of the HSI indicator, only showing the essential elements in a compressed format.

Synthetic Vision (Garmin SVT)

The Synthetic Vision (SVT) option of the G1000 NXi system offers the pilot a significant improvement in situational awareness. The basic G1000 system simply depicts the bottom of the Attitude Indicator in brown and the sky in blue. Garmin's SVT option replaces the brown screen coloring with a three-dimensional graphical representation of what it "sees" from its view of the databases. The SVT option, as it is referred to, offers not only three-dimensional terrain depiction out of the database, but also obstacles as well. Garmin offers this feature as an add-on to the basic G1000 system. From a situational awareness perspective, this option transforms the flight experience into 3D on the display screen, greatly enhancing safety for the pilot during many otherwise harrowing night or IFR operations.

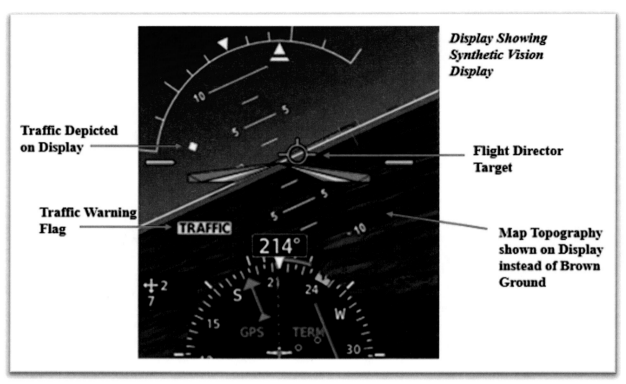

Figure 5.11 – Synthetic Vision (SynVis) of the PFD

Heading Selection Knob

Figure 5.12 – Heading (HDG) bug selection knob

As discussed in chapter three, the HDG or heading selection knob is used to set the heading bug on the G1000 HSI. Turning the same knob on the MFD also moves the HDG bug on the PFD.

PFD OPT Softkey

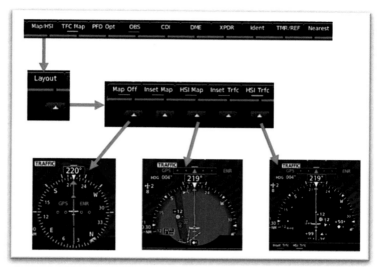

Figure 5.13 – PFD softkey

- o   Selecting the PFD OPT softkey will change the softkey selections offering the normal or the feature view for G1000 to display maps and traffic.
- o   The normal mode is the display mode that is default where it shows the entire HSI.
- o   The feature display mode is where the HSI is displayed in a perspective arc view only showing the top 60% of the HSI. This mode will be very useful for the pilot using Garmin SVT allowing them to see a three-dimensional view of the terrain ahead of the aircraft along the flight plan in the area above the HSI.
- o   The METRIC softkey will change the BARO selection and altitude into metric measurements.
- o   The DFLTS softkey will change selection back to the default selection.

Vertical Speed Indicator (VSI)

Figure 5.14 – Traditional Vertical Speed Indicator vs G1000 Vertical Speed Display

Notice the differences between the traditional instrument and the G1000 representation?

❑ Traditional indicator was a static pressure instrument with an internal vented pressure differential reading to show vertical rates of climb or descent.

❑ The G1000 Vertical Speed readout is set next to the Altimeter tape and shows vertical speed in positive and negative digital feet per minute values.

❑ The VSI in Figure 5.14 reads minus 900 feet per minute descent.

Turn and Bank Indicator

Figure 5.15 – Traditional Turn and Bank Indicator vs G1000 Rate of Turn Indicator

Notice the differences between the traditional instrument and the G1000 display representation?

❑ The traditional indicator was gyroscopically driven, usually with electric power.

❑ The inclinometer was a ball which rolled along a curved tube to show slip and skid.

❑ The G1000 has split up these portrayals into two areas.

❑ The rate of turn is now represented at the top of the HSI and is represented by a magenta trend bar which moves left and right of the top of the HSI.

❑ This rate indicator has two graduated lines which represent ½ standard rate and standard rate or 2-minute turn (3 degrees of turn per second)

❑ The ball function is now portrayed at the top of the Attitude Indicator and is shown by a "trapezoid" which moves right or left to show slip and skid. The pilot should remember to "step on the trapezoid" instead of "step on the ball."

Panel Clock

Figure 5.16 – Traditional panel clock vs G1000 system time display

Notice the differences between the traditional instrument and the G1000 representation?

- ❑ The traditional clock was a stand-alone device which needed a dedicated electrical circuit or internal backup battery to keep it current.
- ❑ The G1000 indicator is located on the lower portion of the PFD panel and derives its timekeeping reference from the atomic clock located in the GPS satellite itself.
- ❑ The clock can be set to local time or GMT (Zulu) time in the settings area of the MFD.

Course Deviation Indicator (GPS)

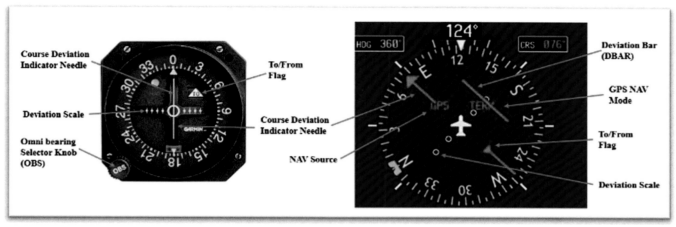

Figure 5.17 – Traditional course deviation indicator (CDI) vs G1000 GPS CDI Indicator and DBAR

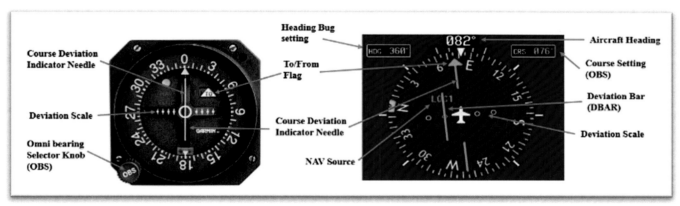

Figure 5.18 – Traditional VOR course deviation indicator (CDI) vs G1000 VLOC CDI Indicator and DBAR

Notice the differences between the traditional instrument and the G1000 representation?

- ❑ The VOR indicator was a stand-alone device which needed a NAV radio to deliver its VHF signal and was tied to the autopilot through the NAV switch. A pilot forgetting to switch the NAV source could make a serious mistake in tracking the wrong course.
- ❑ The G1000 version is superimposed on the compass so a complete view of the navigation picture and progress is shown.
- ❑ CDI Needles are color coded to help depict which NAV source is being displayed.

- o **Green** Represents VOR/LOC needles. A single needle is VOR/LOC1, and a double needle is VOR/LOC2.
- o **Magenta** Represents a GPS course or GPS system derived data.

❑ The DBAR represents the floating portion of the CDI needle and represents the relative position to the desired course.
❑ The G1000 indicator is located on the HSI and is switched between GPS and VLOC mode through the CDI softkey. (Figure 5.19)
❑ The deviation bar always shows the orientation to the desired course radial.
❑ The OBS course is set using the Course/Baro knob on the right side of the PFD.
❑ The pilot can determine which radial they are on by bumping the course knob which centers the CDI. This is a handy feature the pilot might use often.

Figure 5.19 – PFD, OBS, and CDI control softkeys

❑ The course needle is set automatically when in GPS modes to point directly to the next GPS waypoint and the DBAR shows where that course is relative to the current position.
❑ The course needle is set manually by the CRS knob for VOR just like an OBS selector knob on a traditional CDI indicator and the DBAR shows where that course is relative to the current position.
❑ Toggle from GPS to NAV/LOC1 to NAV/LOC2 by pressing the CDI softkey below the indicator.
❑ Toggle from 360 degree to Arc view perspective by pressing PFD.
❑ GPS courses are always shown in Magenta.
❑ VOR and LOCALIZER courses are always shown in Green with VLOC1 being a single Green and VLOC2 being a double Green DBAR line.
❑ When the ADF is added to representation, it is shown with the Bearing Pointers.
❑ Needle always points to the station to avoid back-course indications when orientation to station is reversed.
❑ 360 HSI presentations will show the heading indicator in a 360° format. This will also allow for BRG 1 and BRG 2 to be displayed.
❑ ARC HSI will show the heading indicator in an arc format. About half of the heading indicator is shown in ARC mode and the BRG 1 and BRG 2 cannot be displayed.

Course Selection Knob or (Omni-Bearing Selector –OBS selector knob)

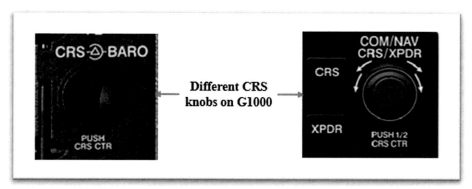

Figure 5.20 – CRS knob used to set OBS course heading used on different models of the G1000

❑ The omni-bearing selector is on the right-hand side of the PFD. It is a small, triangular CRS knob located in the center of the BARO knob.

❑ While using a VOR, the pilot can push the CRS knob and the CDI will center on the radial the aircraft is currently on with a "To" indication.

❑ The OBS key can be used when tracking a GPS to offset the bearing to allow the pilot to fly "around" restricted airspace or to avoid obstacles, mountainous terrain, or large bodies of water.

OBS (Omni-Bearing Selector) Softkey

Figure 5.21 – OBS softkey used to force GPS to obey CRS knob

o The OBS softkey will allow the pilot to select a Bearing/Radial from any airport, navaid or waypoint.

o Once OBS is pressed, the GPS CDI needle is in OBS mode. The Course knob can be turned to select a particular Bearing/Radial and that will be displayed in the course window of the HSI.

o One example where OBS mode will be useful might be to avoid Class B airspace, restricted airspace, TFR, or mountainous terrain.

ADF/DME Selection Box

Figure 5.22 – DME NAV selection box and DME softkey

❑ The G1000 can support the installation of traditional ADF (Automatic Direction Finder) and/or DME (Distance Measuring Equipment) receivers, and these provide the G1000 with the signal necessary to tune. In the US, the GPS function can replicate any ADF or DME functions on published routes or procedures so they are rarely used.

❑ A dedicated DME or ADF receiver would be more practical for use in other countries without robust GPS functionality.

BRG Bearing Selector Rings

Figure 5.23 – Multiple BRG pointer depiction needles and data boxes

❑ BRG1 will display a NAV 1 or GPS CDI needle around the perimeter of the primary CDI selection and show a box to the left of the heading indicator that shows degrees of bearing change. The NAV source could be GPS, VOR/LOC1, VOR/LOC2, or ADF (if installed). It is depicted with a single line pointer.

❑ BRG 2 will display NAV 2 or GPS CDI needle over the primary CDI selection and a box will be to the right of the heading indicator showing degrees of bearing change to that GPS or NAV course. It is depicted with a double line pointer.

Course Deviation Indicator (Glideslope and Glidepath)

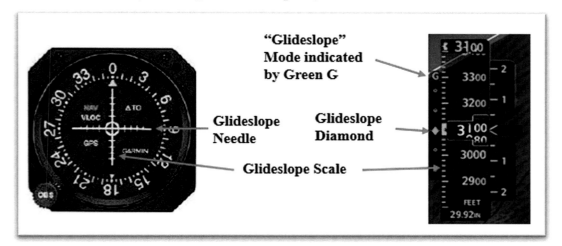

Figure 5.24 – Traditional CDI with ILS Glideslope and G1000 Glideslope Indicator

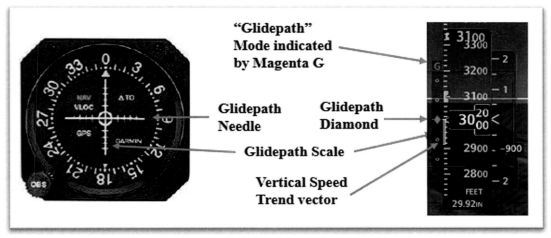

Figure 5.25 – Traditional CDI and G1000 Glidepath Indicator

Figure 5.26 – G1000 Glideslope Indicator with no signal received

Notice the differences between the traditional instrument and the G1000 representation?

- ❑ The traditional indicator was a horizontal CDI needle that went across the face of the VOR indicator.
- ❑ The G1000 glideslope/glidepath indicator is placed near the altimeter for more efficient viewing when pilot is checking altitude during decent.
- ❑ Indicator uses green diamond to represent desired glideslope position so in Figure 5.24 above, the aircraft is on the glideslope of the ILS approach.
- ❑ Indicator uses magenta diamond to represent desired glidepath position so in Figure 5.25 above, the aircraft is on the glidepath of the RNAV/GPS approach.
- ❑ Indicator uses "No GS" to show when the indicator is not receiving the glideslope signal, is too far away from the signal, or is too far from a dependable receiving angle.

The INSET Map

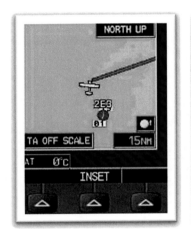

Figure 5.27 – INSET map display with TOPO and TRAFFIC modes

The INSET map is a simplified version of the MFD display map placed on the PFD for situational awareness purposes. It is controlled independently from the MFD moving map with its own controls. It can be turned on and off and has certain features activated and deactivated by softkeys below it on the PFD. It has a separate DCLTR or declutter function from the MFD. Figure 5.27 shows the INSET map in map mode and traffic mode. Figure 5.28 shows the INSET map softkey and shows the various INSET map control softkeys.

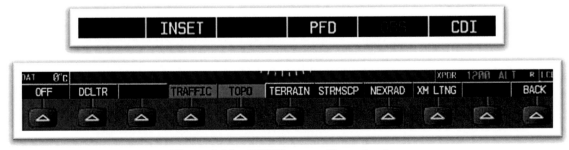

Figure 5.28 – INSET map softkey selections

❑ The INSET Map softkey on the lower left side of the PFD brings up a set of related softkeys.
❑ In general, the INSET Map reflects what is on the MFD moving map but can be displayed at different range resolutions using the PFD RANGE knob.
❑ Softkey selections allow for Terrain, Topography, Traffic, and Weather, if the aircraft is equipped.
❑ A declutter option is available with a DCLTR softkey that removes groups of information from the screen with up to 3 stages of information removed. In general, the screen should be decluttered when in busy terminal areas or when shooting an instrument approach to remove distracting symbols and objects from the screen.

RANGE Knob

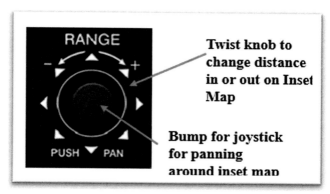

Figure 5.29 – The RANGE knob for map scale and panning

❑ The RANGE knob on the right-hand side of the PFD will zoom the INSET map in or out independently of the large MFD moving map display.
❑ Pressing in on the RANGE knob places the INSET map in the PAN or map pointer mode and can be activated by the joystick function of the RANGE knob.

> *Note: When a waypoint is recognized from the database, it is shown in a highlighted fashion with some limited information about the waypoint listed. This cannot be used to populate Direct To or flight plan menu boxes on the PFD, like it can on the MFD.*

Other Function Boxes and Menus of the PFD

Flight plan Menu Box

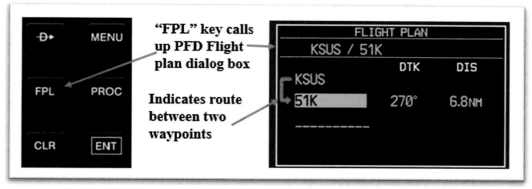

Figure 5.30 – PFD flight plan menu box

The flight plan box on the PFD is very useful for entering a flight plan which could consist of a minimum of 2 and a maximum of dozens of waypoints.

- ❑ The **FPL** key is on the right-hand side of the PFD in the FMS key group.
- ❑ Pressing the **FPL** key will open a box on the lower right-hand corner of the PFD screen.
- ❑ Using the FMS knob, first activate the curser by bumping the FMS knob, then scroll to the desired position, then twist the inner FMS knob to spell the identifier of the desired waypoint, then press ENT to select, and then ENT to confirm the selection.
- ❑ Procedures can be added to this flight plan using the PROC key.
- ❑ The pilot can use the recently used field to highlight and select up to 25 of the most recently used waypoints instead of spelling out waypoints with the twist knob repeatedly.

Direct To Menu Box

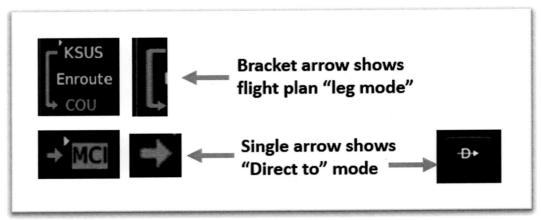

Figure 5.31a – Flight Plan arrow symbology

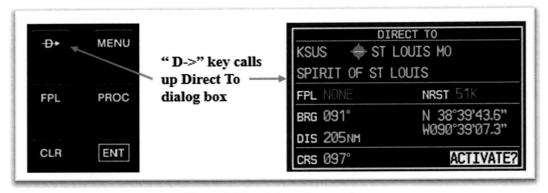

Figure 5.31b – Direct-to menu box

The Direct To box on the PFD is very useful for entering a route which consists of 1 waypoint.

- ❑ The D-> key is on the right-hand side of the PFD in the FMS key group.
- ❑ Pressing the D-> key will create a box on the lower right-hand corner of the PFD screen.
- ❑ Using the FMS knob, first activate the curser by bumping the FMS knob, then scroll to the desired position, then twist the inner FMS knob to spell the identifier of the desired waypoint, then press ENT to select, and then ENT to confirm the selection.

❑ Procedures can be added to this flight plan using the PROC key.
❑ The pilot can use the NRST field to highlight and select up to the 25 nearest airport waypoints instead of spelling out waypoints with the FMS knob repeatedly.

Timer/Reference Menu Box

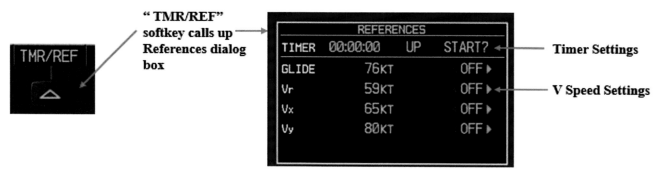

Figure 5.32 – Timer Reference menu box

❑ Can set a count up or count down timer.
❑ Can modify preset airspeed bugs but will denote with asterisk.
❑ TMR/REF softkey will create a box in which a timer can be started or set to count down. Just move the cursor with the outer FMS knob to UP and turn the small knob to select DN, then press ENT.
❑ References to airspeed (Airspeed bugs) for V glide, Vr, Vx, and Vy are also able to be changed in this box but cannot be saved when the aircraft is shut down.

Note: No automatic or programmable audible indication is available to show when a timer expires. If countdown timer is used and it reaches 00:00, then only ALERT flash occurs.

PFD Setup Menu

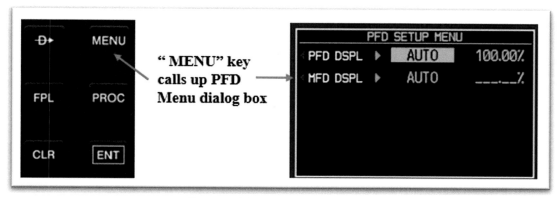

Figure 5.33 – PFD setup menu box

❑ There are two ways to control the brightness of the displays:
❑ Use the aircraft avionics dimming rheostat to brighten/dim the displays or
❑ Manually dim a single display using the PFD Menu setup screen.
❑ On the PFD the brightness of the screens can be controlled manually.
❑ Press the MENU key on the PFD.

❑ Select the brightness mode for the display in question, select manual, press ENT, then turn the inner FMS knob to increase or decrease the brightness of the display. Reverse this process to increase the brightness of the display.

❑ This menu may have to be used in periods of low light such as dawn or dusk.

Note: Displays may flicker if fingers block the light sensor located next to the COM VOL/SQ knob. This is temporary and considered normal.

Procedure Menu Box

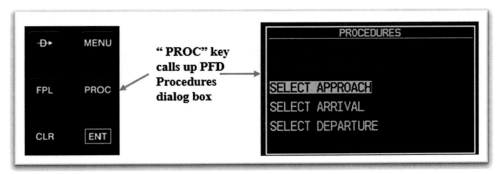

Figure 5.34 – Procedure menu box

This menu box calls up the approaches, arrival procedures, and departure procedures for a particular airport designated in the destination of the Flight plan or Direct To flight plan as an interim destination. Using the Direct To function also allows the pilot to load, activate and to "activate vector to final" an approach procedure at an airport not listed as the destination in the flight plan.

Crew Alert Box

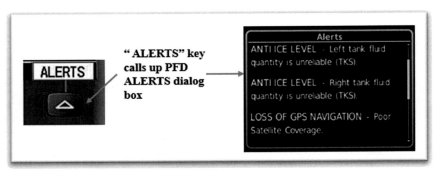

Figure 5.35 – Crew Alert menu box

❑ The far right softkey on the PFD is the warning or alerts key.

❑ When it flashes "warning", "alert", or "caution", that softkey must be pressed and an alerts window will appear on the lower right-hand side of the PFD that will describe what the alert is about.

❑ This is covered in more detail in chapter six.

Note: Because this alert box can hide important information that is needed and there is no audible alert callout to catch the pilot's attention like a warning or caution, they must keep this area of the screen in their scan flow.

Nearest Menu Box

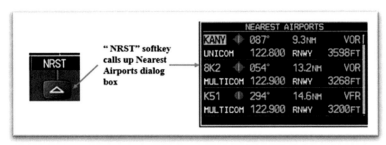

Figure 5.36 – Nearest Menu Box

❑ NRST allows the pilot to select the nearest 25 airports (based upon parameters the pilot can control).
❑ The pilot can also select the frequency and send this to the standby COM highlighted with the blue box by highlighting the frequency and pressing ENT.
   o NRST softkey will create a box which displays the 25 nearest airports to the current position.
   o Move the cursor to the desired airport with the outer FMS knob. Press the **D->** key and press ENT.

The Transponder Control Box

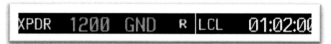

Figure 5.37 – Transponder display box on PFD

This area is described more thoroughly in chapter seven.

❑ A small box located on the bottom right side of the PFD shows the code and the status of the Transponder.
❑ The XPNDR softkey on the bottom of the PFD gives access to change the transponder code.
❑ The code can then be entered manually. If 1200 is desired, the VFR key may be pressed.
❑ Additional modes can also be accessed from this menu.
❑ IDENT softkey can be pressed as requested by ATC.

Note: Double pressing the XPDR key automatically calls up the CODE softkey set.

Data Fields at top of PFD

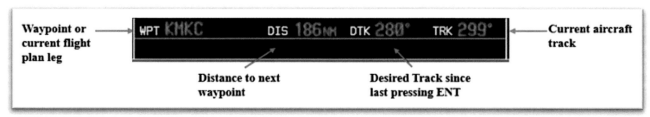

Figure 5.38 – Current waypoint data box bar in the top center of PFD

❑ The data box bar in the top-center of the PFD screen and always depicted in Magenta indicating GPS derived.
❑ Above the flight instruments, the data bar box in the top-center of the screen has information concerning the current course. They are fixed items and cannot be changed.
❑ The pilot should try to get the DTK to match the TRK to correct for the wind.
❑ This is the autopilot's strategy so it makes sense for the pilot, as well.

Autopilot Mode Window

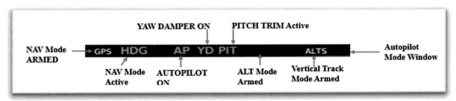

Figure 5.39 – Autopilot Mode data bar on top of PFD

❑ Located under current waypoint data bar on top center of PFD.
❑ This autopilot mode window is the only indication of the status of the autopilot.
❑ Items in Green are ACTIVE which means the autopilot is currently following this mode.
❑ Items in White are ARMED which means the autopilot is preparing to enter this mode when conditions are met.
❑ To change a heading with the autopilot, first bump the heading bug, then twist it to the assigned heading and press the HDG mode of the autopilot.
❑ Autopilot functions will be covered in detail in chapter twelve.

Conclusion

In this chapter, we looked at the main functions of the Primary Flight Display and how it helps the pilot to manage the flight aspects of the G1000 equipped aircraft. By knowing the functions of these menus, keys, knobs, and controls of the PFD, the pilot can most efficiently maintain a proper scan flow and safely operate the TAA aircraft.

Most of the flight instruments and aircraft functions that the pilot has come to know and love in traditional paneled aircraft have been replaced by more efficient and scan friendly portrayals of flight information. By placing information where it is needed when it is needed, the more safely the pilot can operate these aircraft because situational awareness is enhanced. This may take some getting used to, but once it is mastered, the pilot will find that the G1000 is very logical in its layout and a pleasure to fly.

Remember
❑ Most of the primary flight instruments work as expected except for some logical portrayal improvements.
❑ The PFD should always be kept in the pilot's primary scan to catch anomalies.
❑ Keep an eye on the Alert area to observe messages that may have no audible tone.
❑ Set HDG and ALT bugs as reference for all piloting activities.
❑ Watch the DBAR in the HSI as a reference to where the aircraft is in relation to the desired course.

❑ Use autopilot to the pilot's advantage, but monitor it as part of the scan flow to identify anomalies.
❑ Most of the information that will change during the flight will be in the HSI as this provides all lateral guidance to the autopilot in terms of both HDG and NAV reference.
❑ Use the **FPL** key to create flight plans instead of the D-> key except when ATC directs the aircraft to a particular waypoint.

Chapter Debriefing:

We have now covered G1000 Primary Flight Display and along with the knowledge of knobs, keys, and controls learned in chapter two, the pilot should be better prepared to operate most functions of the system using the PFD.

❑ If the pilot understands that the knobs, keys, and controls of the Primary Flight Display are the primary way for the pilot to control various instruments, menu, submenus, and functions, then they should see that the PFD is a very capable unit providing much more timely and relevant information than traditional instruments!
❑ If the pilot understands that the PFD is a very powerful tool for maintaining safe flight, then they will also understand there is a logical flow to accomplish a desired task on the PFD.
❑ If the pilot understands that this system offers a way to integrate the flying tasks with the navigation tasks, then they will also understand that knowing how to get the advanced features out of the system quickly will prevent them from becoming fixated on the display screens keeping operations safer.

If the pilot not only understands these key areas, but also can correlate these major points into their everyday flying skills and apply these skills to the operation of the G1000 aircraft, then they are ready to take the quiz and then move to chapter six!

The Chapter Quiz Scenario

This Chapter Quiz Scenario (CQS) is designed to create a real-world flight situation and use the new knowledge of the PFD to answer some situational questions about how to safely operate their aircraft. The pilot can then determine whether they "understand" and can even "correlate" the material covered with their existing aeronautical knowledge and are prepared to use this information in a way which will enhance operational safety while using the G1000 equipped aircraft.

In this chapter quiz, the pilot will be asked to demonstrate their understanding of the G1000 system Primary Flight Display (PFD) on a flight from Kansas City Downtown airport (KMKC) at an altitude of 2500 feet VFR with ATC flight following to Roosterville, Missouri (0N0), a non-tower-controlled airport. This information is entered into the PFD Flight plan menu box. Consider the following questions about this scenario:

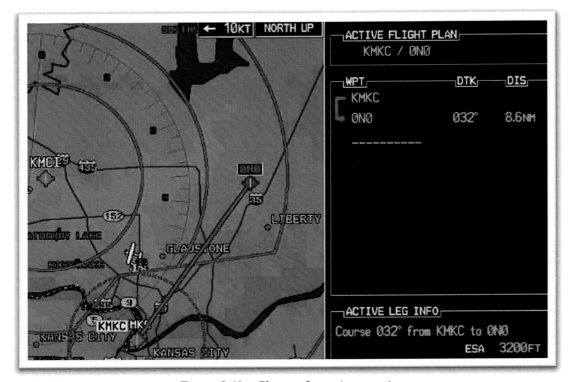

Figure 5.40 – Chapter five quiz scenario

Question 1: While en route to the destination, ATC advises the pilot to make a 30-degree heading change to the right. How would this operation be completed on the G1000 aircraft, if the auto pilot was already engaged in NAV mode?

    a) Use the CRS/BARO knob to set in the new heading in CRS mode.

    b) Bump the HDG knob to center the heading bug, then select HDG mode on the autopilot, then turn the HDG Heading knob right 30 degrees.

    c) Change the heading of the aircraft while carefully scanning for traffic, then make the change on the HDG bug of the autopilot.

Question 2: TC issues a clearance to the pilot to squawk code 4632 and asks them to IDENT. How would this be completed on the G1000?

    a) On the MFD, press the XPNDR softkey twice, press 4632 softkeys, then press ENT.

    b) On the PFD, press the XPNDR softkey, press the CODE softkey, press 4632 softkeys, then press IDENT.

    c) Use the FMS knob to navigate to the Transponder page and enter the requested information.

Question 3: As the pilot continues the flight to the destination, ATC advises them to "remain clear of Class B airspace ahead". Which procedure is correct on how to use the G1000 PFD to help thm?

    a) Adjust the range scale to show the Class B airspace, then use the OBS key with the CRS knob to create an offset course around the airspace.

    b) Adjust the range scale to show the Class B airspace, then add another waypoint to the Flight plan creating a diversion around the airspace.

    c) Both A and B are correct.

Question 4: As the pilot continues the flight to the destination, an airport is observed ahead. Which procedure is correct on how to use the G1000 PFD to help them identify this airport?

    a) Press in the PFD RANGE knob, activate the joystick pointer, and move the pointer on the INSET MAP until the airport highlights on the airport.

    b) Press the NRST softkey on the PFD and look find at the airport on the NRST Menu box.

    c) Both A and B are correct.

Question 5: As the pilot continues the flight to the destination, they decide to dial up a VOR to watch their progress along the route of flight. How can they do this and not lose the NAV lock on the autopilot that is set to tracking the GPS course in the flight plan?

> a) Key in the frequency of the VOR using the NAV frequency selection knob, press the toggle key to make it active in NAV 1 or NAV 2, then on the PFD, press the CDI softkey to read the course on the HSI.
>
> b) Key in the frequency of the VOR using the NAV frequency selection knob, press the toggle key to make it active in NAV 1 or NAV 2, then on the PFD, press OBS and turn the CRS knob to see what radial the aircraft is on.
>
> c) Key in the frequency of the VOR using the NAV frequency selection knob, press the toggle key to make it active in NAV 1 or NAV 2, then on the PFD, press the PFD softkey and then activate BRG pointer 1 to create another pointer on the HSI.

Question 6: As the pilot passes the halfway point to the destination, they decide to see what approaches are available in case the weather deteriorates. What is the best way to do this on the PFD?

> a) Press MENU and select ACTIVATE APPROACH.
>
> b) PRESS PROC and select APPROACH.
>
> c) Press the APPROACH softkey.

Question 7: The weather finally deteriorates, and the pilot decides to proceed to the nearest alternate airport to land and wait. What is the best way to do this on the PFD?

> a) Press NRST softkey and select the closest suitable airport using PROC.
>
> b) Press NRST softkey and select the closest suitable airport using MENU.
>
> c) Press the NRST softkey, bump the curser, scroll down to the NRST field and press D-> and then ENT-ENT.

Grading Criteria:

The pilot will know when they have completed this chapter when they get all the answers correct and demonstrate a solid understanding of the material. When the exam is complete, grade the answers with the answer key in the back of this handbook. Incorrect answers should be researched by going back to the appropriate reference area in the chapter or the Garmin Cockpit Guide that comes with the aircraft. Once the correct answers have been achieved, proceed to the next chapter. Come back to items in this chapter at any time.

Chapter Six: Crew Alerting System

Chapter Objectives:

The objective of this chapter is for the pilot to demonstrate understanding regarding the Crew Alerting System (CAS) of the G1000 by reviewing the content of this chapter. The pilot will then take the chapter quiz at the end which will check their knowledge about the material covered.

Completion Standards:

When this chapter is complete, the pilot will be able to describe and explain the modes of the Crew Alerting System (CAS) of the G1000. The pilot will know when they have met the completion standards of the chapter when they have correctly answered all the quiz questions at the end of this section. If any questions are scored as incorrect, go back to the appropriate reference area in the chapter or the Garmin Cockpit Guide that comes with the aircraft. When the pilot has correctly answered all the chapter quiz questions, then they may proceed to the next chapter.

Crew Alerting System

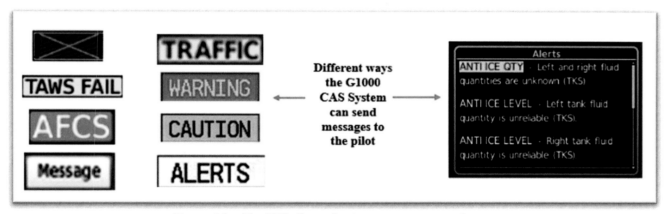

Figure 6.1 – The PFD Crew alerting system message formats

The G1000 is equipped with a system which monitors the LRUs and the systems of the airframe, avionics, and the powerplant and provides real time information regarding the status of these systems. This allows the pilot to make informed decisions about how to cope with a system loss or degradation. Many times, this is the difference between survival and disaster in an emergency because dealing with a pending emergency is always better with time on the pilot's side.

G1000 Faults and Warnings

The G1000 system displays alerts to the pilot in the following ways:

Softkey Annunciation

Figure 6.2 – The PFD Crew alerting softkey

For new alerts, new messages will appear as a blinking softkey, and possibly an audible alert tone, first to catch the pilot's attention. This softkey assumes that something has changed that requires attention. The label indicates the level of the alert (WARNING, CAUTION, and ALERT). When the pilot presses the softkey, they are acknowledging the alert. The softkey then returns to the previous label from the last alert. If the alert softkey is pressed a second time, the text of the message appears.

LRU Failures

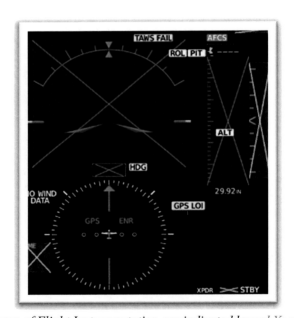

Figure 6.3 – Failures of Flight Instrumentation are indicated by red Xs over the instrument

The pilot needs to know immediately when an LRU has failed or is providing invalid data to the system. When this is a failure of a critical flight instrument, the G1000 must alert the pilot in a way that is unmistakable with a red X. Sometimes this can be resolved by resetting a circuit breaker, even resetting the avionics master switch. A complete reset of the electrical system master switch may seem drastic, but in a dire situation, the pilot may have to try anything to get control back. While trying to resolve critical instrument failures such as these with red Xs, the pilot should fly the aircraft with the standby instruments. The pilot should be aware that certain LRU failures will disable functions of the autopilot and that manual control of the aircraft may be required.

Annunciation window

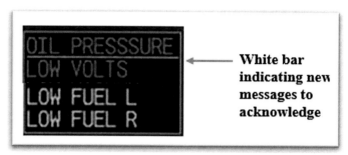

Figure 6.4 – The PFD annunciation window

This window displays colored messages about the system issue. The system uses three different colors: Red, Yellow, and Green. The annunciation window is located on the right side of the display, to the right of the vertical speed and altitude tape. There is room for multiple messages to be displayed at any one time with the warnings on top, yellows next, then greens. There is a white horizontal line that separates the annunciators that are acknowledged from those that are not. Also, the higher the priority of the alert will be the higher the position on the screen. If a problem is resolved, the G1000 will clear the message from the screen.

Alerts Window

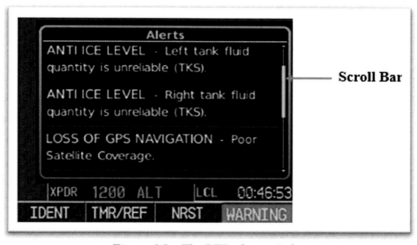

Figure 6.5 – The PFD alerts window

The Alerts window displays text alert messages. There is room for many messages to be displayed in the window and the scroll symbol on the right side indicates that there are more messages to be viewed. To display the alerts window, the pilot must press the ALERTS softkey. Pressing the ALERTS softkey a second time removes the alerts window. When the window is displayed, the pilot may use the outer FMS knob to scroll through the list of alerts that are displayed.

Engine System Annunciations

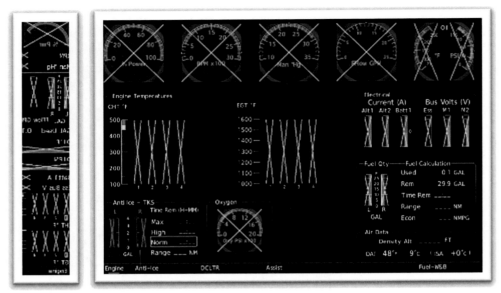

Figure 6.6 – The Engine Information System (EIS) failure annunciations

A large Yellow X appears over engine instruments when a failure of the sensor that provides information to the GEA LRU. These will be discussed more in detail later in the engine management; chapter nine.

Pilot Alerting Message Lights and Tones

The G1000 system uses three alerting systems to warn pilots of failures or to provide information. These levels of alerting are WARNING, CAUTION, and ALERT.

Figure 6.7 – The warning

Definition: <u>Warning</u> -*An aircraft condition which requires the immediate attention of the pilot and if left unresolved, may cause a serious breach in operational safety.*

Annunciation Window Text	Alerts Window Message	Audio Alert
OIL PRES LO	Oil pressure is below 25 psi.	Continuous Aural Tone
FUEL PRES LO *	Fuel pressure is below 14 psi.	Continuous Aural Tone
FUEL PRES HI *	Fuel pressure is greater than 35 psi.	Continuous Aural Tone
ALTERNATOR	Alternator failed. Battery is only electrical source.	Continuous Aural Tone
STARTER ENGD	Starter is engaged.	Continuous Aural Tone
DOOR OPEN	Canopy and/or rear door is not closed and locked.	Continuous Aural Tone
TRIM FAIL	Autopilot automatic trim is inoperative.	Continuous Aural Tone

Figure 6.8 – Warning examples (Courtesy Garmin)

The Warning alert is something that requires immediate attention from the pilot. The warning alert is also accompanied by an annunciation in the annunciation window on the right portion of the PFD display. The text that appears in these windows is RED for a warning. There is a continuous aural tone generated in the their audio system to attract the pilot's attention. If the pilot presses the WARNING softkey it acknowledges the presence of the warning and silences the aural tone.

Note: The pilot should always refer to the Garmin Pilots Cockpit Reference Guide included with the aircraft to determine the best course of action to resolve a system failure.

Figure 6.9 – The caution advisory

Definition: **Caution** *-An aircraft condition which requires the imminent attention of the pilot and if left unresolved, may develop into a warning which could cause a serious breach in operational safety.*

Annunciation Window Text	Alerts Window Message	Audio Alert
L FUEL LOW	Left fuel quantity is less than 3 gallons.	Single Aural Tone
R FUEL LOW	Right fuel quantity is less than 3 gallons.	Single Aural Tone
LOW VOLTS	On-board voltage is below 24 Volts	Single Aural Tone
PITOT FAIL	Pitot heat is inoperative.	Single Aural Tone
PITOT OFF	Pitot heat is off.	Single Aural Tone

Figure 6.10 – Caution examples (Courtesy Garmin)

The Caution alert indicates that an abnormal condition exists on the aircraft that may require the pilot to intervene. The caution alert is also accompanied by an annunciation in the annunciation window, which appears in the color yellow. Also, for a caution the pilot will see a flashing caution softkey and will hear a single aural tone in their audio system. Pressing the softkey acknowledges the caution alert.

Note: The pilot should always refer to the Garmin Pilots Cockpit Reference Guide included with the aircraft to determine the best course of action to resolve a system failure.

Figure 6.11 – The Alert

Definition: **Alert** - *An aircraft condition which requires the attention of the pilot whose action is left to their own discretion.*

Alerts Window Message	Audio Alert
PFD FAN FAIL – The cooling fan for the PFD is inoperative.	None
MFD FAN FAIL – The cooling fan for the MFD is inoperative.	None
GIA FAN FAIL – The cooling fan for the GIAs is inoperative.	None

Figure 6.12 – Alert examples (Courtesy Garmin)

The Alert message is used to provide general information to the pilot. An advisory alert does not show up in the annunciation window but do show up as a softkey that flashes ADVISORY. When the pilot presses the ADVISORY softkey it acknowledges the presence of advisory and displays the text message in the Alerts window. There is no audio tone for the pilot.

Note: Cooling fan advisories have been known to occur when operating at high altitudes or high-density altitudes or when cooling vents have impeded cooling airflow. Cooling fan failures are not generally considered inflight emergencies but the pilot should not initiate a flight with a cooling fan inoperative.

Safe Operating Annunciation

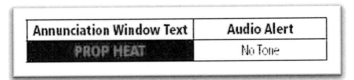

Annunciation Window Text	Audio Alert
PROP HEAT	No Tone

Figure 6.13 – Safe annunciation examples (Courtesy Garmin)

Some aircraft use this to inform the pilot that a system is operating within the safe limitations. These only appear in the annunciation window in green text.

G1000 SYSTEM ANNUNCIATIONS

The pilot can use the Aux-System Status page on the MFD to show the status of all LRUs in the system. Green checks show the pilot an LRU is functioning normally, and a red X indicates that an LRU has failed. Please refer to chapter fourteen for a more specific description on how to deal with these situations.

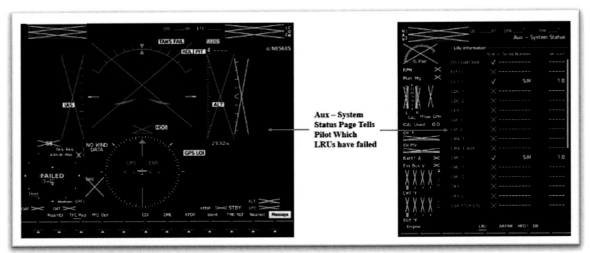

Figure 6.14 – System failure annunciations and the Aux – System Status page

Conclusion

In this chapter, we looked at the crew alerting system as a way for the pilot to understand whether the G1000 system is operating correctly and to what extent they might have to deal with system degradation or failure. An important point is that the pilot must always keep the crew alerting panel within their scan flow. Many pilots have fallen victim to the trap that a message light is blinking, and they are too slow to notice it or react to it giving up precious time they may have needed to execute a viable option. When a system fails such as a cooling fan, pull the circuit breaker (if one is provided) and wait for up to one minute and retry the circuit breaker to see if the system resets. Inflight cooling fan failures do not constitute an emergency unless other failures are also present.

Remember

- ❑ A **blinking** message indication must be acknowledged by the pilot.
- ❑ **Green** messages are just alerting the pilot that a system is operating normally.
- ❑ **White Alert** messages contain information that the pilot probably needs to know.
- ❑ **Yellow caution** messages imply a degrading condition and if not dealt with may eventually lead to a red warning.
- ❑ **Red Warnings** mean that something has failed that needs to be addressed immediately.

Chapter Debriefing:

We have now covered the Garmin G1000 crew alerting system and the pilot should now see that a technically advanced aircraft (TAA) requires a thorough knowledge of the warnings, alerts, and cautions, to properly detect and respond to system annunciations in a timely manner before they turn into a safety or operational issue.

- ❑ If the pilot understands that the G1000 crew alerting system uses a variety of flashing softkeys, message boxes, and color codes to tell them about system status, then they will understand why it is so important to keep this area of the PFD in their scan flow.
- ❑ If the pilot understands that the differences between the colors of messages indicate the level of severity, then they will also understand that addressing a problem when it first appears as an Alert is a far safer technique than waiting until it is a Warning.
- ❑ If the pilot understands that the G1000 uses an information monitoring system to determine whether data is valid before displaying it on the screen, then they will understand that the system automatically removes invalid or suspect data from the screen to prevent them from using the data until it is deemed accurate.

If the pilot not only understands these three areas, but also can correlate these major points into their everyday flying and apply these skills to the operation of their G1000 aircraft, then they are ready to take the quiz and then to move to chapter seven!

Chapter Six Quiz: Crew Alerting System

The Chapter Quiz Scenario

This Chapter Quiz Scenario (CQS) is designed to suggest a real-world flight situation and use the new knowledge of the G1000 crew alerting system to answer some situational questions about how to safely operate the G1000 equipped aircraft. The pilot can then "correlate" the material just covered with existing aeronautical knowledge which will enhance operational safety while operating the G1000 equipped aircraft.

In this chapter quiz, the pilot will be asked to demonstrate their understanding of the G1000 system crew alerting system on a flight from Roosterville, Missouri airport (0N0) to Clay County airport (KGPH), a tower-controlled airport. Consider the following questions about this scenario:

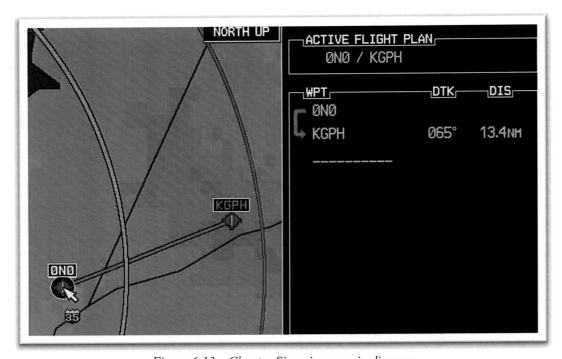

Figure 6.13 – Chapter Six quiz scenario diagram

Question 1: While flying enroute, the pilot notices a red flashing softkey in the bottom right corner of the PFD. What level of alert is being displayed?

    a) **CAUTION**

    b) **WARNING**

    c) **ADVISORY**

Question 2: What should the pilot do next with the red flashing softkey in order to determine their options?

   a)   Press the CLR key to see if the system resets.

   b)   Look on the PFD next to the Vertical Speed indicator to see what system has failed.

   c)   Press the ADVISORY key on the MFD to get a status of LRUs.

Question 3: What are the three levels of ALERTS used in the G1000 system?

   a)   CAUTION, DANGER, ALERT

   b)   WARNING, ALERT, CAUTION

   c)   ALERT, ADVISORY, CAUTION

Question 4: How is a WARNING acknowledged by the pilot?

   a)   Looking at the screen and pressing enter.

   b)   Pointing at the WARNING alert with the RNG knob pointer.

   c)   Pressing the WARNING softkey.

Question 5: How will the G1000 system display the information when a system or component fails?

   a)   A red X over the failed component removing all information from the item deemed inaccurate.

   b)   Removing the component from the display.

   c)   There is no warning of this.

Question 6: Where will the pilot be able to look up the status of a failed component?

   a)   The MFD Aux – System Status page.

   b)   The PFD MENU box.

   c)   The SD Card can be removed to show the failure data.

Grading Criteria:

The pilot will know when they have completed this chapter when they get all the answers correct and demonstrate a solid understanding of the material. When the exam is complete, grade the answers with the answer key in the back of this handbook. Incorrect answers should be researched by going back to the appropriate reference area in the chapter or the Garmin Cockpit Guide that comes with the aircraft. Once all correct answers have been achieved, proceed on to the next chapter. Come back to items in this chapter at any time.

Chapter Seven: G1000 Transponder

Chapter Objectives:

The objective of this chapter is for the pilot to demonstrate understanding regarding the G1000 Transponder and its functions by reviewing the content of this chapter. The pilot will then take the chapter quiz at the end which will check their knowledge about the material covered.

Completion Standards:

When this chapter is complete, the pilot will be able to describe and explain functions and modes of the G1000 Transponder. The pilot will know when they have met the completion standards of the chapter when they have correctly answered all the quiz questions at the end of this section. If any questions are scored as incorrect, go back to the appropriate reference area in the chapter or the Garmin Cockpit Guide that comes with the aircraft. When the pilot has correctly answered all the chapter quiz questions, then they may proceed to the next chapter.

The GTX Digital Mode S Transponder

Figure 7.1 – Garmin GTX Transponder LRU control box

The GTX Transponder functions from within the confines of the Primary Flight Display. It has no separate control box or knobs within the cockpit other than on the PFD. In addition to the basic transponder mode C functions, the Mode S Transponder supports specific ATC interrogations and data exchange due to a specific unique code assigned to that aircraft. Newer G1000 installations also feature a GTX 335/345R remote control Transponder LRU to support ADS-B in/out functions.

Transponder Functions and Support

Mode A

This is referred to as 4096 transponder mode. This means that the Transponder allows for the processing of 4 digits ranging from the numbers 0 to 7 and has 4096 possible combinations of codes. The VFR squawk code of 1200 is an example of a 4096 code. When the Transponder is set to the "ON" position rather than the "ALT" position, it is generating a mode A signal and only supplies ATC the transponder code. This information is encoded on the radar signal and sent back to ATC as a reply to their radar system interrogation signal. This discrete code will appear on the ATC radar scope to help distinguish the aircraft from others. When ATC issues a special code to put into the Transponder, it is imperative that this is done in accordance with their instructions. Only press IDENT when instructed by ATC.

Mode C

Mode C allows for the automatic encoding of altitude or flight level information calibrated to a pressure altitude setting of 29.92. This information is sent back to ATC radar for display on their radar screens so they can distinguish your aircraft altitude from other aircraft. When the Transponder is set to the "ALT" position, it is generating a mode C signal and supplies ATC the transponder code and the altitude.

Mode S

Mode S Transponders are the current technology level supported in the G1000. While some of the newer G1000 equipped aircraft have the GTX 335R remote mounted Transponder that supports ADS-B "out" functions transmitting the aircraft altitude, speed, and position information to ATC and other aircraft, most aircraft manufacturers install the Garmin GTX 345R remote mounted Transponder which supports all those functions plus ADS-B "in" data which allows other traffic to be displayed on the INSET map and MFD map pages. Mode S Transponders with ADS-B receive weather information from the Flight Information Systems (FIS-B) service. The weather products transmitted via FIS-B include Airmen's Meteorological Information (AIRMETs), Significant Meteorological Information (SIGMETs), Convective SIGMETs, METARs CONUS NEXRAD, Regional NEXRAD, NOTAMs, PIREPs, Special Use Airspace (SUA) Status, Terminal Aerodrome Forecast (TAFs), and Winds & Temperatures Aloft. The G1000 displays these weather products using a few different screens on the Multi-function Display and these functions will be covered in chapter ten.

> *Note: Pilots should understand the configuration of the G1000 aircraft they fly so they can properly determine the limitations of the traffic advisories their systems will display. Because ADS-B is still not required of all aircraft, pilots should remain vigilant for aircraft in their vicinity using visual surveillance of their surroundings.*

Transponder Display

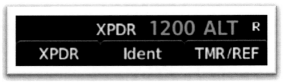

Figure 7.2 – Garmin GTX Transponder display on PFD

The Transponder status is in the bottom right corner of the PFD. The squawk code and the status of the Transponder is shown. GND will be shown if the Transponder is in ground mode, and ALT will automatically appear when the aircraft exceeds liftoff speed, and the display will switch to green digits indicating the Transponder is active. If the Transponder does not switch to altitude encoding, then it can be turned on from the Transponder softkeys depicted in figure 7.3.

> *Note: Transponder always starts up squawking code from the last flight.*

Transponder Operating Modes

Figure 7.3 – Garmin GTX Transponder PFD softkeys

ALT Mode

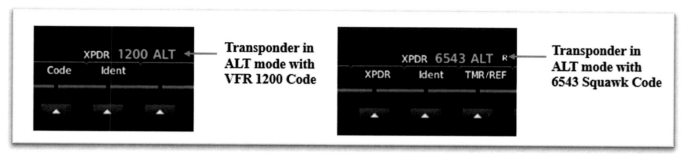

Figure 7.4 – Garmin GTX Transponder in ALT mode

Alt - Transponder is operating and is sending "Mode A" and "Mode C" information to ATC. ALT is automatically selected as soon as the aircraft is operating at a groundspeed greater than the aircraft liftoff speed. If it is operating at less than liftoff speed, then the aircraft remains invisible to airborne radar and aircraft operating TCAS. It is however in Ground mode so it would be visible to ATC ground surveillance RADAR.

ON Mode

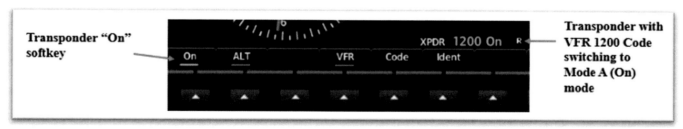

Figure 7.5 – Garmin GTX Transponder squawking 1200

On – Transponder is operating in "Mode A" but is not sending "Mode C" information, so ATC is not receiving any altitude information. ATC could instruct an aircraft to "Turn off Mode C" when the aircraft is generating incorrect or faulty Mode C altitudes.

Standby Mode

Figure 7.6 – Garmin Transponder in standby mode

Standby – Transponder is not sending or receiving any information to ATC. It is disabled. ATC could instruct an aircraft to "Squawk Standby" when flying in formation with other aircraft.

GROUND Mode

Figure 7.7 – Garmin GTX Transponder squawking 6543 in GROUND mode

Ground - Transponder is operating and is sending GROUND tag Mode C information to ATC. This tells the ATC equipment that the aircraft is still on the ground and reduces RADAR screen clutter and controller workload by not mixing traffic alerts with other aircraft that may already be airborne above them. Special Ground Control RADAR at certain facilities will be able to paint the aircraft in the taxiway system so that they can schedule and sequence traffic releases to departure control based upon terminal release of pending traffic.

PFD Transponder Softkey Control Keys

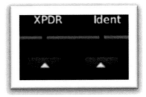

Figure 7.8 – Garmin GTX Transponder PFD softkeys

This is the screen that we see as a default on all PFD softkey selection options. This is the main point of entry into all Transponder functions. The XPDR softkey takes the pilot to other options. The IDENT softkey is used by the pilot when instructed to IDENT by Air Traffic Control (ATC).

Garmin Display Unit (GDU) Transponder Control

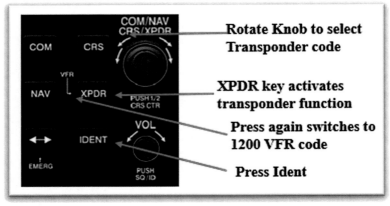

Figure 7.9 – Garmin Control Unit (GCU) Transponder control functions on Perspective Plus

If the aircraft is equipped with a Garmin Control Unit (GCU) such as on a Cirrus aircraft, there are Transponder control functions located on the GCU. Press the XPDR key to enter transponder control mode. Press the XPDR key again to switch to 1200 VFR mode or a second time to switch back to the previous code. The pilot can rotate the inner knob to dial in the first two digits of the assigned Transponder code. Then turn the outer knob to move the cursor to the second two digits. Now use the inner knob to sequentially dial in the last two digits. The Transponder will timeout after 10 seconds of pilot inactivity if the operation is not complete returning to the previous Transponder code.

Note: It is much easier to enter a transponder code using the numeric keypad of the GDU than to use the COM/NAV/CRS/XPDR knob located on the GCU.

PFD Transponder Functions

Figure 7.10 – Garmin GTX XPDR softkey

To enter the Transponder control functions, press XPDR. This converts the PFD softkeys into the set 2 Transponder control softkeys.

Note: Pressing XPDR twice (double pressing) is a shortcut straight to the code softkey set

Figure 7.11 – Garmin GTX Transponder set 2 softkeys

Press VFR to squawk the universal **VFR code 1200**. Since this is a complete action, the PFD screen immediately returns to the main PFD softkey set 1.

Figure 7.12 – Garmin GTX Transponder VFR softkey

When operating on an IFR flight Plan or when receiving flight following from ATC, they issue a discrete transponder code. To enter that specific code assigned by ATC, we press the CODE softkey.

Figure 7.13 – Garmin GTX BKSP backspace key

The code can then be entered manually. The BKSP softkey will clear any mistakes made on the code. Make sure to press the final of the 4-digit codes. Failure to enter all four digits within 10 seconds will result in a timeout and the transponder code will return to the previously set code.

Note: Failure to enter the remaining digits of the 4-digit code within a reasonable timeframe may result in a function timeout and the system will revert to the previous code.

Figure 7.14 – Garmin GTX BACK key

The BACK softkey will return to the previous PFD menu softkey set.

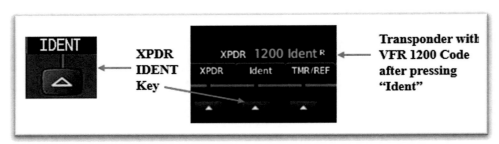

Figure 7.15 – Garmin GTX Transponder IDENT softkey

The IDENT softkey should only be pressed when requested by ATC. The IDENT softkey is also displayed on the default PFD menu and is located on the GCU on aircraft with this LRU installed.

Entering ATC Assigned Transponder Codes

Figure 7.13 – Garmin GTX transponder code softkey

Figure 7.14 – Garmin GTX transponder code softkey set 3

Pressing the Code softkey in Transponder softkey set 2 brings up the Code keyboard set 3. The pilot can enter the code issued by ATC here. Any errors of input, the pilot can use the Backspace key to erase an errant code and key in the correct code. Remember that there are only 4 digits to a code. Once 4 digits are entered the code keyboard disappears and returns to Transponder code set 2. If IDENT is entered after the 4 digits are entered, then the screen returns to the main PFD softkey set 1.

> *Note: The Transponder function times out after approximately 10 seconds of pilot inactivity and will return to the previous code.*

- ❑ The XPNDR softkey on the bottom of the PFD gives access to additional softkeys which change the transponder code and change the operating mode of the Transponder.
- ❑ The VFR softkey will automatically change the squawk code to 1200.
- ❑ Pressing the CODE softkey will display the corresponding numbers to enter a different squawk code when assigned by ATC.

Conclusion

In this chapter, we looked at the operation of the G1000 Transponder with its controls on the PFD. The pilot will find that operating this unit is essentially the same as the Transponders on traditional aircraft with the exception that many of the functions are automatic. The operation of the TIS-B and ADS-B traffic reporting is sent to the G1000 displays and is self-contained within the system, but the display of that information is spread out across the rest of the system in terms of audible and visual Traffic Alerts and display boxes when enabled. We will cover this in much more depth in chapter ten.

Remember

- ❑ The Transponder functions exclusively on the PFD and is driven solely by softkeys unless a GCU is installed.
- ❑ The mode S features of the Transponder function only when the ATC radar facility provides mode S signal support.
- ❑ Pressing the XPDR key twice in a row brings up the CODE softkey set.
- ❑ Pressing IDENT acknowledges all keystrokes and codes, and goes back to the home PFD softkey set.
- ❑ The Transponder always starts up with the squawk code from the last flight – always check this in the startup flow!

Chapter Debriefing

We have now covered the area of the G1000 Transponder system and the pilot should have a good understanding of its operation modes and how they are different from a traditional Transponder.

- ❑ Now that the pilot understands that the G1000 Transponder operates like other traditional Transponders, they will understand that it is easy to use and very flexible!
- ❑ Now that the pilot understands that the G1000 Transponder offers mode S functionality that depends upon special equipment at the ground radar facility, they will also understand that this mode S can create a false sense of security until it has data latency errors and delays.
- ❑ Now that the pilot understands that this Transponder is controlled exclusively from the PFD, then the pilot will also understand why knowing that the XPDR and IDENT softkeys are available in

nearly every PFD screen so that they have ready access to its controls regardless of where they are in the PFD operation.

If the pilot not only understands these three areas, but also can correlate these major points into their everyday flying and apply these skills to the operation of their G1000 aircraft, then they are ready to take the quiz and then to move to chapter eight!

Chapter Seven Quiz: Garmin GTX Transponder

The Chapter Quiz Scenario

This Chapter Quiz Scenario (CQS) is designed to suggest a real-world flight situation and use this new knowledge of the G1000 Transponder to answer some situational questions about how to safely operate the G1000. The pilot can then determine whether they "understand" and can even "correlate" the material covered with their existing aeronautical knowledge and are prepared to use this information in a way which will enhance the operational safety when flying the G1000 equipped aircraft.

In this chapter quiz, imagine a VFR flight on a cross country from Clay County Regional airport (KGPH) airport back to Kansas City International Airport (KMCI). Consider the following questions about this scenario:

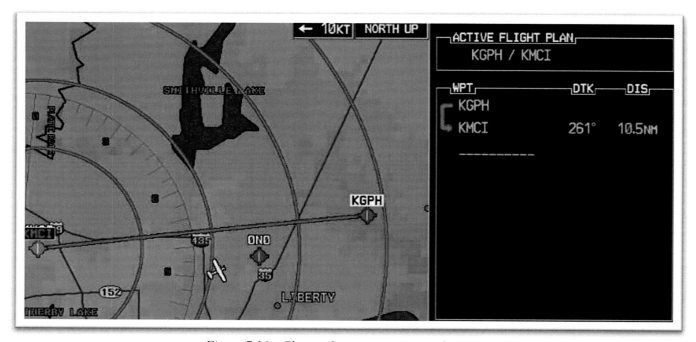

Figure 7.16 – Chapter Seven quiz scenario diagram

Question 1: How does the pilot activate the ALT mode after takeoff and how do they verify that it is properly sending mode C Altitude to ATC?

    a) **Activate ALT by pressing XPDR and CODE prior to takeoff.**

    b) **The G1000 will automatically turn the ALT on after liftoff and the ALT readout will appear in the Transponder status window in Green.**

    c) **We can check ALT readout on the airspeed tape on the PFD screen to make sure that ALT was turned on at 30 knots.**

Question 2: During the flight, ATC requests the pilot to IDENT. What must be done to IDENT?

    a) Press the **IDENT** key **on the PFD softkey that is available in all modes of PFD operation.**

    b) Press the **XPNDR** key **on the MFD.**

    c) Press the **XPNDR** key **then the IDENT** key **on the MFD.**

Question 3: The pilot has contacted ATC and requested flight following and has been instructed to "squawk 2146". How does the pilot comply with ATC instructions?

    a) Press **XPDR** and then the **IDENT** key twice.

    b) Press the **XPNDR** softkey on the PFD twice and enter the proper code but do not press **IDENT.**

    c) Press the **MAN SQ** key on the audio panel and turn the **FMS** knob to enter the proper code.

Question 4: How does the G1000 system show traffic and provide alerts of traffic conflicts?

    a) **Uploads traffic from RADAR signal.**

    b) **Downloads traffic from GDL 69 datalink.**

    c) **Displays ADS-B traffic from the GTX 344/345R Transponder.**

Question 5: What code will appear in the Transponder display window when the aircraft is first powered up with the avionics master switch?

    a) **A blank code.**

    b) **A code of 1200.**

    c) **The code that was used from the last flight.**

Grading Criteria:

The pilot will know when they have completed this chapter when they get all the answers correct and demonstrate a solid understanding of the material. When the exam is complete, grade the answers with the answer key in the back of this handbook. Incorrect answers should be researched by going back to the appropriate reference area in the chapter or the Garmin Cockpit Guide that comes with the aircraft. Once all correct answers have been achieved, proceed on to the next chapter. Come back to items in this chapter at any time.

Chapter Eight: G1000 Audio Panel

Chapter Objectives:

The objective of this chapter is for the pilot to demonstrate understanding regarding the G1000 Audio Panel by reviewing the content of this chapter. The pilot will then take the chapter quiz at the end which will check their knowledge about the material covered.

Completion Standards:

When this chapter is complete, the pilot will be able to describe and explain functions and modes of the G1000 Audio Panel. The pilot will know when they have met the completion standards of the chapter when they have correctly answered all the quiz questions at the end of this section. If any questions are scored as incorrect, go back to the appropriate reference area in the chapter or the Garmin Cockpit Guide that comes with the aircraft. When the pilot has correctly answered all the chapter quiz questions, then they may proceed to the next chapter.

The G1000 Integrated Audio Panel Overview

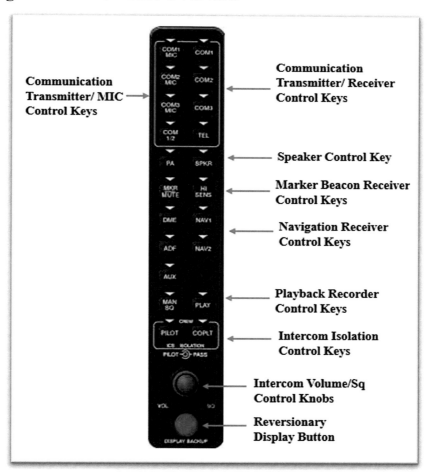

Figure 8.1 – The GMA 1347D Audio Panel functional overview

This audio panel shown in Figure 8.1 is installed on many G1000 aircraft installations and is typically installed between the PFD and the MFD. On larger aircraft that have three screens consisting of a PFD for the pilot and the copilot, there will be two audio panels installed next to each PFD, so each pilot has ready access to its functions.

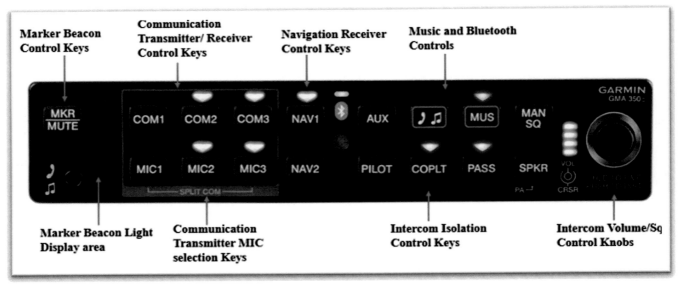

Figure 8.2 – The GMA 350C Audio Panel functional overview

This audio panel configuration shown in Figure 8.2 is installed on some G1000 installations such as the Cirrus SR20 and the SR22. Cirrus chose to install this audio panel to take advantage of existing pilots' comfort with traditional audio panels among other reasons. The functions of this horizontal audio panel are similar to the ones that will be described below for the GMA 1347D vertical audio panel.

This GMA 1347D digital audio panel is similar to many modern audio panels except that it controls digital signal communications between the PFD and the MFD display units and it features a Bluetooth controlled audio system for digital streaming. When a selection is made, the light above that option will illuminate in the shape of a triangle ▼ pointing at the function. When a particular function is active, that light blinks ▼.

The Audio Panel is divided into several groups depending upon the functions that it performs.

The G1000 GMA 1347D Audio Panel Functions

Communication (COM) Audio Controls

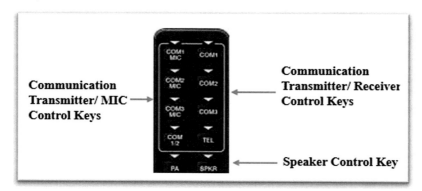

Figure 8.3 – The GMA 1347D Audio Panel COM control key group

This control group facilitates the operations of COM 1, COM 2, the combination of both in split COM mode, and controls which COM radio is active on the microphone.

- ❑ Transceiver audio selector keys (COM 1, COM 2, COM3) - These keys select the desired transceiver audio. More than one radio may be monitored at one time. The ▼ light above the active source will be illuminated.
- ❑ Transmitter (AUDIO/MIC) selection keys (COM 1 MIC, COM 2 MIC, COM3 MIC) - These keys select the desired transmitter and then receive audio for that transceiver. The audio is automatically selected for the appropriate transmitter when the key is depressed. There is no need to depress the audio key for the selected transmitter. Only one transmitter can be selected at any one time (exception: COM ½)
- ❑ Split COM key (COM 1/2) -Pressing the COM 1/2 key selects the split COM function. During split COM operation, the COM 1, COM 1 MIC, COM 2 and COM 2 MIC keys are active. When the COM 1/2 key is selected, COM 1 is used by the pilot for transmission and COM 2 is used by the copilot. The COM 1 MIC ▼ annunciator blinks when the pilot's microphone is keyed and the COM 2 MIC annunciator blinks when the copilot's microphone is keyed. In this mode, both the pilot and the copilot can transmit simultaneously over separate radios. The pilot can still monitor COM3, NAV 1, NAV 2, DME, ADF, AUX and MKR audio as selected, but the copilot is only able to monitor COM 2. Split COM mode is cancelled by pressing the COM ½ key again.
- ❑ Dedicated telephone interface key (TEL) - The GMA 1347D contains a dedicated telephone interface. It is controlled by the TEL key but only works if an "Air to Ground" telephone system is installed.

Navigation (NAV) Audio Controls

Figure 8.4 – The GMA 1347D Audio Panel NAV control key group

This control group allows the pilot to direct the operations of NAV 1, NAV 2, DME, ADF, and Auxiliary audio that might be connected to the system separately from the G1000. The ▼ light above the active source will be illuminated.

- ❑ Aircraft radio audio selector keys (NAV 1, NAV 2, ADF, DME, AUX) - By pressing the DME, ADF, AUX, NAV 1, or NAV 2 one can select and deselect the radio source. Selected audio can be heard over the headset and or speakers. These audio keys can be selected individually or together in any combination.
- ❑ Passenger address key (PA) - By pressing the PA key the passenger address function is activated. When the PA function is activated the Push-to-talk (PTT) must be used to deliver PA announcements over the headsets.
- ❑ Speaker key (SPKR) - Speaker audio is selected by the pilot by pressing the SPKR key. The speaker audio is automatically muted when the PTT switch is keyed. Adjustment of the speaker volume by the pilot is not available.

Intercom Controls including Cockpit Recorder

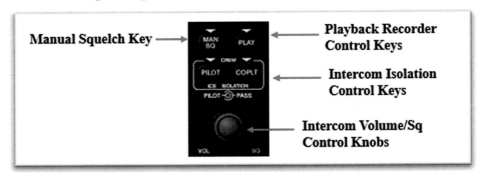

Figure 8.5 – The GMA 1347D Audio Panel Intercom control key group

This control group allows the pilot to direct the operations of the cockpit intercom, the isolation of the pilot and the copilot from the rest of the passengers, and the cockpit voice recorder which automatically records all incoming communication transmissions in discrete memory blocks for a total of up to 2 ½ minutes.

Figure 8.6 – The GMA1347 Audio Panel VOL/SQ knob

❑ Volume/squelch knob (VOL/SQ) - Intercom volume can be adjusted by turning one of the concentric knobs located near the bottom of the audio panel. The small knob adjusts the pilot's ICS volume. The large knob adjusts the ICS volume for the copilot and passengers. Pressing the VOL/SQ knob switches between volume and squelch adjustment (after pressing the MAN SQ key). When the unit is in volume adjustment mode, the VOL indicator on the lower left of the VOL/SQ knob is lit and volume can be adjusted. When the unit is in squelch mode, the SQ indicator on the lower right of the VOL/SQ knob is lit and squelch level can be adjusted.

❑ Intercom manual squelch key (MAN SQ) - Manual Squelch mode can be activated by pressing the MAN SQ key. This allows the listener to override the automatic squelch system, which might be required when there is unusual noise in the cockpit such as the window being opened. Pressing the VOL/SQ knob toggles between volume and squelch adjustment. When the unit is in squelch mode, the SQ indicator on the lower right of the VOL/SQ knob is lit and squelch threshold level can be adjusted. The small knob adjusts the pilot's squelch level, the large knob adjusts the copilot and passenger squelch level.

Additional Options Available

❑ AUX - The GMA 1347D provides for an entertainment input which allows audio from outside sources to be played over the intercom system. There are two types of playback: Muted music and Unmuted music. (Note: Requires either a Bluetooth device to stream media or a stereo audio cable to connect a playback device to the aircraft to function independent of the GDL69 datalink.)
  o Muted music is available to the pilot and copilot during normal intercom operations. It is muted anytime there is audio from the aircraft radio, marker beacons, or intercom system. – Unmuted music is available only to the passengers and is never muted.
❑ Some aircraft models have passenger music volume controls installed.

Figure 8.7 – The GMA 1347D Playback recorder

❑ Digital recording playback key (PLAY) - The GMA 1347D provides a digital clearance recorder with playback capability. The length of playback is up to several minutes of COM signal recording. Each separate COM radio transmission is recorded in separate memory positions.
❑ Signals from all the selected COM radios are recorded and can be played back in reverse order. After the recording time limit is reached, the recorder begins recording over the stored memory positions, starting from the oldest one. These digital recordings are automatically cleared upon power off.
  o Each time the play key is pressed the next oldest recording position will be played until the storage limit is reached. While in playback mode the annunciator is illuminated above the PLAY key.

o The ▼ light above the active source will flash during playback.
o Pressing the Marker Mute key stops playback.
o Any new incoming COM transmissions automatically stops playback and recording starts again.
o All recorded data is lost after shutdown and power is turned off to the system.

Figure 8.8 – The GMA1347D intercom isolation keys

❏ Intercom system (ICS) isolation keys (PILOT, COPLT) - Four isolation modes are available: ALL, PILOT, COPILOT and CREW.
o When only the PILOT key is selected: The pilot can hear the selected radios, and muted music. The passengers can hear unmuted music, and the copilot and passengers can communicate with each other.
o When only the COPLT key is selected: The copilot is isolated from everyone else. The pilot and passengers can hear the selected radios and communicate with each other. In this mode, the pilot can hear muted music, and the passengers can hear unmuted music.
o When both the PILOT and COPLT keys are selected: Both the pilot and copilot can hear the selected radios and communicate with each other, while the passengers can only communicate with each other and hear unmuted music.

Reversionary Backup Controls

Figure 8.9 – The GMA 1347D Reversionary mode key

Reversionary mode key (DISPLAY BACKUP) - This control key is located on the bottom of the display and controls the operation of the G1000 Display Units from either normal mode or reversionary mode. In reversionary mode, the screens display identical information. This includes engine instrumentation but forces the removal of the moving map display on the MFD and the INSET display on the PFD.

Figure 8.10 – The GMA 1347D Reversionary mode duplicating screens

In case of a display failure, the Reversionary mode can be activated by pressing the DISPLAY BACKUP located at the bottom of the audio panel or between the GDUs on a Cirrus. The Reversionary mode operation displays important flight and engine information on both the PFD and MFD. While in reversionary mode, the INSET map cannot be displayed on the PFD on the left side as the engine controls go there. The Inset map will move to the right side of the PFD until another menu box is required by pressing FMS keys. Additionally, the MFD will not function in moving map mode but it will display the Inset map on the far right lower corner.

Note: In case of power loss to one of the GDU display units, the remaining GDU will automatically default to reversionary mode.

Operating the screens in the Reversionary mode occurs in the following circumstances:

❑ Automatic reversion by the G1000 computer when it senses that the PFD is not in service or has suffered a power loss.
❑ Manual reversion, by pressing the red key when the pilot determines that something is wrong with the PFD display and the computer did not detect it.
❑ Manual reversion, by pressing the red key when the pilot determines removing the MFD information enhances flight safety such as operating in the traffic pattern with a flight instructor, etc.
❑ During takeoff and landing placing the engine instrumentation in front of the pilot.

Marker Beacon Controls

Figure 8.11 – The GMA 1347D Audio Panel COM control key group

This control group allows the operate of the audio portion of the marker beacon receiver.

- ❑ Marker beacon receiver audio select/mute key (MKR/MUTE) - The receiver detects the three (3) marker tones, outer, middle, and inner, and illuminates the appropriate marker beacon indicators located on the upper left of the altimeter tape on the PFD. The outer marker is indicated with a blue indicator, the middle marker with an amber indicator and the inner marker with a white indicator. When the MKR/MUTE key is selected, the annunciator light illuminates, and the audio signal can be heard over the speaker or headsets during marker reception.
- ❑ The GMA 1347D provides a marker audio muting capability. When the MKR/MUTE key is illuminated and a marker beacon tone is received, pressing the MKR/MUTE key mutes the audio but does not affect the annunciators. The audio returns when the next marker signal is received.
- ❑ Marker beacon receiver high sensitivity key (HI SENS) - The HI SENS function is used to receive a weak or earlier indication of the marker beacon during an approach. HI SENS can be pressed for increased marker beacon signal sensitivity.
- ❑ The marker beacon display light on the PFD cannot be turned off.

Conclusion

In this chapter, we looked at the functions of the GMA1347D Audio Panel and how it controls the communications of the Audio system in the aircraft and directs the audio of the NAV and COM system. The functions of the GMA 350C audio panel work in a manner similar as the vertical GMA 1347D. We also learned about the Reversionary Display key which controls the display unit behavior in the event of an emergency or any time the pilot wants to limit the information on the screen, such as when entering the traffic pattern or when flying with a flight instructor.

Remember

- ❑ Autopilot cannot be used if the GMA 1347D is disabled or turned off due to the FAA requirement to hear audible alarms.
- ❑ The ▼ light above an item indicates that it is active.
- ❑ The ▼ light blinking above an item indicates that it is active.
- ❑ The Reversionary display key is an important part of the emergency response to display failures.

Chapter Debriefing:

We have now covered the area of the GMA 1347D Audio Panel and the pilot should now understand how this system controls the audio of the entire G1000 system.

- ❑ Now that the pilot understands that the G1000 uses the GMA 1347D (or the GMA 350C on certain aircraft) as a control of digital audio information flow between the display units, they will also understand that recognizing the main groups of keys on the audio panel can ensure that they do not accidentally disable a radio that they meant to listen to.
- ❑ Now that the pilot understands why the Red Reversionary key is their first line of defense in reducing distracting information in the cockpit when they need to concentrate, then they should also understand that the system can do the same thing automatically if it detects a display unit LRU failure.
- ❑ Now that the pilot understands that the cockpit playback recorder records all incoming radio transmissions, then they should understand that pressing the PLAY key repeatedly will allow them to move backwards to review previous ATC transmissions in order of receipt.

Now that the pilot understands these key areas about the audio panel, they should be able to correlate these major points into their everyday flying skills and apply these skills to the operation of the G1000 aircraft. It's time to take the quiz and then to move to chapter nine!

Chapter Eight Quiz: The G1000 Audio Panel

The Chapter Quiz Scenario

This Chapter Quiz Scenario (CQS) is designed to portray a real-world flight situation and use the pilot's new knowledge of the G1000 to answer some situational questions about how to safely operate their aircraft. They can then determine whether they can correlate the material covered with their existing aeronautical knowledge and are prepared to use this information in a way which will enhance operational safety while flying the G1000 equipped aircraft.

In this chapter quiz, the pilot will be asked to demonstrate their understanding of the Garmin GMA 1347D Audio Panel and the role it plays in this flight scenario from Kansas City International Airport (KMCI) to Kansas City Downtown airport (KMKC). Consider the following questions about this scenario:

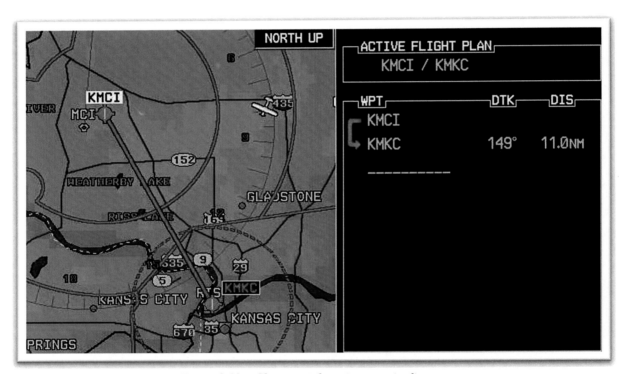

Figure 8.12 – Chapter eight quiz scenario diagram

Question 1: As the pilot approaches their destination airport, they want to listen to the ATIS while maintaining contact with approach control. How is the second frequency selected on the audio panel?

    a) Pressing the COM/MIC key for the other radio.

    b) Pressing the COM key for the radio tuned to ATIS.

    c) Pressing the MKR/MUTE key.

Question 2: Before the flight, the pilot wants to listen to ATIS on the speaker. How is this accomplished?

 a) *Pressing the COM key.*

 b) *Pressing the ADF key.*

 c) *Pressing the SPKR key on the audio panel.*

Question 3: During the flight, the pilot wishes to isolate their passengers so they can talk and concentrate uninterrupted. How is this accomplished on the audio panel?

 a) *Pressing the MKR/MUTE key.*

 b) *Pressing the PILOT key in the intercom section of the audio panel.*

 c) *Turning down the Passenger intercom volume.*

Question 4: During the flight operation in the destination terminal area, the pilot desires to reduce the distraction caused by the MFD. How do they change the MFD into the PFD?

 a) *Using the PA key.*

 b) *Using the HI SENS key.*

 c) *Pressing the Red Reversionary backup key.*

Question 5: The pilot received ATIS information on their COM radio a moment ago, but neglected to make a note of the wind speed. Other than tuning the frequency back in again, how else can they get this information?

 a) *Press the PLAY key on a portable voice recorder.*

 b) *Using the HI SENS key to listen to the ATIS more clearly.*

 c) *Pressing the PLAY key repeatedly until they hear the ATIS in playback mode, then press MKR MUTE when they have heard what they need.*

Grading Criteria:

The pilot will know when they have completed this chapter when they get all the answers correct and demonstrate a solid understanding of the material. When the exam is complete, grade the answers with the answer key in the back of this handbook. Incorrect answers should be researched by going back to the appropriate reference area in the chapter or the Garmin Cockpit Guide that comes with the aircraft. Once all correct answers have been achieved, proceed on to the next chapter. Come back to items in this chapter at any time.

Chapter Nine: Engine Indications and Management

Chapter Objectives:

The objective of this chapter is for the pilot to demonstrate understanding regarding the G1000 Engine Indicating System (EIS) and indications by reviewing the content of this chapter. The pilot will then take the chapter quiz at the end which will check their knowledge about the material covered.

Completion Standards:

When this chapter is complete, the pilot will be able to describe and explain functions and modes of the G1000 Engine Indicating System (EIS). The pilot will know when they have met the completion standards of the chapter when they have correctly answered all the quiz questions at the end of this section. If any questions are scored as incorrect, go back to the appropriate reference area in the chapter or the Garmin Cockpit Guide that comes with the aircraft. When the pilot has correctly answered all the chapter quiz questions, then they may proceed to the next chapter.

The Engine Management and Monitoring System

In normal G1000 operation, the engine indicators are stacked on the left-hand side of the MFD, and also appear on the PFD any time the system is operating in reversionary or emergency backup mode. These instruments have the same basic look and feel as their traditional counterparts, but are organized to optimize space and take advantage of the crew alerting system on the PFD.

The G1000 always uses the color paradigm:

GREEN means things are good or within an acceptable range.

Yellow (Caution) requires investigation and could go either way – but don't ignore it.

RED (Warning) means trouble and requires immediate decision making on your part.

VOLTS 0.0 or **▼5** where the triangle turns yellow or red means a parameter is out of normal range and needs your attention – do not ignore!

The engine Monitoring quadrant can take several different views and has evolved over the aircraft model years and software revisions of the G1000. Older aircraft used primarily sidebar views of data and newer versions used full page data views when pressing the **Engine** softkey:

ENGINE Sidebar or normal mode using color banded slider gauges to show current relative operating parameters for each gauge using the color codes shown above and the sliding triangle pointer which shows where the reading falls within the colored arc. When something is out of the green range, the triangle pointer turns a color as noted above and it may place the cylinder number in the triangle, as well. When something such as the triangle pointer blinks, it needs attention.

SYSTEM Page or detailed view changes many of the sliding-colored scale pointers into enlarged, graphic, or numeric displays telling the pilot exactly what the reading is. When something is out of the green range, the triangle pointer turns a color as noted above and if it refers to a particular cylinder of the engine, it may place the cylinder number in the triangle, as well. When something such as the triangle pointer blinks, it needs attention.

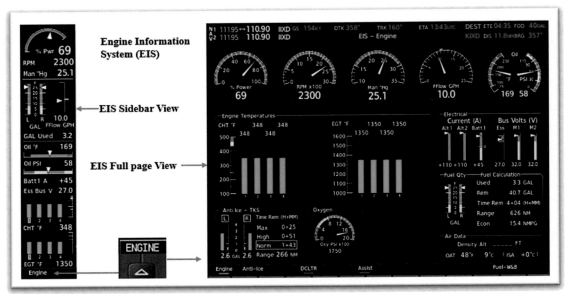

Figure 9.1 – Engine Information System (EIS) data views

These two views are available to the pilot on many G1000 equipped aircraft. The sidebar view is available on the MFD or the PFD when Reversionary mode is active. The EIS full page view is available when the pilot presses the **Engine** softkey on the MFD.

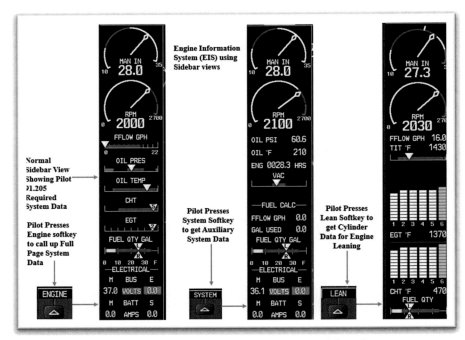

Figure 9.2 – Engine Information System (EIS) Sidebar data views

This engine monitoring system data can be broken into several information groups as needed by the pilot.

Engine Performance

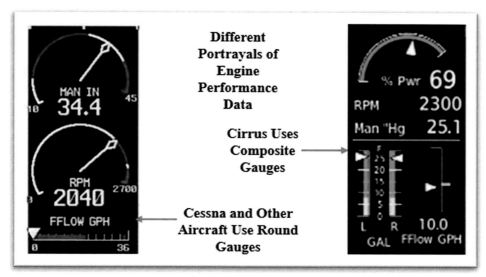

Figure 9.3 – Engine performance group

This portion of the monitoring system can vary from aircraft model to aircraft model depending upon if there is a constant speed propeller or even single engine versus multiengine.

❑ **Manifold pressure** (where applicable) in Inches/Hg – This is the primary way we set power with the throttle on a constant speed propeller equipped aircraft such as Piper, higher horsepower Cessna, Mooney, and Diamond aircraft.

❑ **Percent of Power** – Cirrus aircraft use a "Percent of Power" gauge to set power which is a computed value combining manifold pressure and RPM.

❑ **Engine speed in RPM** – Many of the aircraft mentioned above will set this value using the Propeller control. Aircraft with a fixed pitch propeller will not have a Manifold Pressure gauge and throttle settings will be set with this indicator. Examples of this type of aircraft would be a Cessna 172 and Piper Pilot.

❑ **Fuel-Flow** – Shown in Gal/Hour of the G1000 aircraft will have this feature driven by a fuel flow transducer to help the pilot control their fuel consumption rate and control the aircraft range.

Internal Engine Operating Parameter

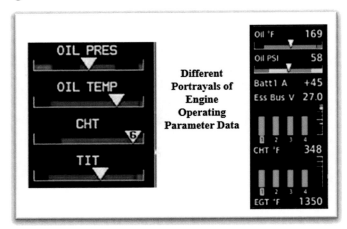

Figure 9.8 – Internal engine parameters

This portion of the monitoring system can vary from aircraft model to aircraft model depending upon if there is a turbocharger, a vacuum pump, and other factors.

- ❑ **Oil Pressure** - shows whether value is in yellow, green, or red range.
- ❑ **Oil temp** - shows whether value is in yellow, green, or red range.
- ❑ **Cylinder Head Temperature** (CHT) indicating hottest cylinder with the triangle shows whether value is in yellow, green, or red range.
- ❑ **Exhaust Gas Temperature (EGT)** - indicating temperature per each cylinder with the horizontal or vertical slider with triangle.
- ❑ **Turbine Inlet Temperature (TIT)** – Only for Turbocharged aircraft to help avoid over temping by setting mixture to achieve right operating temperature- shows whether value is in yellow, green, or red range.

Fuel Quantity Monitoring

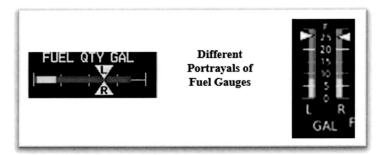

Figure 9.9 – Fuel quantity gauges

This portion of the monitoring system can vary from aircraft model to aircraft model depending upon if there are auxiliary fuel tanks, and other factors.

- ❑ Fuel quantity in Gallons or Liters from each measurable tank
- ❑ Fuel Quantity should always be verified by the pilot prior to takeoff.

❑ These values can vary during flight depending upon slip/skid conditions or after extended turns such as during maneuver training.

❑ Area above top of green on fuel gauges indicates unreadable fuel above top of fuel indication sending unit in fuel tanks.

❑ Low wing aircraft require the pilot to switch tanks during flight to keep fuel balanced from all wing tanks.

Notice: When fuel tank levels drop to certain values, a "Low Fuel" Crew Alerting System indication will appear in yellow, then eventually red.

Most aircraft have other data available such as:

❑ Gallons Remaining
❑ Gallons Used
❑ Endurance
❑ Range

Caution: This measurement system is only required to be accurate when the gauges are empty.

Fuel Range Ring Management

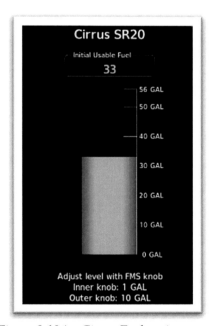

Figure 9.10A – Cirrus Fuel setting screen

Different aircraft manufacturers use different approaches to setting fuel onboard. Cirrus uses this cylinder portrayal to set fuel on board. Notice that the pilot can set this either accurately based on verification of fuel levels or they can set it inaccurately. This does not have any effect on fuel gauges which represent the true value of what is in the tanks. It is recommended that a pilot not show fuel as full unless they have personally verified that the tanks are full prior to flight.

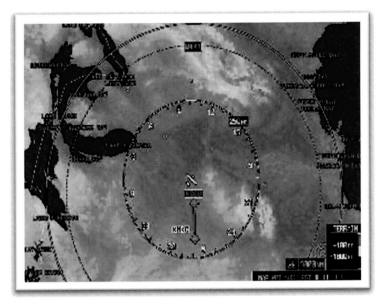

Figure 9.10B – Fuel range ring

The Fuel Range Ring feature of the G1000 uses the fuel level set by the pilot and the fuel burned from the fuel flow transducer to estimate how far the aircraft can fly in any direction considering winds before reaching the 45-minute reserve (dashed line circle) and fuel tanks empty (solid lined circle). The pilot can change the fuel reserve circle to be any value, but it is advised to set it no less than 45-minute reserve for all operations. Settings on other G1000 aircraft other than the cylinder portrayal used on the Cirrus would have softkeys for the pilot to adjust fuel onboard. Examples of these softkeys are:

- ❏ INCR FUEL – increase fuel for purposes of measurement on the Fuel Range ring on the MFD.
- ❏ DEC FUEL – decrease fuel for purposes of measurement on the Fuel Range ring on the MFD.
- ❏ RST USD – reset fuel used for purposes of measurement on the Fuel Range ring on the MFD.

Caution: The Fuel Range Ring measurement system is not in any way connected to how much fuel is in the fuel tanks. Only press reset when you have verified that the tanks are full. If the manufacturer provides for an INC and DEC function, then adjust fuel after verifying exact amount in tank.

Electrical System Monitoring

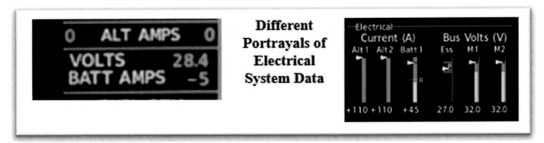

Figure 9.11 – Electrical System Portrayals

The electrical system portion of the monitoring system can vary from aircraft model to aircraft model depending upon if there is a standby battery or even multiple batteries and other factors. The important factors that the pilot needs to know is whether the electrical system has sufficient voltage to sustain aircraft flight. Voltage is measured in volts. Another element that is presented to pilots is electrical current draw and that is measured in amps. If desired voltage on a 24-volt electrical system is below 28 volts then the system may not be producing enough power. Typically, when system voltage drops below battery voltage of 24 volts, a Crew Advising System caution light appears. Other aspects of the electrical system that will be presented to pilot's are:

❑ Main (M) and Essential (E) bus Voltages – relative to a 24-volt battery and a targeted 28 volt charging voltage – Note Maximum voltage is 32 volts – Anything higher than this and the G1000 system components may sustain heat damage internally. The system attempts to maintain system voltage at 28 volts.

❑ Main (M) and Essential (E) Bus Amperage or current – Positive Amps charging is good. Negative Amps means the system is drawing off the battery and may mean the alternator is not producing enough power to sustain the system and the battery will discharge.

❑ Voltage and Amperage together represent the whole story about the integrity of the electrical system.

Definition: <u>Critical Idle Speed</u> – The speed at which when idling with electrical equipment on, the alternator and the charging system provides a positive current charge as reflected by the Ammeter.

❑ Every aircraft has a critical idle speed. Determine the critical idling speed for the aircraft and try not to let it idle below that. This may be different at night or in IFR weather than it is for day VFR due to variances in power consumption.

❑ Extensive engine idling with the throttles pulled all the way back to the stop will result in battery discharge since the alternator cannot spin fast enough to keep the system operating with heavy loads and still keep the battery at full charge.

Important: Never attempt takeoff with a discharging ammeter, or with a battery that has not had a chance to operate at or above the critical idle speed for a period long enough to regain pre-starting capacity.

Engine Leaning

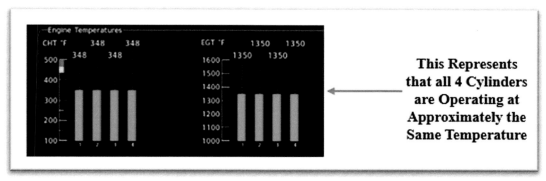

Figure 9.12 – Engines Leaned for Cruise

When the pilot changes altitude and levels off, the cruise checklist is performed, and the engine(s) are leaned for the new altitude. Press **Engine**, then **Assist** to lean the engines using the engine temperature

---

assist function. As the mixture is leaned, the EGT temperatures of the cylinders will rise until one peaks. The pilot then wants to either richen the mixture by 50 degrees for "rich of peak" operations or continue to lean the engine for "lean of peak" operations. The pilot should consult the aircraft manual for proper leaning techniques for their engine but in general, engines with cylinders with varying or inconsistent temperature ranges should be leaned to rich of peak of the hottest cylinder to prevent cylinder damage.

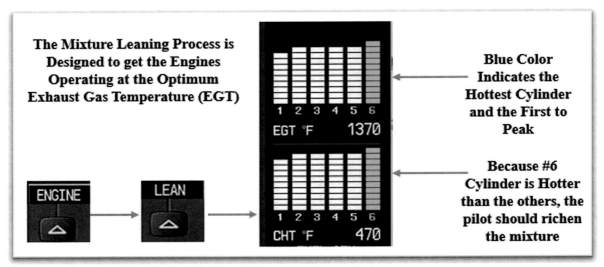

Figure 9.13 – Fuel leaning screen

Pressing the LEAN or ASSIST softkeys accesses additional functions as follows:

CYL SLCT – allows display of the absolute value of the cylinder head and exhaust gas temperatures for the selected cylinder indicated by a blue numeral above that cylinder.

ASSIST – enables the lean assist function. As the mixture is leaned the exhaust gas temperatures will be shown to increase. The hottest cylinder is displayed in blue. The first cylinder that decreases in EGT is the leanest cylinder. Once this peak is reached a hollow blue box will be displayed on the graph. At that time the temperature differential will be displayed below the graph with the peak temperature as the zero-degree reference point. Richen the mixture to the value recommended by the engine manufacturer.

Example: The pilot levels off in cruise and starts the leaning process. The recommended cruise mixture is 50-degrees. F rich of peak EGT. Press the ENGINE, LEAN, and ASSIST softkeys. Start reducing the mixture slowly. As the leanest cylinder reaches peak EGT the hollow box will appear along with the temperature differential. Now richen the mixture until the temperature differential reaches the proper value (-50deg F).

Conclusion

In this chapter, we looked at the engine monitoring and management systems in order to thoroughly understand the features available that were not on traditional aircraft. Follow the color coding literally and relate them to a traffic light. Red is never good, and the pilot should be prepared to take immediate decision-making action when it appears on critical engine monitoring equipment.

Remember

❑ The fuel gauges show the quantity of fuel in each tank. If one tank becomes low, an amber caution will appear. If a tank drops below a predetermined minimum, the fuel gauge will flash red and the Crew Advisory System will display a red warning.

❑ If the MFD were to fail, the engine stack will be shown on the left side of the PFD.

❑ The engine indicators will change color if there is an alert or warning with a particular system. For example, if the oil pressure was too low or too high, the indicator will begin to flash with a yellow color.

❑ Engine Gauge color shading legend:

> ❑ **GREEN** means things are good or within an acceptable range.
> ❑ **Yellow** requires investigation and could go either way – but don't ignore it.
> ❑ **RED** means trouble and requires immediate decision making on your part.
>
> ❑ **VOLTS 0.0** or where the triangle turns yellow or red means a parameter is out of normal range and needs your attention – do not ignore!

❑ Fuel gauges do not match the fuel range ring unless they are properly calibrated and verified.

❑ Take care of the aircraft battery and charging system by monitoring the critical idle speed to ensure the alternator is sufficiently charging the battery before takeoff.

❑ Never attempt takeoff with an operating parameter in the red range or when an indication is out of limits or has a red X.

❑ Keep the engine instrumentation within the scan flow.

Chapter Debriefing:

We have now covered the area of the G1000 engine monitoring and control screens and the pilot should have a much better understanding about how the G1000 places information on the screen and how it uses colors to represent concepts of normal and abnormal engine and operating indications.

❑ Now that the pilot understands that the G1000 uses color coding to represent normal and abnormal parameter indications, they will also understand that they can use the SYSTEM softkey to display more detailed indications and get the system to produce more information about the indication in question.

❑ Now that the pilot understands that a yellow or red indication on a monitoring system indicates that there may be a problem, they should also understand that not always does this mean it is a dire emergency and that there are options to diagnose a bad sending unit sensor by cross checking other indicators and see if the problem is a real emergency.

❑ Now that the pilot understands that the G1000 is a digital system representing many sensors which are driven by software and computers, then they will also understand that software updates may come along from the manufacturer or Garmin that may change the way these systems appear or behave, after updates.

Now that the pilot understands these key areas about the engine information system (EIS), they should be able to correlate these major points into their everyday flying skills and apply these skills to the operation of the G1000 aircraft. It's time to take the quiz and then to move to chapter ten!

Chapter Nine Quiz: Engine Indications and Engine Management

The Chapter Quiz Scenario

This Chapter Quiz Scenario (CQS) is designed to portray a real-world flight situation and use the pilot's new knowledge of the G1000 engine information system (EIS) to answer some situational questions about how to safely operate their aircraft. They can then determine whether they can correlate the material covered with their existing aeronautical knowledge and are prepared to use this information in a way which will enhance operational safety while flying the G1000 equipped aircraft.

In this chapter quiz, the pilot will be asked to demonstrate their understanding of the G1000 engine monitoring system and some of the engine system monitoring chores that they have to perform using information on this flight scenario between Kansas City Downtown airport (KMKC) to Cedar airport in Olathe, Kansas (51K), a non-tower-controlled airport. Consider the following questions about this scenario:

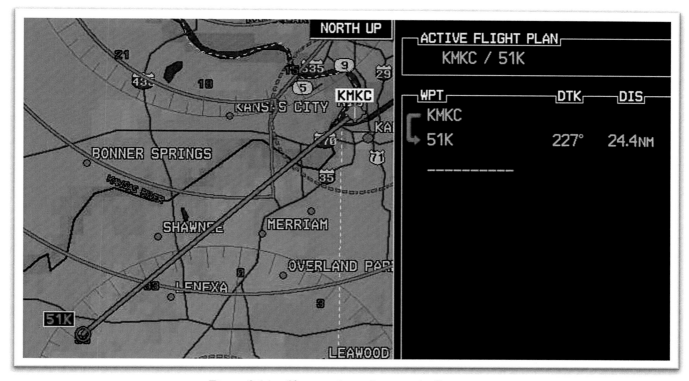

Figure 9.14 – Chapter nine quiz scenario diagram

Question 1: During this flight the MFD display unit fails. Where will the pilot be able to view the engine indicators?

   a) They will be displayed on the left side of the PFD.

   b) They will not be visible unless you press the Display Backup key on the GMA 1347D.

   c) They will be on map page 3.

Question 2: While enroute the pilot wants to look at the fuel remaining in a numeric format. What softkey will give them this information?

    a) *Press the FMS cursor and move it onto the fuel gauges.*

    b) *Press the ENGINE softkey and then the SYSTEM softkey.*

    c) *Press the INSET softkey on the PFD to display the information in the PIP screen.*

Question 3: During the engine run-up, the pilot needs to look more specifically at the EGT gauge to lean the mixture. How is this done?

    a) *Pressing the ENGINE softkey, then the SYSTEM softkey.*

    b) *Moving to AUX page 5*

    c) *Pressing the CODE softkey*

Question 4: When using the lean assist function, which softkeys are pressed to navigate to the correct screen?

    a) *ENGINE then SYSTEM.*

    b) *LEAN then ENGINE.*

    c) *ENGINE then LEAN then ASSIST.*

Question 5: As the pilot approaches the destination, they notice that the fuel range ring only shows 15 minutes of fuel remaining, but the fuel gauges still show plenty of fuel. What could have caused this disparity between the two systems?

    a) *The fuel gauge sending unit has developed a problem.*

    b) *The fuel range ring reset key was not pressed the last time that the aircraft was fueled.*

    c) *The fuel flow transducer has developed a sending fault and should be followed by a caution on the PFD crew alert system.*

Grading Criteria:

The pilot will know when they have completed this chapter when they get all the answers correct and demonstrate a solid understanding of the material. When the exam is complete, grade the answers with the answer key in the back of this handbook. Incorrect answers should be researched by going back to the appropriate reference area in the chapter or the Garmin Cockpit Guide that comes with the aircraft. Once all correct answers have been achieved, proceed on to the next chapter. Come back to items in this chapter at any time.

Chapter Ten: Multi-function Flight Display (MFD)

Chapter Objectives:

The objective of this chapter is for the pilot to demonstrate understanding regarding the G1000 Multi-function Flight Display (MFD) by reviewing the content of this chapter. The pilot will then take the chapter quiz at the end which will check their knowledge about the material covered.

Completion Standards:

When this chapter is complete, the pilot will be able to describe and explain functions and modes of the G1000 Multi-function Flight Display (MFD). The pilot will know when they have met the completion standards of the chapter when they have correctly answered all the quiz questions at the end of this section. If any questions are scored as incorrect, go back to the appropriate reference area in the chapter or the Garmin Cockpit Guide that comes with the aircraft. When the pilot has correctly answered all the chapter quiz questions, then they may proceed to the next chapter.

The Multi-Function Display (MFD) uses the right GDU on smaller aircraft and is the middle display on larger aircraft like a King Air. The MFD displays the most thorough information of the G1000 system and will be the focus of much of the pilot's attention during planning and flight. The information is separated into page groups that can be navigated once the pilot understands how to use the FMS knob. The MFD has a number of key areas and features of its screen. The pilot must become very familiar with the groups and symbols on the MFD to avoid distraction delays trying to find information.

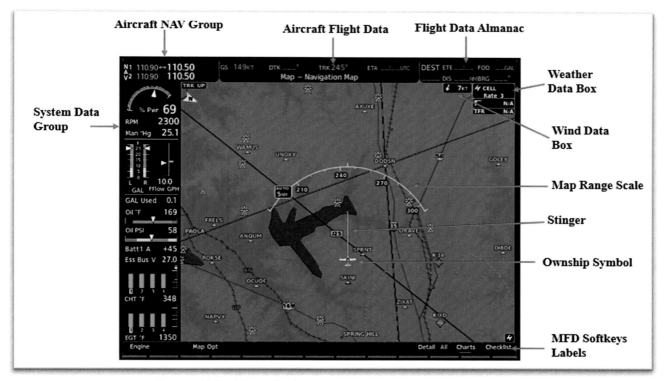

Figure 10.1 – The Multi-function Display in Map Page 1 or Home

The MFD has a full set of Page Groups that are subdivided into Pages. The pilot must become familiar with these Page Groups and what is contained on the Pages within them to avoid hunting for information which will cost them time they sometimes do not have. The main page of the MFD is the main map page. It is considered Home. It can always be reached by pressing the CLR key for two seconds or can be reached by pressing the Home key on the GCU, if installed.

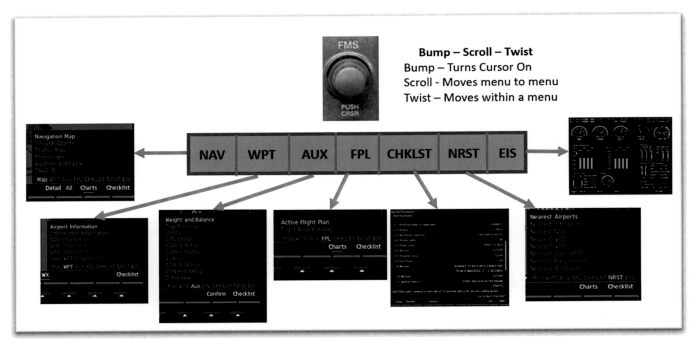

Figure 10.2 – Multi-function display Menu Navigation

Page Groups

Page Groups are shown in the bottom right-hand corner of the MFD. Think of these Page Groups as "chapters" with "pages" within the chapters. When the pilot scrolls the outer FMS knob, the system calls up these Page Group menus. Each different aircraft manufacturer may have a different set of Page Group menus for their aircraft. The menus shown in figure 10.2 above are for a Cirrus but should be representative of most others. Navigation will always be first and Engine (EIS) are usually last, but again, this can vary. In the following sections, we will detail each Page Group and the various Pages or submenus beneath it. Some of the Page Groups have softkeys associated with them and some have softkeys that will call up the menu such as Checklist.

Note: *Page Group menus are only called up if the cursor is not active on another MFD function. Remember, if the Cursor is blinking in any screen, bump the FMS knob to turn it off. Then the Page Group menus will respond to scrolling the FMS knob outer ring.*

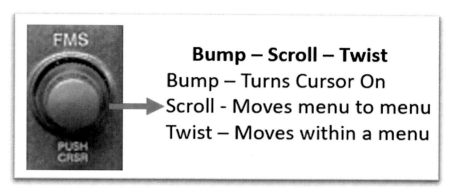

Figure 10.3 – FMS knob navigation

The different page groups are labeled as:

NAV – (Navigation) This Page Group shows all the various modes of the moving map. The moving map shows the main map (Home) and additional information including aeronautical data, traffic, topography, terrain, and weather data.

WPT - (Waypoint) This Page Group shows information on select waypoint types. The pilot can search for waypoints or can click on ones within other Page Groups and data will be presented using these menu pages.

AUX - (Auxiliary) The Page Group provides for many auxiliary functions including GPS system status, LRU Status, RAIM, trip statistics, programmed events and timers, and setup screens.

FLTPLN - (flight plan) This Page Group provides information about the current flight plan and stored flight plans.

NRST - (Nearest) Shows information on the nearest airport, VOR, NDB, Intersection, user waypoint, ARTCC, Center, and FSS.

CHKLST – This Page Group calls up the checklist menu which allows the pilot to select various checklists as instituted by the manufacturer. Some manufacturers have not implemented checklists in their G1000 implementations and therefore this function would not be present on those aircraft.

EIS – (Engine Information System) – This option calls the EIS page rather than a menu. There are softkeys associated with the EIS group which control a variety of options for the pilot.

MAP Page Group indications

Some G1000 implementations use a Page Group indication to help the pilot determine where they are in terms of Page Group navigation.

Figure 10.4 – Map group page 1

Use the outer FMS knob to select the page group desired and use the inner FMS knob to select the page needed within the group. The default MFD navigation page is Map Page 1, also called "home".

Figure 10.5 – Home Key on GCU Returns to Map Page 1 (Home)

Page Group 2 –Map

Page Group 1 Navigation Map - Home

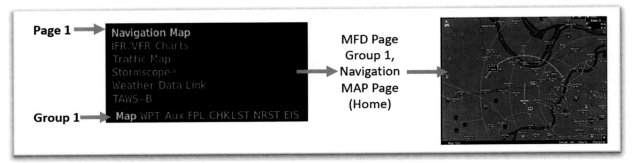

Figure 10.6 – Home Key Group 1 Page 1

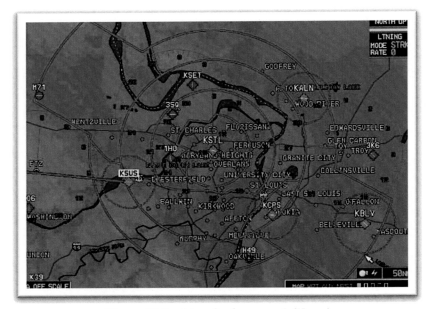

Figure 10.7 – Map display page 1 (Home)

The moving map on the MFD will give the pilot the most overall information in a single full-page screen. The map will be centered on the airplane icon also known as "ownship". When the screen is divided into other menus or data, the pilot should know that they are not on the Home screen map page 1.

Available items shown on the moving map are:

- o Navigation map display
- o Flight plan and current flight plan leg
- o Airports
- o Airspace symbols
- o NAVAIDS
- o Airways
- o Land data Icons for map overlay functions
- o Names of cities, facilities, airports, airspace, water features, highways etc.
- o Zoom range legend (lower right corner above page group icon)
  - o To change the range of the navigation map turn the RANGE knob to the right or left to display the range desired as indicated in the zoom range legend
- o Wind Vector
- o Map Orientation (North-up or Track-up)
- o Track vector
- o Stinger – where the aircraft will be in 60 seconds.
- o Topography features, coloring, and scale
- o Terrain, terrain coloring, and terrain scale
- o Obstacles

To clear up the screen when there is too much information displayed, press the declutter softkey.

Figure 10.8A – De clutter softkey

To return to the previous menu, press the BACK softkey.

Figure 10.8B – Back softkey

To change any of the features displayed on the map, press the MAP OPT softkey at the bottom of the screen. A new set of softkeys is displayed.

Figure 10.9 – Map softkey

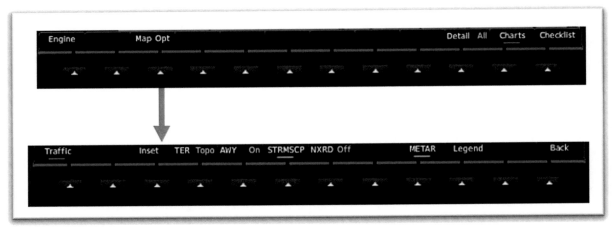

Figure 10.10 – MAP OPT overlay softkey selections

INSET – This softkey turns on several INSET functions for the MFD menu. These are different INSET functions than were discussed on the PFD INSET map. The two are not connected but the functions are similar.

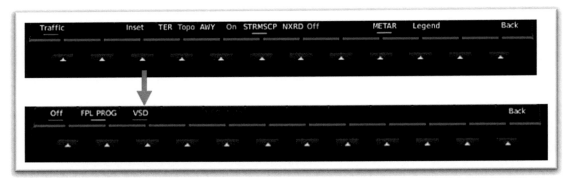

Figure 10.11 – INSET softkey selections

FPL Progress

FPL Progress is a mode where an INSET table is displayed on the bottom of the MFD so the pilot can track the progress as they proceed along their route of flight. There are no other options with this display mode. This window can be opened or closed by the **FPL** Prog softkey.

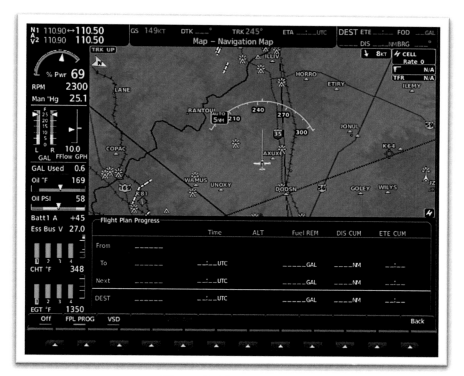

*Figure 10.12 – **FPL** Progress mode*

VSD

VSD is a mode where an INSET table is displayed on the bottom of the MFD so the pilot can track their vertical profile in relation to their current altitude and the terrain below them. This is a very interesting mode, and the pilot will find it very useful when proceeding along unfamiliar terrain. There are several options in the VSD mode.

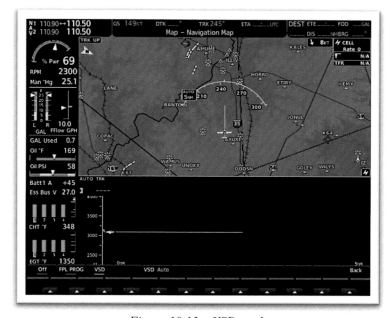

Figure 10.13 – VSD mode

VSD can be set to **FPL** (Flight plan mode) or it can be set to auto mode. If the pilot selects **FPL** mode and there is a flight plan active, it will show the flight plan leg as described below. If no Flight plan is active, then the screen shows a "no active flight plan" in the window which might be confusing to the pilot. If left in the Auto mode, it will show the aircraft flying at its current altitude in relation to its target altitude set by the ALT mode of the autopilot or set in the flight plan leg mode. It is recommended that the pilot leave this in Auto mode.

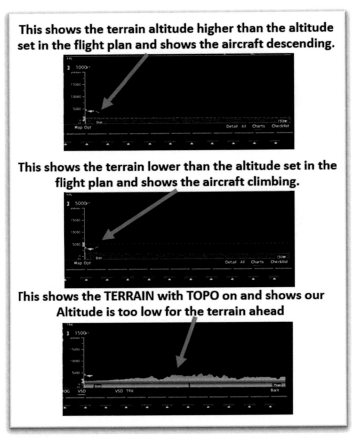

Figure 10.14 – Different depictions of VSD mode

TERRAIN

The TERR (Terrain) softkey has several different modes and options. Pressing this softkey will toggle between TOPO and TERRAIN modes. Pressing TOPO will turn on the topographical information, including all map elevation coloring. Turning this to TERRAIN mode turns on the terrain and obstacles coloring mode. The two modes are mutually exclusive. Only one mode can be on at any time.

When TOPO is turned off, the moving map display will appear black and when it is on, the coloring of the Map is the same coloring as a sectional chart. This is called Topography and the various color groups represent altitudes above mean sea level or MSL. Below 1000 feet, sectional charts, and thus the TOPO screen will appear Green. As the topography of the land rises, such as going into mountainous areas, the sectional chart starts turning a darker color. The main map of the G1000 will change to that corresponding color.

Figure 10.15 – TOPO elevation scale

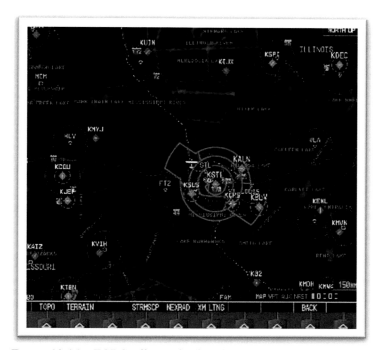

Figure 10.16 – TOPO off map display shows black map background

A terrain awareness display showing terrain features and highlighting those within both 100'(red) and 1000'(yellow) of the aircraft current altitude. The screen show TERRAIN as green if between 1000 ft and 2000 ft. Turn this function on and off the same way as TRAFFIC and TOPO with the TERRAIN softkey.

Figure 10.17 – TOPO/Terrain Color Scale

TERRAIN mode coloring is as follows: Terrain and obstacles are between 100 and 1000 ft of the aircraft's current altitude is shown in yellow and terrain within 100 ft is shown in red. The diagram below shows the aircraft is heading toward higher elevation within 6 nautical miles and they must climb.

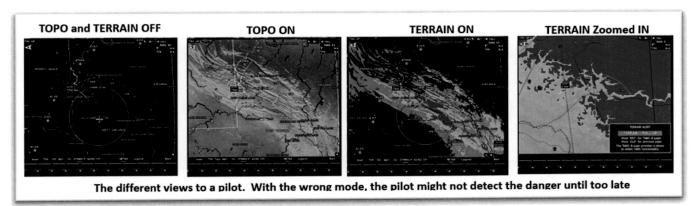

Figure 10.18 – TOPO/Terrain display page versions

The view format is selected by using the softkeys. The range can be changed by turning the RANGE knob. Certain properties of the map will turn on and off depending upon how they were set up in map options.

Figure 10.19 – RANGE knob

The pointer can be moved around the navigation map by pushing the range "joystick" in the desired direction of movement. The map will automatically pan to display the area of the map around the pointer. The pointer can be used to select most main map features. Once an airport is selected by the pointer, the airport type, services available, elevation, distance and bearing to the station are displayed. Additional information is available when the pilot presses enter by going into Waypoint mode.

TRAFFIC

Figure 10.20 – Map overlay softkeys

The TRAFFIC softkey will turn on the TIS-B or ADS-B traffic overlay on the moving map. Traffic will be shown on the Map 1 page. You can turn the overlay on or off by pressing the MAP softkey, then the

TRAFFIC softkey. When the TRAFFIC box is grey, the overlay is turned on. Even with this softkey off, traffic conflicts will be shown to the pilot on the PFD in terms of an audible and visual Alert.

STRMSCP

Press the STRMSCP softkey to turn the overlay of Stormscope on or off. If it is on, the STRMSCP box will be grey.

Figure 10.21 – STRMSCP softkey

At the top right side of the MFD on the moving map, a lightning strike box will appear when Stormscope is activated.

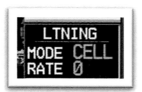

Figure 10.22 – LTNING mode display

This box will give information on the rate of the lightning strikes, current lightning mode, current strike rate and fault messages.

NEXRAD

Press the NEXRAD softkey to activate the overlay of NEXRAD weather on the moving map. Doing this, however, will turn off TOPO, STRMSCP, and XM LTNG.

Figure 10.23 – NEXRAD radar overlay

Additional Information

By pressing the RANGE knob, you enable the pointer to move around the map and highlight items of interest. The pointer can be moved around the navigation map by pushing the range "joystick" in the desired direction of movement. The map will automatically pan to display the area of the map around the pointer. The pointer can be used to select most nav map features. In the example below, once an airport is selected by the pointer, the airport type, services available, elevation, distance and bearing to the station are displayed.

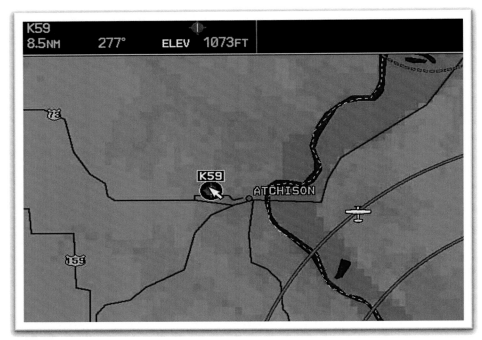

Figure 10.24 – WPT selection with pointer

Group 1 Page 2 VFR/IFR Charts

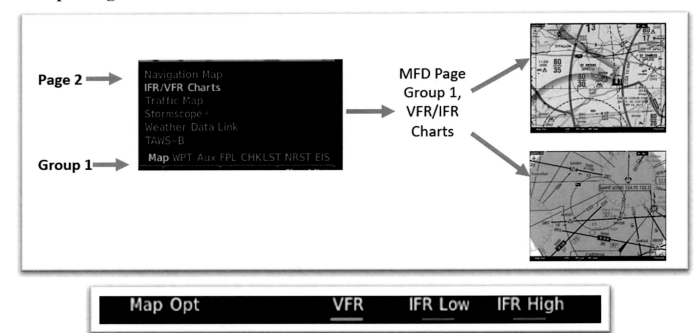

Figure 10.25 – VFR/IFR Chart display

Group 1 Page 3 Traffic Map

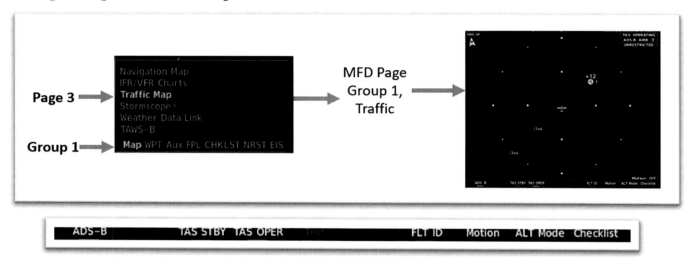

Figure 10.26 – Traffic display and option softkeys

On aircraft that have both TIS-B and ADS-B installed, the aircraft will portray a more complete traffic picture. ADS-B is air to air traffic and TIS-B displays traffic from ground RADAR sources. The traffic alert can be turned on and off by turning the small knob to MAP page 2 and pressing the softkeys at the bottom of the screen. Press the OPERATE softkey to turn on the TIS-B or press STANDBY to turn off the TIS-B. The ring shows the range in which traffic is shown, use the RANGE knob to zoom in or out.

Group 1 Page 4 Stormscope

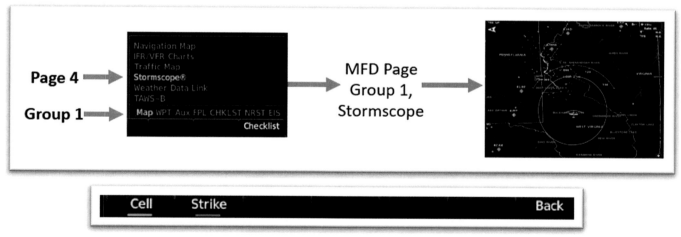

Figure 10.27 – Stormscope and option softkeys

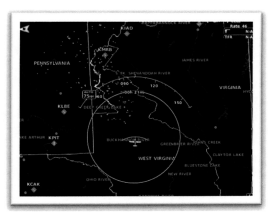

Figure 10.28 – Stormscope display

The range of the Stormscope can be adjusted by twisting the range knob and the display can change the view from CELL mode to STRIKE mode. The pilot can press the CLR softkey to clear strikes to give them a better view of recent strikes and even an idea of storm movement.

Group 1 Page 5 Weather Data Link

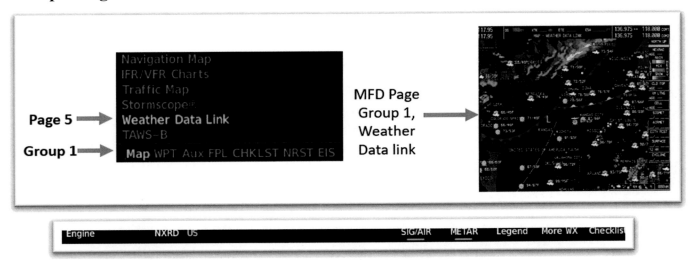

Figure 10.29 – Weather Data Link display page

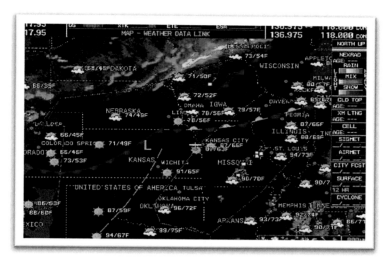

Figure 10.30 – Weather Data link display

NEXRAD Weather uses XM Satellite service and FIS-B data sources to download weather information such as radar, cell movement, storm tops, cloud tops, lightning, SIGMETS and AIRMETS, METARS, surface analysis charts, freezing levels, winds aloft from 3000 feet to FL420, flood warnings and cyclones. There's also a legend to decode all the symbols on the map. The pilot can bump the range key and use the joystick to find all the weather information on the map.

Figure 10.31 – FIS-B Data legend

Figure 10.32 – METAR and TAF stations

Notice the arrow on the airport symbol for KSPI? At the top of the page, the pilot can see where it says Press "ENT" to view METAR and TAF textual information. Press the ENT key to view the information for the desired airport.

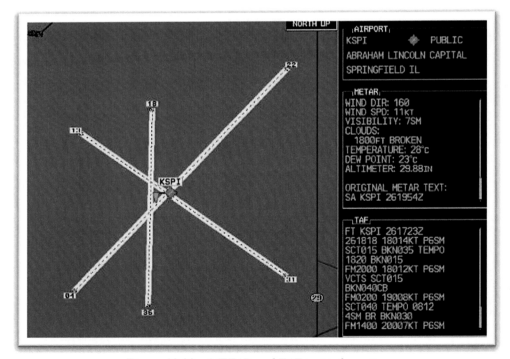

Figure 10.33 – METAR and TAF text information

Another example of some of the information that is provided is AIRMET information. As in the previous example, the pilot bumps the range key, and then uses the joystick to move the pointer over an area that contains an AIRMET. You can see in the figure the large area that the aircraft is in is outlined with an AIRMET.

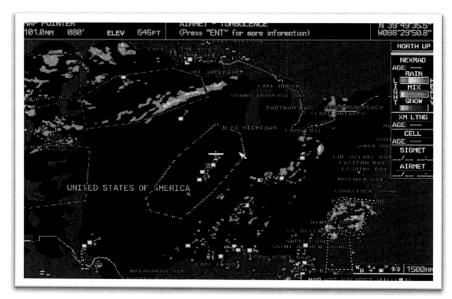

Figure 10.34 – AIRMET area display

By pressing ENT, the pilot can view the textual description of the AIRMET.

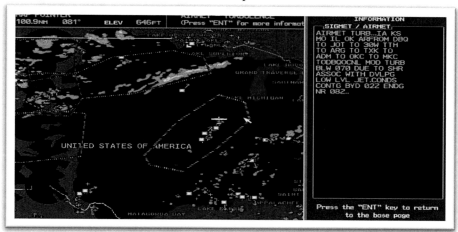

Figure 10.35 – AIRMET text information

Group 1 Page 6 Terrain Awareness and Warning System (TAWS)

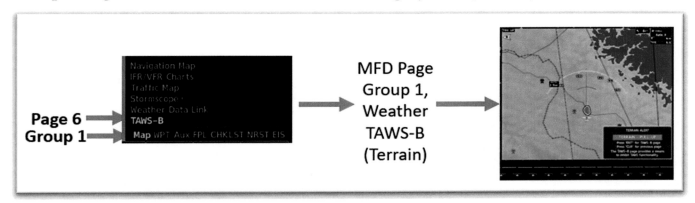

Figure 10.36 – Terrain Awareness and Warning (TAWS-B) information

The Map page 6 shows Terrain Awareness and Warning System (TAWS-B) terrain and obstacles within 1000 ft of the aircraft's current altitude which is shown in yellow and terrain within 100 ft shown in red.

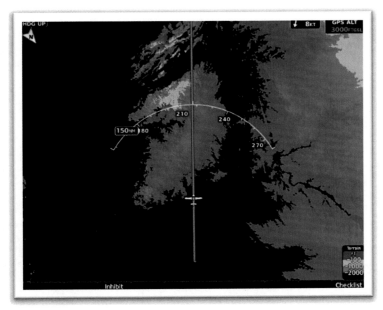

Figure 10.37 – Terrain display page

The view format is selected by using the softkeys. The range can be changed up to 200 NM by turning the RANGE knob. Map displays to show surrounding terrain, current aircraft location, Range rings, and Color scale.

Page Group 2 – Waypoint

Waypoint is the second Page Group in the MFD. The waypoint group will display information on the current destination airport, intersection, NDB, VOR, user waypoint, and Visual Reference points.

Group 2 Page 1 Airport Information

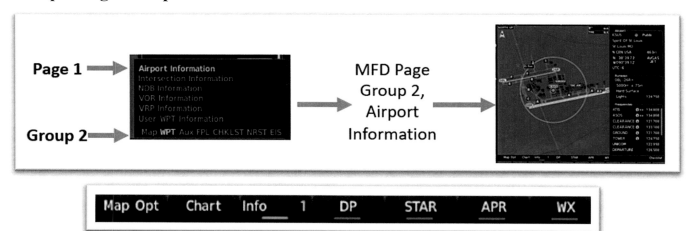

Figure 10.38 – Airport Information display page

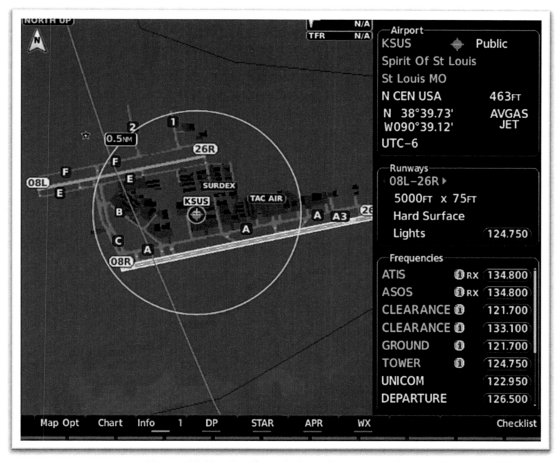

Figure 10.39 – Display of selected waypoint KSUS

The airport page will list information on the airport selected as a destination or the departure airport can be listed. It will be displayed on the right-hand side of the MFD screen, and a map of the runway layout is displayed. The top box will display the airport name, location, elevation and type of airport. (public, controlled, fuel services) information on the different runways such as length, hard surface, and orientation is listed. The list of frequencies includes ATIS, ASOS, clearance delivery, etc. The softkeys on WPT Page 1 can be selected to provide other information such as Departure procedures (DP), Arrivals (STAR), and Instrument Approaches (APR), as well as weather. Charts published for this airport are also readily available on a softkey. The **D->** option is always available in this page.

Waypoint Page 2: Intersection Information

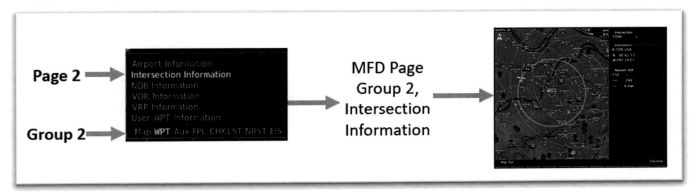

Figure 10.40 – Display of intersection information

Figure 10.41 – WPT page 2 Intersection waypoint TONII

The second page displays intersection information such as LAT/LONG, Nearest VOR radial and distance. There are no softkey options available with Page 2. The **D->** option is always available in this page.

Waypoint Page 3: NDB

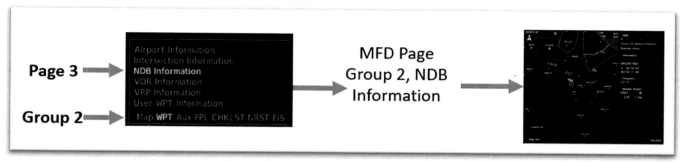

Figure 10.42 – Display of NDB information

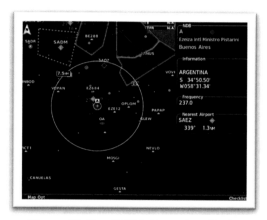

Figure 10.43 – NDB information display

NDB information, type, location, frequency, and nearest airport. There are no softkey options available with Page 3. The **D->** option is always available in this page.

Waypoint Page 4

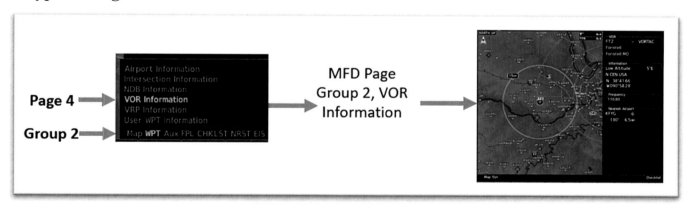

Figure 10.44 – VOR information display

VOR information- VOR type (VORTAC), low altitude, frequency, location, and nearest airport., There are no softkey options available with Page 4. The **D->** option is always available in this page.

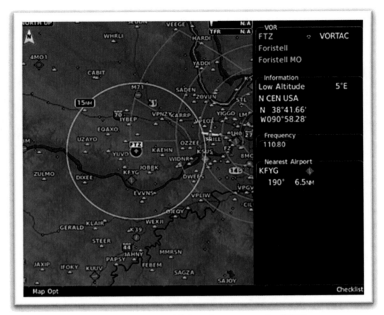

Figure 10.45 – VOR information for FTZ

Waypoint Page 5: Visual Reporting Point (VRP)

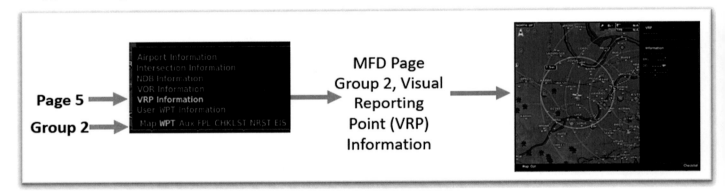

Figure 10.46 – Visual Reporting Point (VRP) display

Visual Reporting Point (VRP)

VRPs are used near congested airports and in terminal areas and are depicted on VFR charts with a flag. ATC uses these as a funnel point for inbound traffic. The pilot can use this function if ATC advises them to report over a particular VRP. The D-> key is always available to use to aid the pilot in navigating to that point.

Figure 10.47 – Visual Reporting Point (VRP) display

Waypoint Page 5: User Defined

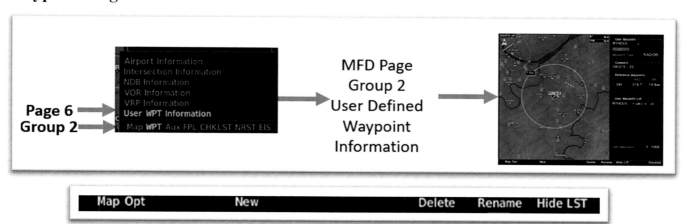

Figure 10.48 – User Defined waypoint display

Figure 10.49 – User defined waypoint MYHOUS

User Waypoint allows a specified point to be created anywhere using Lat/Long or VOR radials and distance. The waypoint list displays all of the user waypoints that have been created and stored. Examples of when a pilot might create User Defined waypoints could be locating uncharted airports, property, points of interest, and reference points to navigate around controlled airspace. Once they are created, they can be called up in flight plans.

Page Group 3 – Aux

Aux is the third Page Group in the MFD. The AUX group is filled with important utility functions that can play an important role for the pilot defining functions, data, and determining system status within the G1000 system.

Group 3 Page 1 Weight and Balance

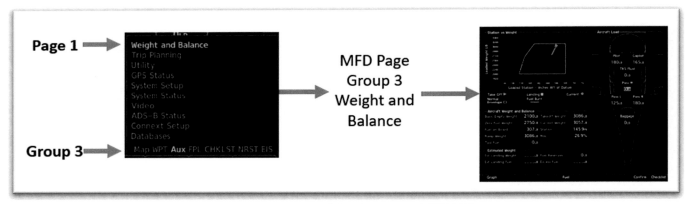

Figure 10.50 – User defined waypoint MYHOUS

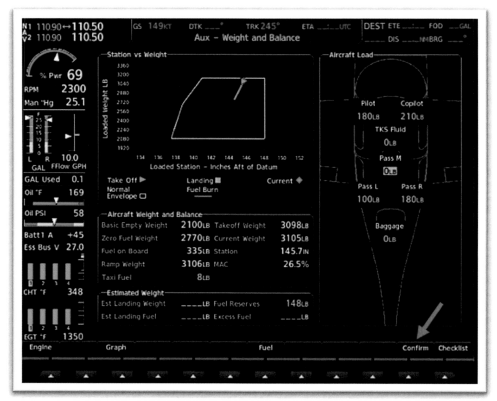

Figure 10.51 – Aircraft weight and balance page

Aux Page 1 is the Weight and Balance page, and this page may not be in all manufacturer's aircraft. It is in the Cirrus, and it is a very useful, so it is worth depicting here in this handbook. The pilot enters in the weights of passengers, baggage, and the fuel that was loaded from the fuel planning page or by pressing the fuel softkey. The result is that it depicts the weight and balance envelope representing the aircraft loading for that trip. The pilot must press the CONFIRM softkey on this screen. The Perspective Plus on the Cirrus will not respond to the pilot pressing ENTER on the PFD or the GCU.

Group 3 Page 2 Trip Planning

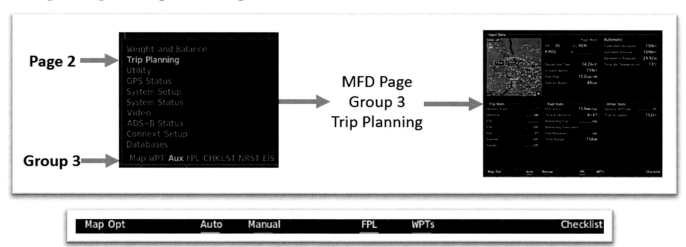

Figure 10.52 – Trip Planning page and softkeys

Figure 10.53 – Trip Planning page and softkeys

On the Trip Planning page, the user can calculate trip statistics for direct-to, point to point or flight plan navigation. This page allows the user to view DTK, DIS, ETE, ETA, and ESA for the selected type of navigation. For normal calculations the user should press the AUTO softkey so that the calculations can be made for that particular type of navigation. If the MAN softkey is pressed the system clears all of the data and the screen can be used as an inflight electronic flight computer. Two other softkeys are present on the trip planning page. The **FPL** softkey is used when the user wants to calculate trip data for a stored flight plan. The WPTs softkey is used for either direct to or point to point navigation.

Group 3 Page 3 Utility

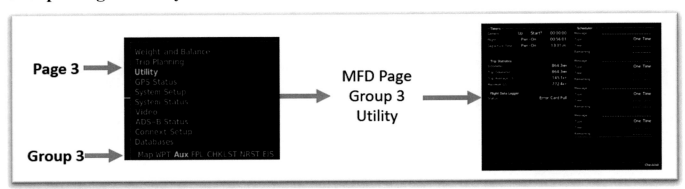

Figure 10.54 – Utility page

Figure 10.55 – AUX Utility page

The Utility page is used to set and display three items. These are the timers, trip statistics, and the scheduler. There are three windows separating this data. The scheduler is used to set reminders about anything the pilot wants to be reminded of, such as switching fuel tanks or checking engine gauges. Bump the softkey to determine fields available and scroll from field to field and press enter. Once an item is set in this page with its reminder time interval, the reminder will appear in the Alerts window of the Crew Alerting System. There are no softkeys associated with this page.

Aux Page 3 – GPS Status

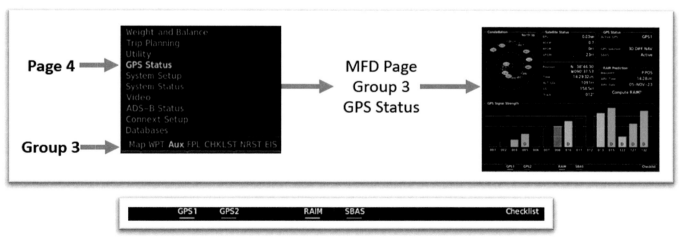

Figure 10.56 GPS – Status page and softkey options

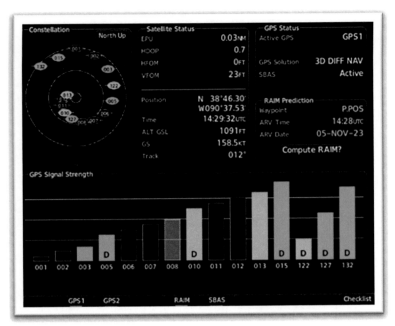

Figure 10.57 – Aux page 3 GPS status

The GPS status page includes information about the GPS constellation and the strength of the satellite locations to the aircraft. Included on this page are satellite status, RAIM prediction, and signal strength. RAIM prediction can be used to determine if RAIM will be available at the time of arrival of this or for a future trip. A RAIM check is required for non WAAS installations or when WAAS is not in service. For G1000 installations with WAAS enabled, RAIM prediction is not required. There are several other softkeys associated with this page, allowing the selection of GPS 1 or GPS 2 and either a RAIM or SBAS. SBAS allows the pilot to select different geostationary systems. WAAS is in the US, EGNOS is in Europe, and MSAS is in Asia. Leaving these selected allows the pilot access to full GPS functionality across the globe.

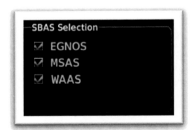

Figure 10.58 – SBAS selection softkey

Aux Page 4 – System Setup

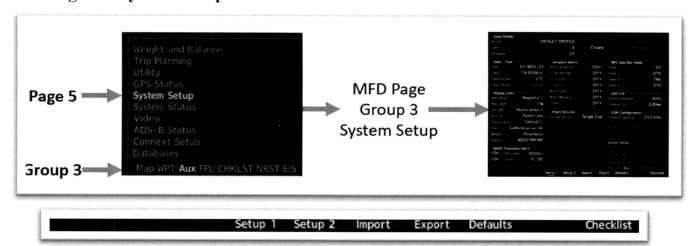

Figure 10.59 – System Setup selection softkey

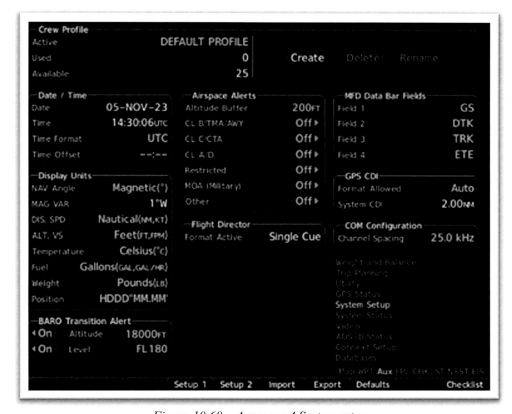

Figure 10.60 – Aux page 4 System setup

The System setup page displays information about the setup of the system defaults, measurement units, and Profiles. This includes the system Date/Time, the display units, map datum, airspace alerts, audio alerts, the MFD data bar fields, GPS CDI, communication channel spacing, and nearest airport. This page allows the pilot to set up this information to customize it to display the type of information that they desire. Keep in mind that although the pilot may select the MFD data bar fields, the fields in the PFD data bar are not changeable. There are several softkeys displayed on this page allowing the pilot to have 2 different setup groups, import and export selections to other aircraft for standardization of a fleet of aircraft, and an option to return to the manufacturer default settings.

> *Note: Some of these system settings are very powerful and affect the behaviors of the map and alerts that the system might send to the pilot regarding airspace areas and boundaries. The pilot should take care in changing these settings without considering the impact on flight operations in busy airspace.*

Map Setup

On the MFD display, many features can be changed, such as the orientation of the moving map display. Press the MENU key on the MFD,

and select Map Setup.

Figure 10.61 – Map setup menu

Use the FMS knob and cursor to tab and select different menu items.

Figure 10.62 – FMS knob

Turn the large knob to select what item you would like to change, then press ENT.

MAP

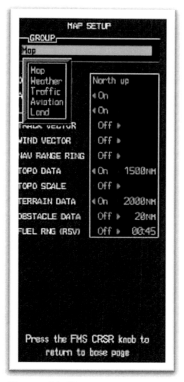

Figure 10.63 – Map setup menu

Orientation of the map: North Up, Track Up, DTK Up. This is a pilot preference item. Most pilots prefer Track up or Direct Track (DTK) up. The default is North up.

Figure 10.64 – Map orientation setup

These features can either be turned on or off using the FMS knob:

- Auto Zoom
- Land Data
- Track Vectors

- Wind Vectors
- Nav Range Ring
- Fuel Range Ring Reserve

Many of these items come turned off by default. It is recommended that Auto Zoom, wind vectors and track vectors all be turned on. The reserve ring can be set for any amount of reserve. The dashed line will show the range with reserve left. The solid green circle will show the range with the amount of fuel left.

WEATHER

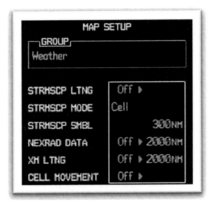

Figure 10.65 – MAP setup weather group

These items are also pilot preference and come turned off by default. It is recommended that NEXRAD be turned on and set cell movement to on. Storm scope can be turned on or off as well as adjusted for range sensitivity. Sensitivity range of the storm scope, Cell Movement, and NEXRAD radar depiction can also be set here.

TRAFFIC

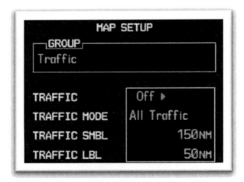

Figure 10.66 – MAP setup traffic group

- The pilot can turn the traffic on or off. It is recommended that this be turned on.
- Range can be changed.

AVIATION

Figure 10.67 – MAP setup aviation group

This area is another area of pilot preference. Make sure that the airspace groups are turned on at least at the 100 - 200NM range so pilots can see the upcoming areas and plan routing accordingly. Range of small and large airports shown on map, or they can be turned off completely. Airspaces, waypoints, and runways can also be changed.

LAND

Figure 10.68 – MAP setup land group

This item is a pilot preference selection. Pilots who fly high or lots of IFR may prefer to turn these items off to avoid screen clutter. Pilots who fly low and lots of VFR may need to keep these on. Items that can be turned on or off:

- Freeway, National and Local Highways, local roads, Railroads, cities, states, river and lakes

Aux Page 6 – System Status

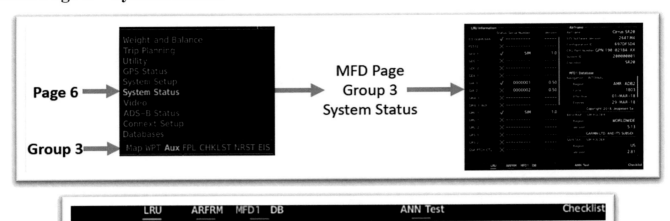

Figure 10.69 – System status display and softkeys

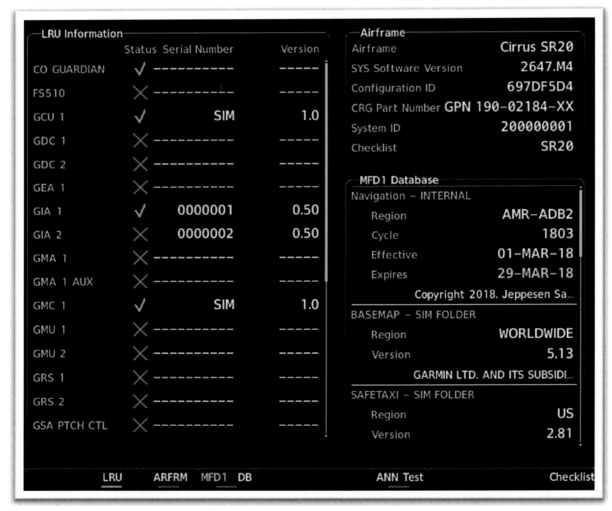

Figure 10.70 – System status

The System Status page displays the status of each LRU in the system. Either a check mark for operational or a red X for non-operational can be seen on this page. Also displayed on the page is the serial number and software version of each component. There are several softkeys present on this screen. The ARFRM softkey is used to verify the aircraft manufacturer airframe matches the software versions. The ANN softkey allows the pilot to test all the alert, caution, and warning lights throughout the system. There is also a DBASE softkey for viewing the status of the database information, including expiration dates.

Aux Page 7 – Video Enhanced Vision System

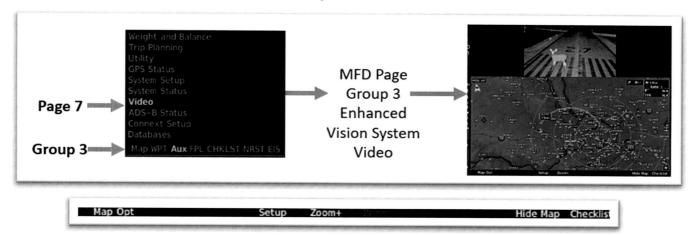

Figure 10.71 – Enhanced Vision System Video display

Figure 10.72 – Enhanced Vision System Video display (image courtesy Cirrus Aircraft)

The Garmin Enhanced Vision System (EVS) is an option installed on certain aircraft that includes a Forward Looking Infrared (FLIR) camera mounted on the aircraft that allows the pilot to see live video images even in the dark and display them on the MFD screen. There are several softkeys associated with this system. Setup allows the pilot to configure the video image and zoom allows the pilot to zoom in and out on the image.

Aux Page 8 – ADS-B Status Page

Figure 10.73 – ADS-B status display page

This Aux page item shows the status of the ADS-B system to the aircraft. There are no softkey options.

Aux Page 9 – Connext Setup Page

Figure 10.74 – CONNEXT setup page

Connext and Flightstream are two different communication technologies that work with the G1000 to link portable devices like phones and iPads to the system. If a Connext or Flightstream SD card is inserted in the bottom MFD card slot, this function will initiate, and options will be available to the pilot to connect their devices via Bluetooth. Once a connectable device is identified, it will require a pairing on both the G1000 and the device itself. Once both devices are verified, the devices are connected and able to share data between the devices with compatible middleware software such as Garmin Pilot and Foreflight. This technology works quite well and facilitates moving route changes back and forth from the pilot's handheld. Devices that have been connected are listed in the box on the screen and are available for future connections. The pilot can remove any device using the remove softkey. Because this system uses an advanced version of Bluetooth 5, it can maintain multiple connection threads to different devices at once. This is particularly useful as both the right and left seat pilots can simultaneously connect their devices to the G1000 allowing enhanced situational awareness.

Aux Page 10 – Database Setup Page

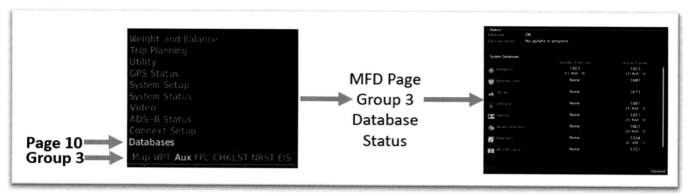

Figure 10.75 – Database status page

Aux Page 11 – XM Information Setup Page

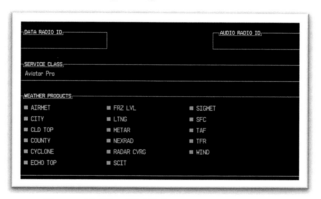

Figure 10.76 – XM Subscription status page

The XM entertainment page is displayed here if the aircraft is equipped with a GDL LRU and a subscription is established with Sirius/XM. To set up this service, the pilot will need the radio ID number associated with the GDL datalink LRU. On this page the pilot can select any of the XM radio stations for inflight entertainment and weather based upon the subscription purchased. There are softkeys for RADIO and INFO. The INFO softkey is used to display what type of XM information is available including the weather features. This is also a volume softkey, which when pressed brings up softkeys displaying a +, - and MUTE. This is where the volume for the XM radio is set. When the radio is on the system plays the audio until either a radio transmission or an intercom transmission interrupts the signal. At no time will entertainment radio take priority over any ATC transmission.

Page Group 4

Flight Planning

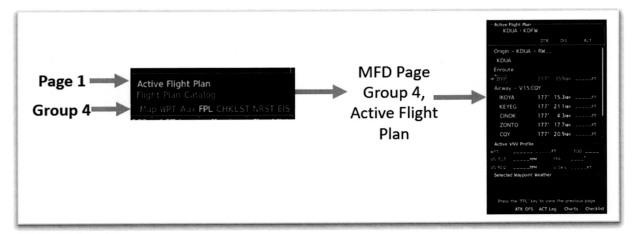

Figure 10.77 – Active flight plan page

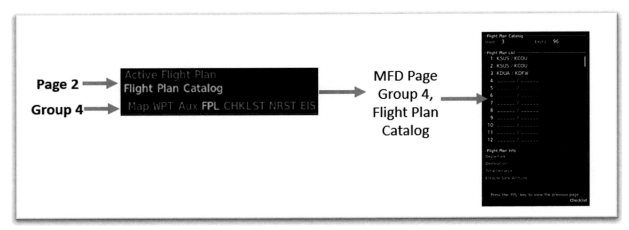

Figure 10.78 – Flight plan catalog status page

Flight planning options on this menu are the same as by pressing the FPL key on the FMS. These will be detailed in chapter eleven.

Page Group 5 – Checklists

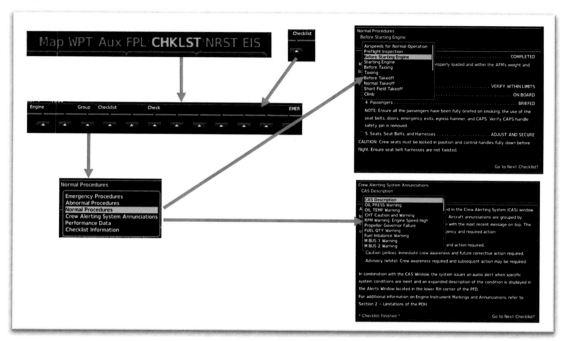

Figure 10.79 – Checklist Menu system

The checklist system has not been implemented on all airframes. This section represents the Cirrus checklist system. The pilot has access to many different checklist groups ranging from airspeeds, preflight and normal procedures to a full complement of abnormal and emergency checklists. As the pilot presses enter on each item in the checklist sequence, the color changes to green indicating that item is complete. If the pilot needs to leave the checklist to take care of other chores, the completed vs incomplete items remain when they return. The pilot should note that the checklist cannot be modified by the pilot. If there are items the pilot wants to insert in the checklist (such as turn on landing lights), they will need an auxiliary checklist other than the on-screen checklist provided and maintained by the manufacturer.

Page Group 6 – Nearest

Nearest Page 1 –Nearest Airport

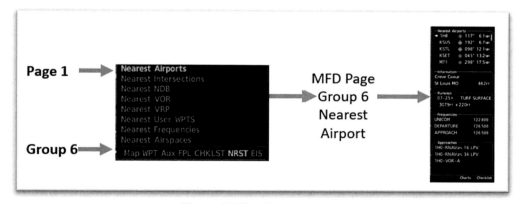

Figure 10.80 – Nearest Airport

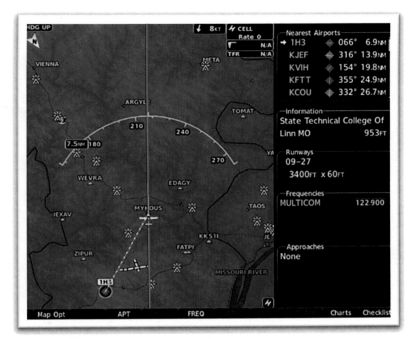

Figure 10.81 – Nearest Airport map details

The NRST airport page will list the nearest 25 airports to the aircraft's current position. The airports are listed by identifier, type of airport and whether it has fuel available, the bearing to the airport and the distance. The Information list will give Lat/Long, field elevation and location of the airport. Runway information includes type of surface, length, and width. Frequencies listed include ATIS or ASOS, clearance, approach, ground tower, etc. Approaches can be view for the airports as well.

Softkeys will allow the pilot to select APT, FREQ, APR. Select the appropriate softkey to select a specific frequency, look at another runway, or to view instrument approaches. For a diversion, the pilot can highlight the airport and press the D-> "Direct to" key on the FMS group and the Flight plan will initiate guidance to the airport. It also will provide the pilot the option to hold at that airport.

Nearest Page 2 –Nearest Intersection

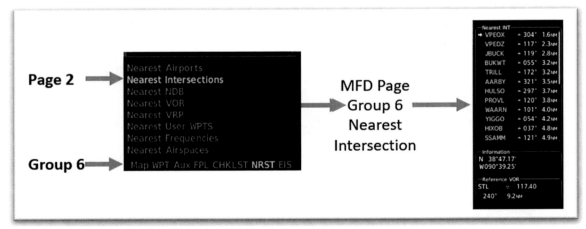

Figure 10.82 – Nearest Intersection details

The list of nearest intersections will be listed with the name of the intersection, the bearing to it, and the distance from it. Information will be Lat/Long reference VOR will give the information on the VOR that identifies the intersection. For a diversion, the pilot can highlight the airport and press the D-> "Direct to" key on the FMS group and the Flight plan will initiate guidance to the airport. It also will provide the pilot the option to hold at that fix.

Nearest Page 3: NDB

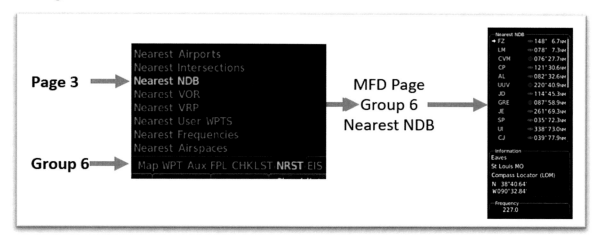

Figure 10.83 – Nearest NDB details

Nearest NDB lists the closest NDBs to the aircraft's current position. The name and type of NDB and the frequency is given. For a diversion, the pilot can highlight the airport and press the D-> "Direct to" key on the FMS group and the Flight plan will initiate guidance to the airport. It also will provide the pilot the option to hold at that NDB.

Nearest Page 4: VOR

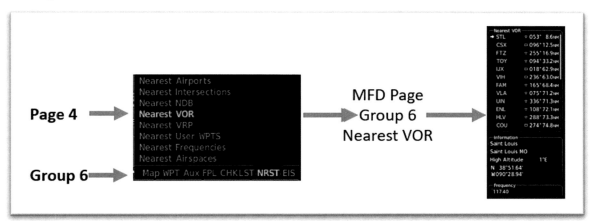

Figure 10.84 – Nearest VOR details

The nearest VORs are listed by identifier, type, bearing to station, and distance. Lat/Long information and the area in which it is located is given in the information box. The frequency for the VOR can be selected by press the FREQ softkey and the pressing ENT when the frequency is highlighted. The frequency will then appear in the standby blue box the NAV frequency. For a diversion, the pilot can highlight the airport and press the D-> "Direct to" key on the FMS group and the Flight plan will initiate guidance to the airport. It also will provide the pilot the option to hold at that VOR.

Nearest Page 5: VRP

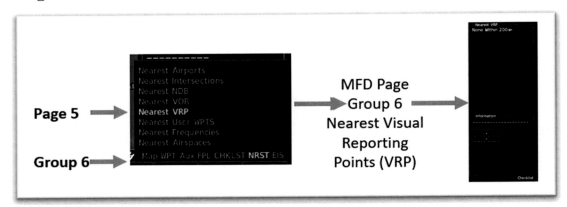

Figure 10.85 – Nearest VRP details

The nearest Visual Reporting Points (VRP) waypoints will be listed by name, bearing and distance to the station. VRPs are common in higher traffic density areas and ATC typically looks for inbound VFR traffic to report over these points. The VRP reference information will be the identifier for the VRP, the radial and distance from the VOR or terminal airport attached to. For a diversion, the pilot can highlight the airport and press the D-> "Direct to" key on the FMS group and the Flight plan will initiate guidance to the airport. It also will provide the pilot the option to hold at that VRP.

Nearest Page 6: User Defined Waypoint

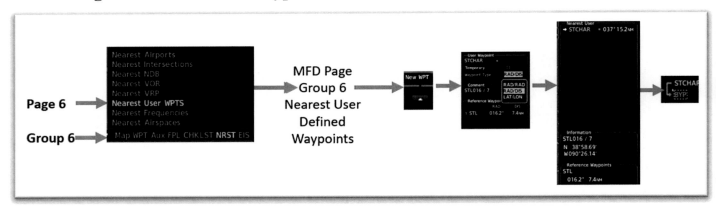

Figure 10.86 – User defined waypoint creation and use in a flight plan

This option allows the pilot to identify the nearest User Defined Waypoints stored in the system. A pilot can press the D-> "Direct to to" key in the FMS group and then the system will initiate guidance to that point.

Nearest Page 7: Nearest Frequencies

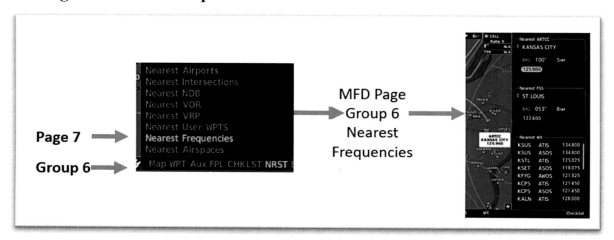

Figure 10.87 – Nearest frequencies page

The nearest ARTCC will give information on the closest frequency to get the Air Route Traffic Control Center. FSS frequencies are shown with the name of the Flight Service Station, the distance and bearing from it and the frequencies available at your present position. Nearest weather frequencies can be selected to listen to local airport conditions from ATIS, ASOS, and AWOS. The softkeys, ARTCC, FSS, and WX allow the pilot to choose which type of frequency they would like to select.

Nearest Page 6: AIRSPACE

Figure 10.88 – Nearest Airspace

The nearest airspace will show airspace data that can be of concern to the pilot. The alerts, controlling agency, vertical limits and frequencies are provided. The softkey for ALERTS and FREQ allow the pilot to select the alert or the frequencies of the controlling agency for that airspace.

Page Group 7 – Engine Information Screen

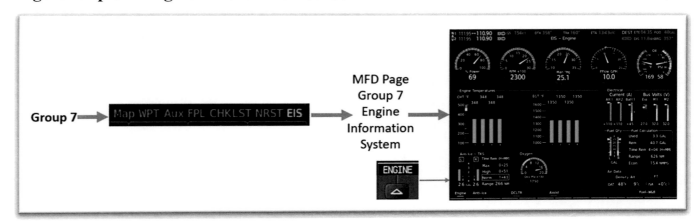

Figure 10.89 – Engine Information System (EIS) page

The engine information System (EIS) was described in chapter nine. Please refer to this chapter for more detailed information.

Communication and Navigation Radio Settings

NAV Radio Control Summary

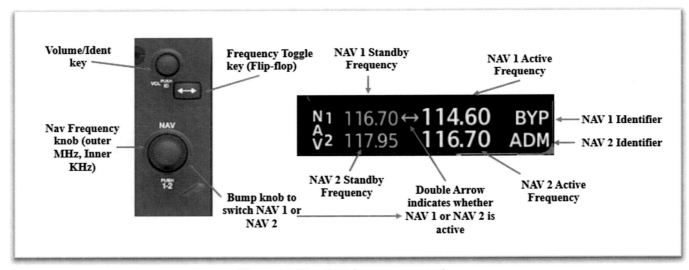

Figure 10.90 – NAV frequency controls

NAV and COM Control Operation like the PFD but located on the MFD.

- ❑ The NAV 1 and NAV 2 controls are located on the upper left-hand corner of the screen. NAV 1 is located and the top row and NAV 2 on the bottom. The active NAV frequencies will be on the right (closest to screen) and standby on the left (farthest from the screen).
- ❑ To change the frequency, the blue box must be around the frequency you wish to change. To move the box from NAV 1 to NAV 2, push the NAV frequency selector knob in.

❑ The NAV frequency selector is located on the left-hand side of the Garmin Display Unit (GDU), the outer knob ring controls MHz and the inner knob ring controls kHz.

❑ To audibly identify a VOR or LOC, make sure the appropriate NAV 1 or NAV 2 is selected on the audio panel. Then press the NAV volume control "in" on the upper left-hand side of the GDU. "ID" will appear in between the standby and active frequency position and the Morse code identifier will be heard.

❑ The VOR or LOC identifier will also be displayed to the right of the active NAV frequency. For example, "STL" will appear if St. Louis VOR is in the active frequency.

❑ The color of the active NAV frequency depends on what is selected as the current CDI needle on the heading indicator. If VOR or LOC 1 is selected, then the active frequency in NAV 1 will be green. And if VOR or LOC 2 is selected as the CDI, the active NAV 2 will be green.

COMMUNICATION Radio Controls (COM)

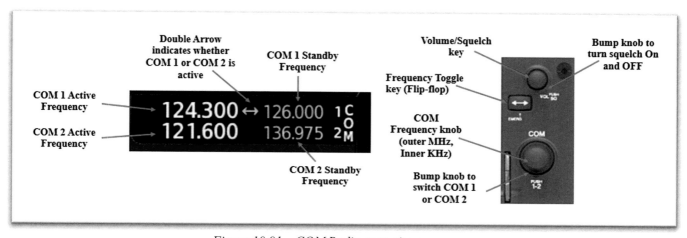

Figure 10.91 – COM Radio operation summary

The COM controls section is for selecting VHF radio communication frequencies such as tower and ground control frequencies. The operation of the COM radios is very similar to that just discussed for the NAV radios. The outer knob ring selects the MHz portion of the frequency in the inner portion of the knob ring selects the KHz portion of the frequency. For instance, to select the COM frequency 136.975, use the outer knob ring to select the <u>136</u> and the inner knob ring portion to select the <u>.975.</u>

Figure 10.92 – COM frequency display box

Figure 10.93 – COM frequency control knob

To select between entering information into COM radio 1 and COM radio 2, the pilot would press in or "bump" the inner portion of the NAV knob. The blue box moves up and down between COM 1 and COM 2.

Figure 10.94 – COM frequency toggle key

Figure 10.95 – COM frequency toggle selected box after flip-flop

Once the pilot places the new desired COM frequency into the blue box, they use the COM toggle select key or "flip-flop" key to move it from the standby position to the active position. They are now free to enter a new frequency into the standby position using the knob or they can select a frequency from the WPT or NRST dropdown menus and press ENT to copy that frequency into the blue box. Some G1000 installations provide a popup window that allows the pilot to specify whether they want the frequency to be sent to COM 1 or COM 2 and whether the pilot wants the new frequency to go to the active or standby position.

Note: Pressing and holding the COM frequency toggle key automatically enters in and selects the emergency frequency 121.5 MHz

Conclusion

In this chapter, we looked at the features and functions of the Multi-Function Flight Display. It is the most robust section of the system and contains the greatest number of menus, options, and softkeys. It also produces the most colorful display and that while the color provides the pilot with very important and relevant information, it is not always the pilot's priority to stare at it instead of doing other things they should be doing to maintain situational awareness and ultimately, control of the aircraft.

Remember

❑ Map page 1 is the default map page. Anytime it is desired to return to that page, simply press and hold the CLR key and the system will automatically return to that page. If flying a Cirrus or other aircraft with a GCU, then press the Home symbol on the GCU.

❑ The vast number of functions that can be used in the MFD can create a distraction for the pilot. Remember not to spend too much time looking at or using the many features of the MFD.

❑ Use the MFD Page Groups and Pages as required to view the status of the system, change the XM radio station, view weather reports and look at NEXRAD radar.

❑ Some pages on the MFD require the use of softkeys to navigate between the information boxes presented on the screen. Besides looking at the blinking cursor, always look at the softkeys to determine proper navigation on the page.

Chapter Debriefing:

We have now covered the most complex area of the G1000 system modules and how to use the MFD to aid in situational awareness by providing information grouped in a high level (Page Groups) then broken down by categories of related information (Pages).

❑ Now that the pilot understands that the G1000 uses the Multi-Function Flight Display (MFD) to perform many of the electronic situational awareness tasks of the pilot's scan flow, they will also understand how distracting the MFD can be to the overall safe operation of the aircraft. The pilot needs to keep their eyes moving!

❑ Now that the pilot understands why knowing the functions of the MFD and where to find certain menus is so important, then they will also realize that if they ever get lost in a menu or a function-screen and quickly need to get back to the top (home), they can just press and hold the CLR clear key and the system will immediately go back to MAP Page 1.

❑ Now that the pilot understands that this system is a digital system featuring many subsystems and sensors which are driven by software and computers, they will realize the importance of keeping the software and the databases current and up to date. Software releases may be released and installed which change some of the basic functions without the pilot being aware.

If the pilot understands these three areas and can correlate these three major points into their everyday flying skills and apply these skills to the operation of the G1000 aircraft, then they are ready for the chapter quiz and then move on to chapter eleven!

The Chapter Quiz Scenario

This Chapter Quiz Scenario (CQS) is designed to offer a real-world flight situation and use the pilot's new knowledge of the G1000 MFD to answer some situational questions about how to safely operate their aircraft. They can then determine whether they "understand" and can even "correlate" the material covered with their existing aeronautical knowledge and are prepared to use this information in a way which will enhance their operational safety while using the G1000 equipped aircraft.

In this chapter quiz, the pilot will be asked to demonstrate their understanding of the Multi-function Flight Display (MFD) and some of the chores that have to be perform using its information in a mountainous terrain flight scenario between Denver, Colorado (KDEN) and Meek County, Colorado (KEEO), a non-tower-controlled airport. Consider the following questions about this scenario:

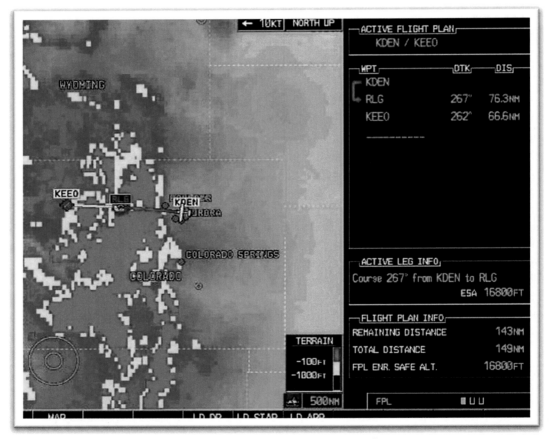

Figure 10.96 – Chapter Ten quiz scenario diagram

Question 1: During this flight, the pilot wants to find the nearest airport on the MFD. How is this information retrieved?

     a) Using the FMS outer knob, scroll to NRST page group

     b) Using the FMS inner knob and moving to map page 4

     c) Pressing the Direct to key

Question 2: On this flight, traffic information appears on the moving map, how does the pilot find a page that will allow to them to get a closer look at the traffic?

     a) Pressing the FMS knob

     b) Turn the inner FMS knob once to the right to get to the Traffic page (MAP page 2)

     c) Pressing the FPL key

Question 3: How many airports does the NRST function display at one time?

     a) 10

     b) 50

     c) 25

Question 4: If the pilot wants to change the MFD map display default information, what screen will allow them to change this information?

     a) pressing the MENU key while on MAP page 1

     b) Pressing the INSET softkey

     c) Selecting AUX page 3

Question 5: The pilot is now flying in the departure terminal area of Denver and they want to turn on the traffic overlay on the moving map display. How do they do this?

     a) Press MENU to select TRAFFIC ON.

     b) Press the MAP OPT softkey on MAP page 1, then press the TRAFFIC softkey.

     c) Select the FPL key and scroll to TRAFFIC on the menu.

Question 6: The pilot is exiting the departure terminal area of Denver and they want to see the NEXRAD weather ahead along the route. How do they do this?

    a)   Press MENU to select NEXRAD ON.

    b)   Scroll the FMS knob to MAP Page 1, twist the inner FMS knob to MAP OPT, press the NEXRAD softkey on the bottom of the MFD to activate the weather.

    c)   Scroll the FMS knob to MAP Page 1, twist the inner FMS knob to WPT, Twist the inside knob to highlight, weather and select NEXRAD.

Question 7: The pilot is now enroute to Meek (KEEO) and they want to see METAR text weather for the destination airport. How do they do this?

    a)   Press MENU to select TAF ON.

    b)   Scroll the FMS knob to MAP Page 1, twist the inner FMS knob to WX, select the TAF/METAR softkey on the bottom of the MFD to activate the weather.

    c)   Scroll the outer FMS knob to view WPT. If there is weather available for the destination, there will be a WX softkey illuminated. Press that key.

Question 8: The pilot is now approaching Meek (KEEO) and they see the red and yellow areas displayed on the screen such as shown on the scenario diagram above. What does this mean and what should they do?

    a)   NEXRAD weather is being used and there is a thunderstorm and heavy rain showers ahead.

    b)   The MAP terrain feature is being used and the terrain ahead is higher than the aircraft requiring the pilot to climb before continuing.

    c)   The NEXRAD and the TERRAIN features are both in use and there are both weather cells and terrain ahead and you should turn around and return to Denver or another alternate airport.

Grading Criteria:

The pilot will know when they have completed this chapter when they get all the answers correct and demonstrate a solid understanding of the material. When the exam is complete, grade the answers with the answer key in the back of this handbook. Incorrect answers should be researched by going back to the appropriate reference area in the chapter or the Garmin Cockpit Guide that comes with the aircraft. Once all correct answers have been achieved, proceed on to the next chapter. Come back to items in this chapter at any time.

Chapter Eleven: Flight Planning

Chapter Objectives:

The objective of this chapter is for the pilot to demonstrate understanding of the G1000 Flight planning function by reviewing the content of this chapter. The pilot will then take the chapter quiz at the end which will check their knowledge about the material covered.

Completion Standards:

When this chapter is complete, the pilot will be able to describe and explain functions and modes of the G1000 flight planning functions. The pilot will know when they have met the completion standards of the chapter when they have correctly answered all the quiz questions at the end of this section. If any questions are scored as incorrect, go back to the appropriate reference area in the chapter or the Garmin Cockpit Guide that comes with the aircraft. When the pilot has correctly answered all the chapter quiz questions, then they may proceed to the next chapter.

Concepts of Flight Planning on the G1000

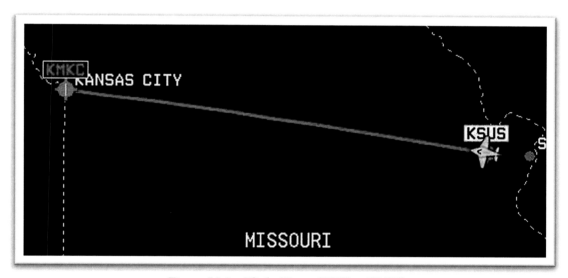

Figure 11.1 – Flight Plan – KSUS to KMKC

> **Definition: <u>Flight Plan</u>** *A sequence of defined waypoints which when connected with lines on a chart constitute a plan of intended action which leads from a point in space (departure point) to another point in space (a destination).*

One of the key advantages of using an integrated system like the G1000 is that information from a variety of sources can be combined to create a logical script of known waypoints to help layout trips with ease. What is even better is that the autopilot can fly this script of waypoints perfectly just like it was a computer running a computer program. When you think about it, it is.

A flight plan, as shown in Figure 11.2 implies that a flight plan consists of at least two known waypoints but may also include an enroute set of waypoints or even Victor airways. Many flight plans could consist of many more waypoints. In fact, the G1000 allows many flight plans to be stored in its database for future use and each of these can contain scores of waypoints each. In the case of Figure 11.2, we have entered a simple flight plan which goes from Spirit of St. Louis Airport, KSUS to Oklahoma City Will Rogers Airport, KOKC. Once we are airborne and engage the autopilot in NAV mode, the autopilot would track this path correcting for winds and would attempt to fly to the destination keeping the CDI needle on the HSI always centered.

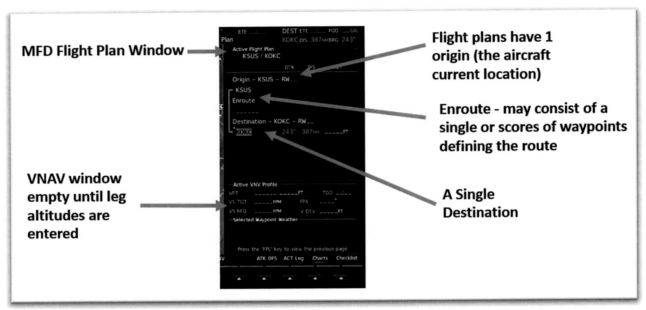

Figure 11.2 – Flight plan page 1

The pilot can enter the flight planning menu on the PFD or the MFD using the **FPL** key. There is a limit as to what can be done from the smaller menu box on the PFD, but in general, the pilot can create, edit, and save flight plans from the PFD but they cannot call-up stored flight plans from the flight plan catalog, nor can they see the specifics of the flight plan on a map as they work to create the route. You get much more flexibility and powerful functions when this type of programming is performed on the MFD. More on this shortly.

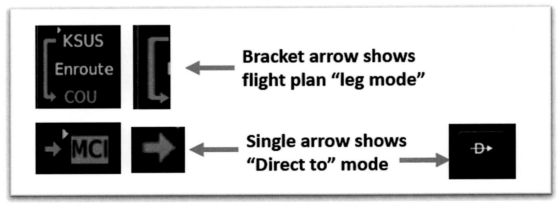

Figure 11.3 – Flight plan leg versus "direct to" leg

Direct To Flight Plan

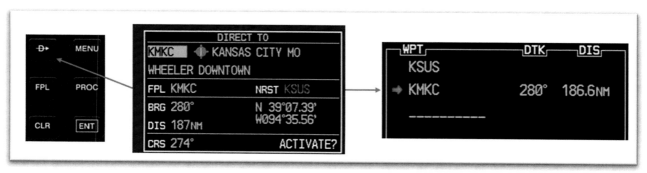

Figure 11.4 – Direct-To menu

A "Direct To" flight plan is what many pilots think of when they program a GPS. Now, there are very practical reasons to use the **D->** key, but in general, the pilot should create flight plans starting with the **FPL** key instead. Among other reasons, using FPL defines a leg between two known points which allows the G1000 databases to offer suggestions and alerts relating to airspace, obstacles, weather, frequencies, and instrument procedures.

To create a Direct To flight plan, we use the **D->** key. The differences are subtle, but the amount of information the system can offer the pilot about the departure point and the arrival point is limited with the Direct To flight plan since it only allows the pilot to input the ultimate destination. We advise the pilot to always use the **FPL** key to create a point-to-point flight plan and then press the **D->** key in certain intentional cases such as when the aircraft is off course and ATC clears the pilot to the destination or next waypoint. We could also use this in cases where we wanted to divert to a waypoint not in the current flight plan.

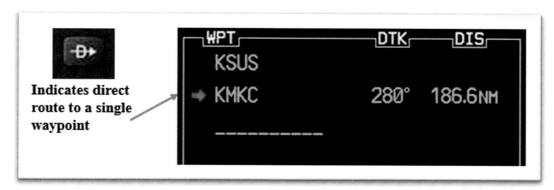

Figure 11.5 – Direct-To a waypoint in active flight plan

Flight Plan Window in MFD

To create a flight plan in the MFD, the pilot presses the **FPL** key which brings up the flight plan window. Bump the FMS knob to start the cursor blinking. The Origin may already be completed if the GPS has initialized and determined its location at a known waypoint database airport. If the Origin is empty or the pilot wants to change the origin to a different waypoint, twist the inner knob of the FMS knob. The pilot then scrolls down to the Destination and fills in that waypoint either using Bump-Scroll-Twist of the FMS knob or by using the keypad on the GCU, if so equipped.

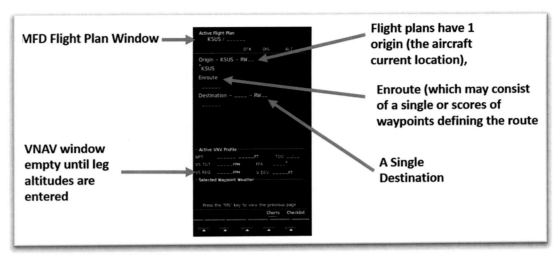

Figure 11.6 – Flight plan page 1

The active flight plan menu group is accessed by pressing the **FPL** key on the MFD or the GCU if equipped. This key brings up the flight plan page 1 as the default.

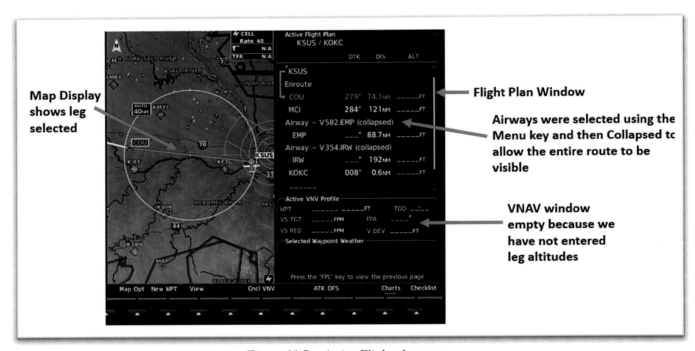

Figure 11.7 – Active Flight plan page

Active Flight Plan

The active flight plan page is where the pilot will spend most of their flying time. This page is used for viewing or editing the current flight plan. Once a flight plan is activated, the Active Flight Plan page shows all the waypoints stored for a flight plan. Also displayed on this page is the distance and desired track to the waypoint for each leg of the flight plan. The active leg is identified by a magenta line on the map and a magenta bracket arrow on the waypoint list. This arrow points from the previous waypoint to the next waypoint. When the active leg is complete the line then moves to the next leg of the flight plan. The active flight plan page shows the estimated enroute safe altitude for the selected leg and or the whole flight plan. The active flight plan page also shows the total remaining distance for the entire flight plan. There are several softkeys associated with the active flight plan page:

Figure 11.8 – Active flight plan softkey options

ENGINE – This quick access to the Engine EIS page is always available throughout the system.

MAP OPT – allows the pilot to customize the map view on the MFD when in the flight plan mode.

Figure 11.9 – MAP OPT Options while in MFD Flight Plan Map mode

NEW WPT – Allows the pilot to create a user defined waypoint and then offers another key to enter it into the flight plan. If they choose to enter it into the flight plan, they first need to scroll the cursor down to the waypoint where they want the new waypoint inserted.

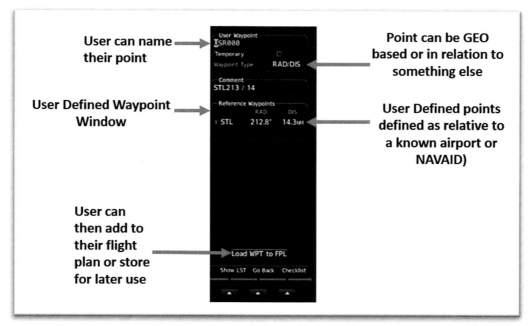

Figure 11.10 – Creating a User Defined waypoint

CNCL VNV – This key allows the pilot to cancel Vertical Navigation (VNAV) mode that the autopilot may have been engaged to follow. An example of this is when a pilot was climbing or descending along a VNAV established route and ATC changed the clearance or the pilot elected to level off.

Figure 11.11 – VNAV softkey options

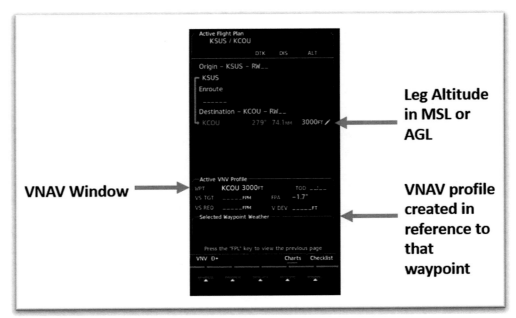

Figure 11.12 – VNAV Active Profile set at 3000 ft MSL

VNAV is a very powerful function of the autopilot and flight plan working together but the elements must be established and programmed by the pilot. Once the parameters are entered, the autopilot will fly these parameters. An example might be that a pilot wants to plan a descent from altitude to arrive at the destination pattern altitude 4nm from the airport. The flight plan VNAV computer will advise the pilot when they reach the Top of descent (TOD) to start that descent to achieve that goal. The TOD and BOD symbols are displayed on the map as arcs. Climbs and Descents work the same way.

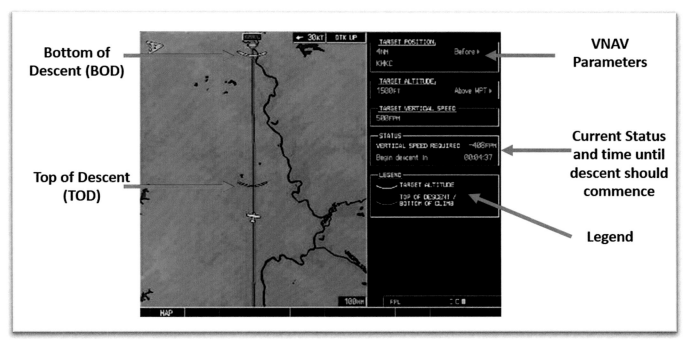

Figure 11.13 –Vertical navigation

This is the vertical navigation page. This page displays information about vertical climb/descent planning and the features related to it. By activating the cursor, the pilot can adjust the following criteria:

- o   Target altitude selectable in 100-foot increments in reference to either AGL or MSL altitudes
- o   Distance in nautical miles from the selected waypoint
- o   Selected waypoint
- o   Rate of descent desired in feet per minute.

Figure 11.14 – Flight plan page 3, Vertical speed required

Also displayed is the vertical speed required to achieve the planned descent/climb.

Two arcs will be displayed on the map shown on this page only. The first arc (dark grey color) is the top of descent/climb point. The second arc (white color) is the programmed target altitude point.

ATK OFS – The Aircraft Track Offset mode allows a pilot to create a flight plan leg offset right or left from the calculated leg route. An example of this might be to fly parallel to a route to avoid weather or an active MOA or even a TFR.

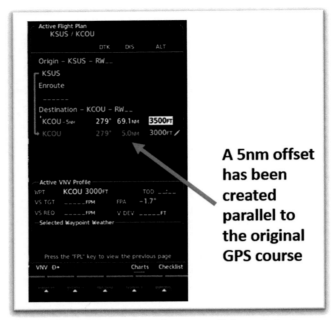

Figure 11.15 – ATK Offset of 5nm parallel to original course

CHARTS – The Charts mode will become very important to the pilot as it allows them to load airport diagrams, approach, arrival, and departure charts on the MFD and will superimpose the position of the aircraft on the chart for superior situational awareness.

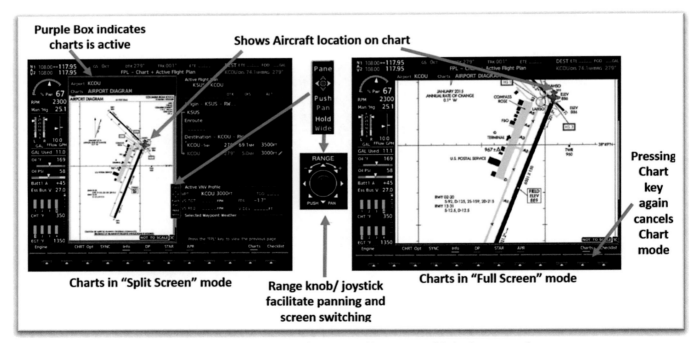

Figure 11.16 – Showing Charts in Full Screen and Split Screen mode

The default mode is Full Screen mode. The pilot can press the MFD or GCU Menu key to select split screen mode. The pilot can then use the Range pointer to pan in or out, up or down, or toggle back and forth from the Chart to the Flight plan. Tilt the Joystick to the right to move the purple box back to Flight plan window and back again to the left to move back to the Charts window.

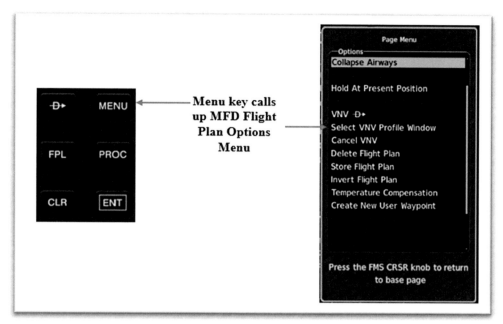

Figure 11.17 – Flight plan Menu screen

The pilot will have to get used to this as it is confusing until they determine which mode they are in and how that will affect the screen scrolling.

Flight Plan Catalog

Figure 11.18 – Flight plan catalog

This is the flight plan catalog page. This page displays stored flight plan information and when the cursor is active, provides softkeys for the following functions:

Figure 11.19 – Flight plan catalog softkeys

NEW – use to create a new flight plan.

ACTIVATE – use to activate a specific flight plan from the catalog.

INVERT – use to invert the sequence of waypoints, often used for the return trip on a specific flight plan

EDIT – used to edit the current or selected flight plan.

COPY – copies a portion of or complete flight plan.

DELETE – use to delete the selected flight plan from the catalog.

IMPORT – Used to import a flight plan created on another G1000 aircraft and stored on the SD card. Some support may be available to create these flight plans on external programs such as Garmin Pilot or Foreflight.

Note: This mode might be useful to a fleet of aircraft to replicate multiple routes across the fleet instead of recreating them on every aircraft.

EXPORT - Used to export a flight plan from the flight plan catalog to another G1000 by writing the flight plan file onto the SD card. Some support may be available to import these flight plans on external programs such as Garmin Pilot or Foreflight.

Note: This mode might be useful to a fleet of aircraft to replicate multiple routes across the fleet instead of recreating them on every aircraft.

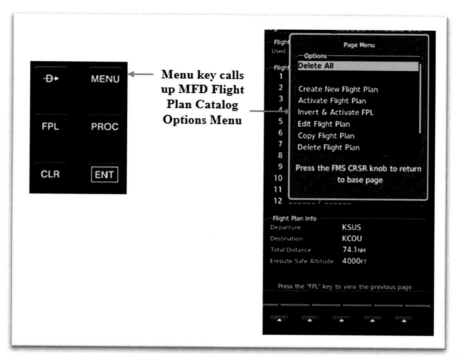

Figure 11.20 – Flight plan page menu options

Figure 11.21 – Empty flight plan catalog

- To enter a flight plan, press the **FPL** key and use the inner FMS knob to display the flight plan Catalog (Flight plan page 2). Press menu to display the catalog options. Use the outer FMS knob to highlight 'Create new flight plan' and press enter. A blank flight plan now appears that will allow the pilot to select waypoints by using the inner and outer FMS knobs and the enter key starting with the origin and ending with the destination. Add Enroute waypoints as needed until the whole route is complete. When finished press the inner FMS knob or the Back key to return to the flight plan catalog.

Note: The pilot can enter legs consisting of Victor airways by entering an enroute waypoint consisting of a VOR identifier. The press MENU. In the menu box will be an option to LOAD AIRWAY. The pilot can specify the on-ramp and off-ramp waypoints along the airway. If a VOR has multiple intersecting airways, it will offer the pilot each choice and then fill the flight plan enroute section in with all the defining fixes that make up that airway.

Figure 11.22 – Flight plan catalog showing 2 stored flight plans

Figure 11.23 – Complete flight plan catalog

Figure 11.24 – Activate flight plan softkey

Figure 11.25 – Activation Confirmation

- To navigate a flight plan, press the **FPL** key and use the inner FMS knob to display the flight plan catalog. Press the inner FMS knob to activate the cursor. Use the outer FMS knob to highlight the desired flight plan and then press MENU to display the catalog options. Use the outer FMS knob to highlight 'active flight plan' and press ENT. Press the ENT again to confirm. A second way to accomplish the same function is to press the softkey which appears once the cursor is activated.

Figure 11.26 – Aux page 1, trip statistics

Additional information valuable to flight planning can be found in the AUX page group on the AUX page. The pilot can use this page to facilitate trip planning.

Direct to page

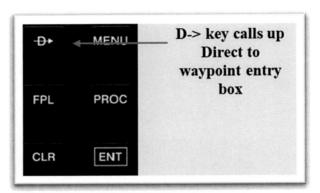

*Figure 11.27 – **D->** key*

Although the G1000 is designed to best be utilized with flight plans, there are many scenarios where the Direct To navigation function is appropriate. The main purpose is to navigate directly to any point in the internal or user defined database.

By pressing the "**D->**" key the pilot may select a waypoint by specifying the identifier, name or location. Bump the FMS knob and scroll to the appropriate field, then select the identifier you would like to go Direct To.

The pilot can also select waypoints that are part of a flight plan, selecting from a list of nearest airports, specifying a course to fly to the waypoint, and activating direct to navigation to the nearest waypoint. This is used in cases where ATC elects to clear the aircraft to a fix or even the ultimate destination skipping other enroute waypoints that may have been identified in the route clearance.

Figure 11.28 – Direct-To data box

If the pilot is navigating with the direct to function, they can cancel the operation by pressing the **D->** key and then pressing the menu key. Highlight 'Cancel Direct To NAV' and press the ENT key.

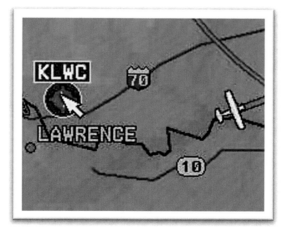

Figure 11.29 – Cursor Direct To

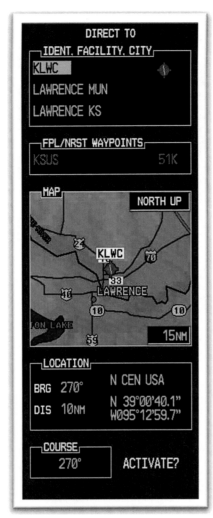

Figure 11.30 – Direct To menu

Figure 11.31 – Direct To a user defined waypoint

Figure 11.32 – Direct To the just created MapWpt

Direct To can also be selected by using the Navigation Map page. Select the navigation map page (Map page 1). Press the Range knob to activate the JOYSTICK to display the panning arrow. Move the JOYSTICK over to a point that the pilot would like to proceed direct to. When the waypoint is highlighted press the **D->** key and then press ENT twice. Doing this operation in an open area, a waypoint called MAPWPT is created, and the GPS will navigate to that point. If it is so desired, the MAPWPT can be renamed to suit the pilot's purpose. This is the same as creating a User defined waypoint.

To use the Direct To function from the active flight plan press the **FPL** key. Next, press the inner FMS knob to activate the cursor. Now, turn the outer FMS knob to select the desired waypoint. Press the "**D->**" key and then press the ENT key twice to select and confirm the choice.

Flight Planning Scenario for the G1000

For this scenario we are going to plan a flight from Spirit of St. Louis (KSUS) to Kansas City Downtown Airport (KMKC).

For the sake of training, this flight will use a Departure procedure, Airway routing and Arrival procedure to better depict all the planning capabilities of the G1000 system.

To begin, press the FPL key to call up the course catalog:

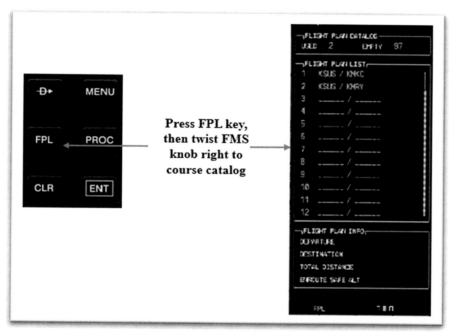

Figure 11.33 – Flight plan catalog, stored flight plans

Figure 11.34 – Flight plan menu options

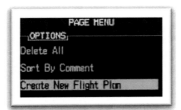

Figure 11.35 – Create new Flight plan

Figure 11.36 – Enter waypoints

Press the **FPL** key on the MFD. Pressing this key brings up the flight planning page 1. Twist the inner FMS knob to display the catalog (flight plan page 2). Press the MENU key to bring up the flight plan catalog options. Scroll the outer FMS knob to highlight 'create new flight plan' and then press the ENT key. A blank flight plan page will appear for the first available storage location. Use the inner and outer FMS knobs to enter the first waypoint identifier and then press the ENT key. The other waypoints are entered in the same fashion.

Figure 11.37 – Menu key

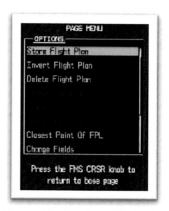

Figure 11.38 – Store flight plan

Our departure airport will be Spirit of St. Louis Airport (KSUS). Our next point will be the Macon VOR (MCM), and then for our last waypoint it will be our destination (KMKC). At this point the inner FMS knob should be used to move to the flight plan catalog page. Press the FMS knob to activate the cursor. Then use the outer FMS knob to highlight the flight plan created. Press the MENU key and select "Store flight plan. The flight plan will be stored in the first empty slot in the flight plan catalog. Press ENT to confirm intention to store the flight plan.

Figure 11.39 – Flight plan key

Figure 11.40 – Flight plan catalog

Figure 11.41 – Menu key

Figure 11.42 – Flight planning menu options

Figure 11.43 – Acknowledge activate flight plan

When it is time to begin navigating a flight plan, press the **FPL** key and use the inner FMS knob to display the flight plan catalog page. Press the FMS knob to activate the cursor. Use the large knob to highlight the flight plan desired. Press the MENU key and highlight 'Activate flight plan' and then press the ENT key. Confirm this action by making sure that OK is highlighted and then press the ENT key. The flight plan is now active and is now displayed in the active flight plan page.

Now that the flight plan is active, we can load Departure and Arrival procedures that may be a part of the ATC clearance/flight plan by pressing the PROC key. Select the appropriate key for either the Departure Procedure or Arrival Procedure. The pilot could also load an approach at this point, but this is not the correct time to do that as the approach will be assigned by ATC in real time and would likely change by the time the pilot arrived. The system will prompt the pilot for some additional information such as which runway will be used for landing. The pilot can skip this since they rarely know prior to departure.

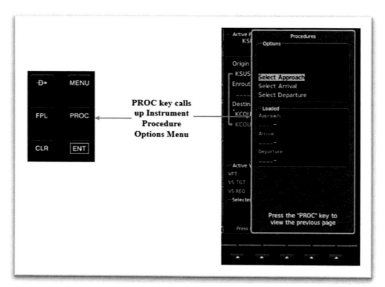

Figure 11.44 – Acknowledge activate flight plan

Figure 11.45 – Departure procedure selection

The pilot should then select the departure procedure if they know it. Many airports do not have them so in these cases, just skip this. If there is a DP for the airport you are departing (Spirit of St. Louis has many), then this is the time to load it into the flight plan. Now load the transition which will be the organized flow that ATC guides aircraft out of a terminal area.

Figure 11.46 – Transition selection

Figure 11.47 – Runway selection

Figure 11.48 – Waypoint sequence

For our example, we will load the OZARK3 departure out of KSUS using the MCM transition. Next, we will load the Braymer Two Arrival. We are given choices for which transition and which runway we were expecting to land on. Once the entry is complete, the pilot can check the sequence of waypoints in both the procedure page and in the active flight plan page. By looking at the Map page adjacent to the flight plan screen, the pilot will be able to tell if the routing is correct. The two most common errors in a flight plan creation are entering the incorrect waypoints and incongruencies caused by loading illogical departure and arrival procedures. The pilot can practice performing these programming tasks on programs such as Garmin Pilot and Foreflight so they have time to study the route to ensure it is ready to fly.

One of the more powerful functions that pilots miss is knowing that they can "invert" the incoming flight plan rather than reentering the trip home as a separate flight plan. The Menu key will allow the pilot to easily invert a flight plan without reentering it.

Note: Remember to store the flight plan into the course catalog before the aircraft is shut down as the active flight plan is deleted on startup.

While using the "active flight plan" page there are many actions that can be accomplished. Some of the features are as follows:

- o Changing the flight plan title
- o Inverting the flight plan
- o Deleting the flight plan
- o Getting information on the closest waypoint in the flight plan
- o Activating a selected leg of the flight plan
- o Loading and deleting Approaches, Departures, and Arrivals

Note: Selection of approach procedures will be covered in detail in the Instrument Procedures section.

Conclusion

In this chapter, we looked at the flight planning functions from within the Multi-Function Display and how the pilot can use them to customize the trip planning of the trips they are going to fly. Once the flight plan is entered, the autopilot will fly the flight plan like a script. The pilot can monitor the status of their flight plan on the MFD or the flight plan window of the PFD.

Chapter Debriefing:

We have now covered the area of flight planning with the G1000 and the pilot should now understand how to develop, store, retrieve, and work with flight plans and how they are operated differently than traditional aircraft.

- ❏ Now that the pilot understands that the G1000 flight planning functions are designed to create a customized agenda for the proposed flight, then they should also understand that they can create, edit, save, retrieve, and invert those flight plans to give them flexibility and save key strokes.
- ❏ Now that the pilot understands when it makes sense to use a "point to point" flight plan leg and when it makes sense to use a Direct To flight plan, then they will also understand why entering a flight plan on the MFD makes sense. The larger screen and increased detail will be preferred over entry on the PFD.
- ❏ Now that the pilot understands that this system of interoperating menus can lead to distraction, they will understand that planning ahead and using the enroute phases of the trip is the best time to plan for the pending arrival at the destination.

Now that the pilot understands these three key areas and can correlate these three major points into their everyday flying skills and apply these skills to the operation of your G1000 aircraft, then it is time to take the quiz and move on to chapter twelve!

Chapter Eleven Quiz: Flight Planning

The Chapter Quiz Scenario

This Chapter Quiz Scenario (CQS) is designed to offer a real-world flight situation and use the pilot's new knowledge of the G1000 flight planning functions to answer some situational questions about how to safely operate their aircraft. They can then determine whether they "understand" and can even "correlate" the material covered with their existing aeronautical knowledge and are prepared to use this information in a way which will enhance their operational safety while using the G1000 equipped aircraft.

In this chapter quiz, the pilot will be asked to demonstrate their understanding of the Garmin flight planning system functions on this flight scenario between Johnson County airport (KOJC) to New Century airport in Olathe Kansas (KIXD), a tower-controlled airport. Consider the following questions about this scenario:

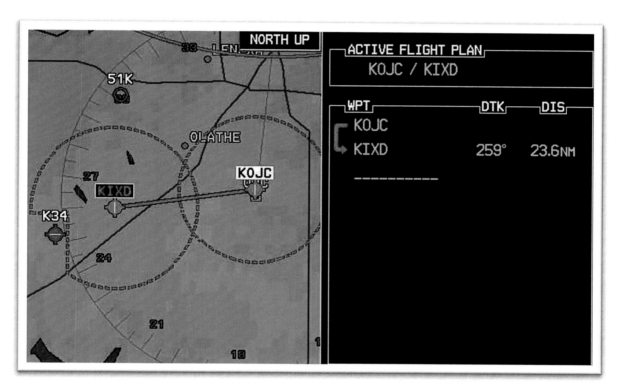

Figure 11.49 – Chapter Eleven quiz scenario diagram

Question 1: If the pilot wanted to create a flight plan for the trip suggested in this scenario, what would be the first key to push?

    a) **MENU**

    b) **FPL**

    c) **Direct to**

Question 2: What page of the FPL menu group is the catalog located on?

    a) **Flight plan page 5**

    b) **Flight plan page 3**

    c) **Flight plan page 2**

Question 3: To cancel a fight plan that has already been activated, what is the sequence to accomplish this?

    a) **Press the FPL key, Press the MENU key, highlight 'delete flight plan', press the ENT key twice**

    b) **Press the FPL key and then pressing ENT key**

    c) **Hold down the CLR key**

Question 4: How can the pilot use the range joystick to navigate direct to a known waypoint?

    a) **Pressing the FMS knob and then the JOYSTICK**

    b) **Bump the RANGE knob, move the cursor to highlight the desired waypoint, pressing ENT, press D->, then pressing ENT twice**

    c) **Pressing the Direct to** key **and then the JOYSTICK** key

Question 5: How would the pilot load a departure procedure into the current flight plan?

    a) **By pressing the PROC key, then select DEPARTURE from the menu, selecting the procedure, and then the desired transition.**

    b) **By going to the active flight plan page and adding each individual waypoint to the flight plan.**

    c) **Press the D-> key and enter the first waypoint of the STAR, the GPS will auto sequence from there.**

Grading Criteria:

The pilot will know when they have completed this chapter when they get all the answers correct and demonstrate a solid understanding of the material. When the exam is complete, grade the answers with the answer key in the back of this handbook. Incorrect answers should be researched by going back to the appropriate reference area in the chapter or the Garmin Cockpit Guide that comes with the aircraft. Once all correct answers have been achieved, proceed on to the next chapter. Come back to items in this chapter at any time.

Chapter Twelve: Autopilot Integration

Chapter Objectives:

The objective of this chapter is for the pilot to demonstrate understanding of the G1000 Autopilot system by reviewing the content of this chapter. The pilot will then take the chapter quiz at the end which will check their knowledge about the material covered.

Completion Standards:

When this chapter is complete, the pilot will be able to describe and explain functions and modes of the G1000 Autopilot system. The pilot will know when they have met the completion standards of the chapter when they have correctly answered all the quiz questions at the end of this section. If any questions are scored as incorrect, go back to the appropriate reference area in the chapter or the Garmin Cockpit Guide that comes with the aircraft. When the pilot has correctly answered all the chapter quiz questions, then they may proceed to the next chapter.

Autopilot Concepts

Definition: **Autopilot** -An integrated mechanical, electrical, or hydraulic system developed to control an aircraft or vehicle with little or no intervention from a human controller.

Autopilots have been in use for over 60 years although their level of sophistication have been steadily increasing in the past several years since Garmin certified its GFC/GMC 500 and GFC/GMC 700 autopilots. Traditional autopilots like the KAP 140 and S-TEC 55 were installed in early model G1000 aircraft. Their inputs were analog and did not seamlessly integrate with digital cockpit systems like the G1000. Figure 12.1 shows the various autopilot controllers the pilot may see in different G1000 aircraft. Note that all autopilot interfaces with the pilot will come through the autopilot controller or interface with the PFD. No autopilot functions controlled by the MFD.

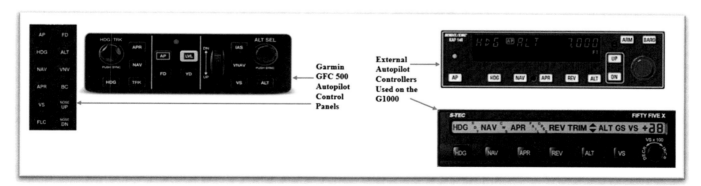

Figure 12.1 – Autopilot Controllers used on the G1000

Traditional autopilot architecture relied on analog interfaces between dissimilar components to function. These two-axis autopilots such as the Bendix/King Honeywell KAP 140 autopilot were installed in the early G1000 aircraft delivered during between 2004 and 2006. This type of system controls the aircraft on the pitch axis through electromechanical servo control over the elevator using the trim system. It controls the aircraft on the roll axis through electromechanical servo control over the aileron system cables. The two-axis autopilot allows the pilot to fly an aircraft virtually hands-free, with sole input on the rudder pedals.

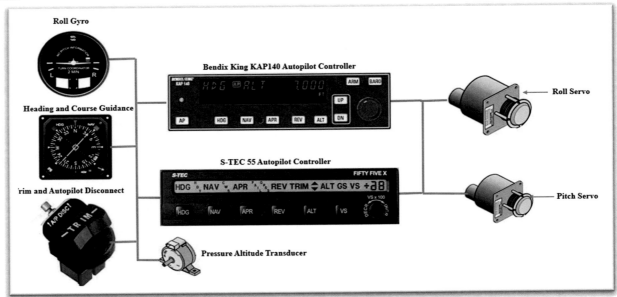

Figure 12.2 – Traditional Autopilot architecture

Modern G1000 autopilot architecture is integrated with a digital data sharing technology that passes precise control inputs and responses back and forth between the various LRUs and the control servos and then displays the status and modes to the pilot with full self-test and system monitoring capability. These digital systems are more dependable and accurate than their traditional counterparts due to the nature of the digital data from the sensors and the speed at which the data is processed.

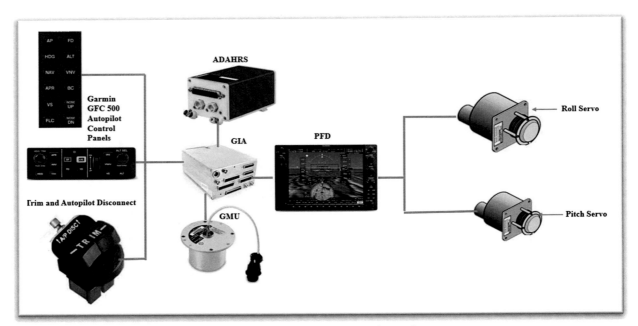

Figure 12.3 – G1000 Digital autopilot architecture

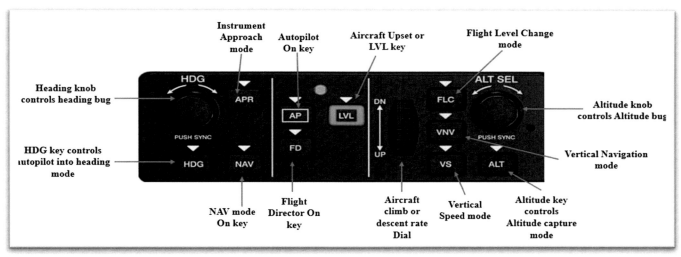

Figure 12.4 – Integrated Garmin Perspective Plus GFC/GMC *Autopilot Control Panel functions*

Modern two and three axis autopilots are certified and installed in most aircraft delivered over the last fifteen years. The two axis versions control the pitch axis through electromechanical servo control over the elevator using the trim system. It controls the aircraft roll axis through electromechanical servo control over the aileron system cables. If equipped, it controls the aircraft on the yaw axis through electromechanical servo control over the rudder cable system and may introduce a yaw damper mechanism to dampen oscillations that may occur through the vertical axis of the aircraft. By introducing a yaw damper, these aircraft truly allow the pilot to be a flight systems manager and eliminate problems with external autopilots by ensuring the complete exchange of all digital information between the G1000 and the autopilot.

While an autopilot may be analog, digital, or a combination, ultimately its performance depends upon its level of digital integration and will depend upon how well it integrates with the G1000 and its digital LRUs and systems.

Autopilot ROLL and PITCH Modes

An autopilot that controls the aircraft along the longitudinal axis usually has three different operational modes; ROLL, HDG, and NAV. When the autopilot is first turned on, it initiates the ROLL and Pitch channels, but requires the pilot to make inputs to specify how they want the autopilot to behave. This prevents inadvertent autopilot modes the pilot was not expecting.

Roll Mode

Figure 12.5 – Roll mode indication of the autopilot

In this mode, the autopilot simply captures the amount of bank the pilot has induced on the wings and does not attempt to maintain any other reference parameter. This is useful as a temporary mode for the pilot to address cockpit chores or address a temporary distraction or situation. If the aircraft wings are level when the roll mode is captured, the autopilot will continue to hold the wings level. This is also considered the default mode since when an autopilot is activated, there is no immediate confirmation that either the HDG or the NAV inputs are valid. The pilot should note that when the autopilot is confused by pilot inputs, it returns to roll mode. In this mode, it does not follow any lateral guidance such as heading or navigation signals. This can be dangerous for an unaware pilot who does not realize that the autopilot dropped back to ROLL mode expecting that it is still following an earlier command.

Heading Mode

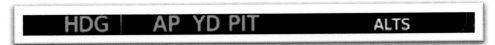

Figure 12.6 – Heading mode indication of the autopilot

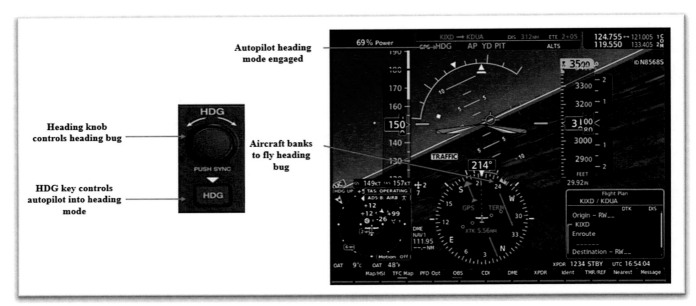

Figure 12.7 – The autopilot in HDG mode

The heading bug selector will select the desired heading that the pilot wishes to hold in flight. Turn the knob right or left to select a heading. If the current heading is desired, just push in the heading selector knob and the bug will center on the current heading. When engaging the autopilot in the heading mode, first center the heading bug on the current heading, then press the HDG key on the autopilot so it will capture the heading bug. Once the heading mode is active, the autopilot will turn the aircraft to desired headings by twisting the HDG knob and moving the heading bug. Keep in mind that the autopilot will be able to turn to any desired heading but keep the heading bug within approximately 150-degrees, or the autopilot will not be able to compute whether or not the operator desires a left or right turn. The heading that the heading bug is on will also be shown in a HDG box to the left of the heading indicator.

NAV Mode

Figure 12.8 – The autopilot in NAV mode

The NAV mode of the autopilot is designed to follow course guidance as selected by the pilot using the CDI softkey on the PFD. The indication in the status window will tell the pilot which NAV source is being used. In the case of Figure 12.8, the autopilot is following GPS. If the GPS symbol were white, it would tell the pilot that the GPS mode is armed but not active. Many times, the pilot must engage Heading mode first and select an intercept angle suitable to capture the course before the GPS or VLOC mode.

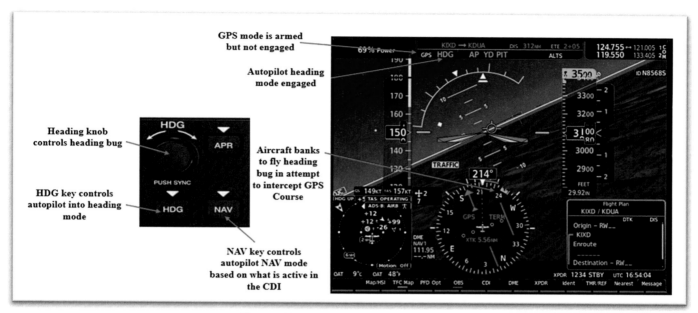

Figure 12.9 – Autopilot in NAV mode

The NAV mode is when the autopilot is set to follow a particular course from a CDI needle. In the case of the G1000, it is following whatever NAV mode is primary in the center of the CDI. If the NAV signal is interrupted, or is deemed not dependable, the NAV mode will automatically exit returning the unit to ROLL mode.

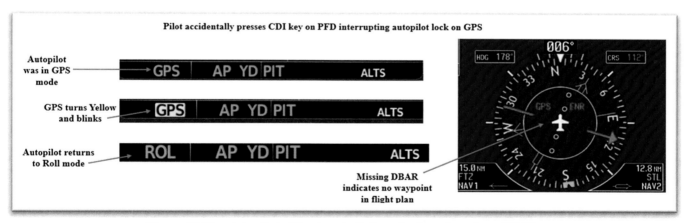

Figure 12.10 – Autopilot will return to Roll mode since there is no DBAR

Notice in the above diagram that there is no DEVIATION BAR needle in the center of the HSI. This indicates that there is no dependable signal, and the autopilot would either not engage in the NAV mode, or if it already was, it falls out of NAV mode back to ROLL mode after flashing yellow caution.

Autopilot PITCH Channel

An autopilot that controls the aircraft along the PITCH channel usually has several different operational modes: Altitude hold, Vertical Speed, Flight Level Change (FLC), Vertical Navigation (VNAV), and Approach which has a pitch and lateral guidance component. The following sections will detail these modes.

Altitude Hold Mode

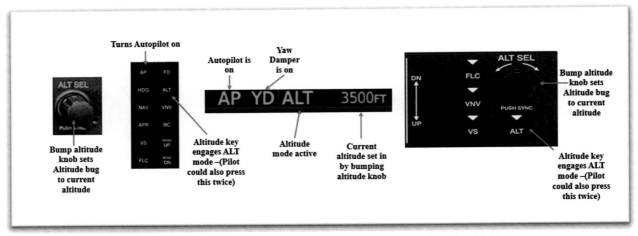

Figure 12.11 – Autopilot set in ALT mode to hold current altitude of 3,500 feet

The Altitude hold mode on most autopilots uses the same logic process. The Altitude hold allows the pilot to select the altitude they are flying simply by pressing the ALT key. Pressing ALT the first time will set the autopilot in the pitch mode and then pressing the ALT key again will tell the autopilot to stay at its current altitude. We can think of this as "stay here" mode.

Here is the recommended sequence:
1. Ensure the autopilot and flight director are on.
2. Bump ALT knob to set at current altitude and then press ALT key or...
3. Press ALT key twice to tell the autopilot to maintain the current altitude.

Altitude Capture Mode

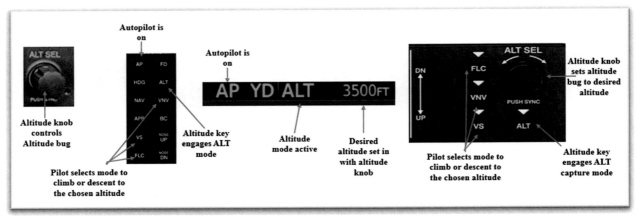

Figure 12.12 – Autopilot set in ALT capture mode at 3,500 feet

This mode is used in conjunction with ALT hold mode. The pilot inputs the altitude they want to hold, and the autopilot requires the selection of another mode to determine how to get to that altitude and then stay at that altitude once it does. Set the altitude bug with ALT knob and then press ALT to set the autopilot in pitch mode. Now select a mode to climb or descend by pressing VS, FLC, or VNAV. This can be confusing to pilots if steps are done out of order. These modes are described in the next sections.

Here is the recommended sequence for setting altitude capture mode:

1. Ensure the autopilot and flight director are on.
2. Turn the Alt knob to set the desired altitude.
3. Now press ALT to tell the autopilot that this is the altitude to maintain.
4. Now the pilot must tell the autopilot how to get there; either vertical speed (VS), Flight Level Change (FLC), or Vertical Navigation (VNAV) modes. Press that key on the autopilot to engage that mode.
5. Now use the up and down keys or the vertical mode dial on the autopilot controller to set the rate at which you want the aircraft to go to the assigned altitude.
6. The autopilot will now start its process of going to that altitude.
7. When the aircraft reaches that altitude, it will level off and maintain the desired altitude in altitude hold mode. It will sound an audible tone when within 200 feet of level off.
8. The process is the same for climbs and descents.

Vertical Speed Mode

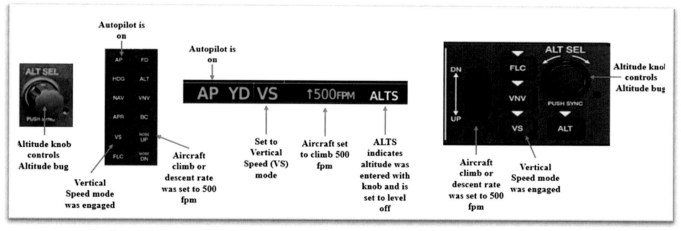

Figure 12.13 – Autopilot in VS mode with 500 feet per minute climb vertical speed set

The current Vertical Speed automatically initializes when the autopilot VS key is engaged. In this mode, the autopilot captures the feet per minute the aircraft is climbing or descending and adjusts the pitch trim to maintain that climb or decent. If the autopilot is placed in the VS mode during level flight, then the vertical speed is set to zero, and the pilot can start a climb simply by pressing the 'UP' key. Each time they press this key, the vertical speed will increase by one-hundred feet per minute. For example, if the pilot wanted to initiate a climb at 500 Feet Per Minute, they would press the 'UP' key five times and the autopilot display screen would show a climb at 100, 200, 300, 400, and then 500 feet per minute and the aircraft will hold 500 FPM until it is told to level off, or it reaches an altitude at which it can no longer climb.

> *Note: In VS mode, the autopilot will continue to climb at the vertical speed selected. This situation can become hazardous as the aircraft may stall trying to maintain the set rate of climb due to diminishing aircraft climb performance. The pilot should watch carefully at higher altitudes and decrease the rate of climb if the airspeed decreases below the best rate of climb speed.*

Flight Level Change Mode

Figure 12.14 – Autopilot in Flight Level Change (FLC) mode indications

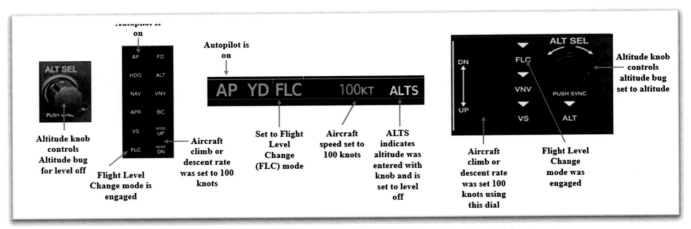

Figure 12.15 – Autopilot in Flight Level Change (FLC) mode with 100 knots set

Flight Level Change (FLC) mode was added by Garmin to match similar functionality in business and commercial jet cockpits. This is a very significant autopilot feature for the pilot to understand and use regularly. The concept is simple: instead of setting a vertical speed using the Up and Dn keys or the dial on the autopilot control panel as they would in VS mode, the pilot sets a speed using a speed bug which appears on the airspeed indicator. By setting a speed, the pilot increases operational safety because the aircraft won't inadvertently stall at higher altitudes as it might using vertical speed mode. Once the pilot sets a speed the autopilot will climb at whatever climb attitude it must to maintain that speed considering the power setting applied. This gives the pilot amazing flexibility in both the climb and the descent profiles.

NAV Mode

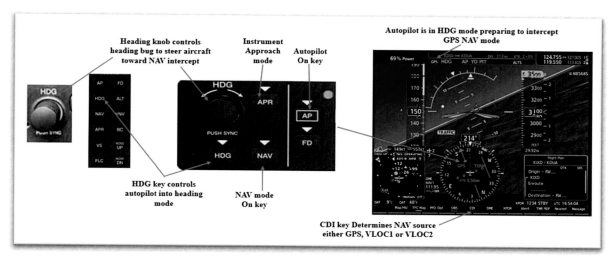

Figure 12.16 – Autopilot in NAV mode tracking GPS needle

The autopilot will track whatever course is shown on the CDI. Depending on what course the pilot wants the autopilot to track, the correct source must be shown on the HSI using the CDI key. To change the NAV function, press the CDI softkey. A magenta needle will be a GPS course, a solid green needle will be VLOC1 and double lined green needle will indicate VLOC2. So, if the pilot were tracking a radial to a VOR that is entered into NAV 1, they should not be displaying a magenta needle on the HSI. If the DBAR is centered or within 1 dot of centered, the autopilot will go directly into NAV mode and intercept the course. If the DBAR is beyond 1 dot from centered, the pilot will need to use HDG mode to steer the aircraft to intercept the course track.

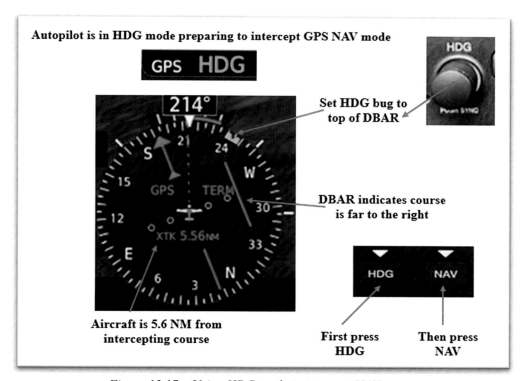

Figure 12.17 – Using HDG mode to intercept NAV course

Approach Mode

The approach mode of the autopilot is a special mode which combines precise lateral and VNAV tracking once the prerequisite parameters are met. Approach mode can be set once all other approach selection selections are made using the PROC key and menu dropdown.

Figure 12.18 – Autopilot indications in APPCH mode

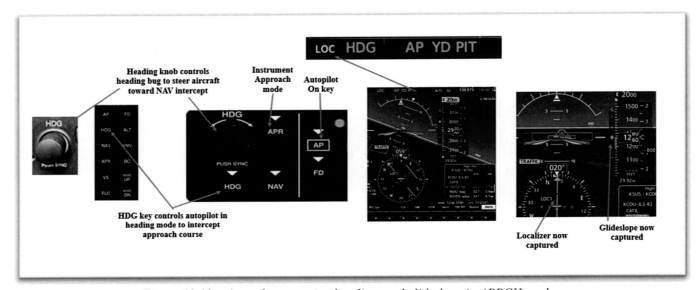

Figure 12.19 – Autopilot capturing localizer and glideslope in APPCH mode

The Approach mode (APR) allows the autopilot to maintain a more accurate adherence to the centerline of the course than in the NAV mode while using VLOC1, VLOC2, or the GPS CDI needles. If executing an approach, make sure the appropriate NAV function is selected in the CDI display. For example, if an ILS overlay approach is selected in the GPS for situational awareness, and the CDI is selected on GPS, it will appear on the CDI but the approach will never arm because the CDI is set for GPS not VLOC.

The operation of the G1000 in Approach mode will be covered in more depth in chapter 13.

Operating the KAP 140

Many early G1000 aircraft were delivered with the KAP 140 autopilot since the Garmin GFC/GMC autopilot had not yet been certified. The following section is for those pilots who encounter this autopilot controller in aircraft they fly.

Figure 12.20 – The Bendix/King KAP 140 autopilot

The KAP 140 autopilot is capable of holding heading, altitude, NAV courses, flying instrument approaches and holding climb and descent rates. While the KAP 140 has some analog connections to the G1000, it does so without the benefit of digital connectivity to the G1000 so there are some caveats to operating with this autopilot.

- o Important! The pilot must enter the current altimeter setting into the BARO key of the autopilot.
- o The autopilot must be turned on by pressing the AP key on the lower left-hand corner.
- o The altitude set knobs on this autopilot do <u>not</u> set the altitude bug on the G1000. They are not connected. All altitude and vertical speed operations are done using the KAP 140 device and the sensors it is connected to.
- o The KAP 140 <u>will</u> interface with and respond to changes in the heading bug and the course needle of the G1000.
- o When the autopilot is turned on, it automatically captures the vertical speed (VS) of the aircraft at that moment and engages roll (ROL) mode which holds the wings level.
- o To hold the current heading, press the heading bug selector on the G1000 display to center the bug. To change heading using the autopilot, turn the bug on the G1000 and the autopilot will turn the aircraft at standard rate to the desired heading. Then press the HDG key on the autopilot and "HDG" will replace "ROL" on the left-hand side of the autopilot screen.
- o When the autopilot is turned on and the vertical speed is captured, it is very important that the pilot makes a note of what vertical speed was captured. When the AP key is pressed and the autopilot is engaged, the vertical speed rate will flash momentarily on the right-hand side of the autopilot screen. If the rate is too high or too low, press the UP and DN keys until an appropriate rate is reached.
- o To have the aircraft climb and level off at a specified altitude, press the AP key to turn the autopilot on. Select the altitude by turning the altitude selector knob on the bottom right-hand corner of the KAP 140, the altitude pre-select will be shown on the right-hand side of the autopilot screen.

> *Note: If the altitude is not armed, the aircraft will only continue to climb or descend through the selected altitude*

- o To hold the current altitude, press the ALT key at any time to make the aircraft level off at the current altitude. This includes during a climb or a descent. If you set a VS of 500 fpm and are climbing, if ALT is pressed, the aircraft will stop climbing and level off at the altitude you were at when you pushed ALT.
- o To operate the NAV function, the desired course must be shown on the HSI. For example, you are tracking the 270-radial TO a VOR. The desired VOR is tuned into NAV 1. The HSI should be displaying a green needle on and reading VLOC1. If the course is within one dot of center when you press the NAV key on the autopilot, then the autopilot will begin tracking that specific course.

- o On the HSI, if the KAP 140 is armed in the NAV mode on NAV 1, and the CDI key is pressed to change the HSI display to NAV 2, the autopilot will default into the ROLL mode. Keep in mind now the KAP 140 is no longer locked on NAV 1 (verified by NAV flashing in the KAP 140 display). If NAV 2 happens to be centered or within one dot on the HSI, the NAV will arm itself again to capture NAV 2. If the autopilot does not arm itself, press the NAV key again to manually arm the KAP 140.
- o APR works similarly to NAV; however, it will capture a glide slope on an ILS and track the localizer.

Autopilot Disarming

While there is only one way to turn on the autopilot using the AP key, there are multiple ways to disconnect it in the event of a situation where the pilot wants/needs to assume control of the aircraft. They are:

1. Press the AP key to turn the autopilot off.
2. Overpowering the autopilot by forcefully moving the yoke.
3. The autopilot disconnect is a red switch on the pilot's yoke.

Figure 12.21 – The yoke mounted autopilot quick disconnect and trim switches

4. Engaging the electric trim on the pilot's yoke will force the autopilot offline,
5. If all else fails, pull the autopilot circuit breaker.

> Note: The autopilot must be tested prior to each flight to ensure proper operation. This is usually stated plainly in the aircraft flight manual and/or the supplement to the AFM concerning the autopilot and should be called out in the checklist.

The TRIM System

The trim system in integrated with the autopilot. If the trim were to become inoperative, the autopilot would also be inoperative. The electric trim works by adjusting elevator trim to reach a desired altitude. If there was not sufficient power, and a vertical speed was selected that was too high, the aircraft would lose airspeed and eventually stall. If the airplane is trying to climb, and the pilot pushed against the yoke, the trim will counteract the forward pressure and continue trimming, which can create a dangerous situation. Trim system runaways are defined as situations where the trim system starts an uncontrolled and uncommanded up or down motion and the pilot must immediately respond to this emergency by disarming the trim system and/or the autopilot that may have initiated it. Pressing the Autopilot disconnect should disable the trim runaway. If it does not attempt to manually overpower with the yoke, then pull the trim and/or the autopilot circuit breaker.

Conclusion

In this chapter, we have covered autopilot operation in a G1000 aircraft. This chapter also has described and given examples of how to operate the Garmin and KAP 140 autopilots and described the procedures of setting up the various modes.

Remember

- ❑ When the pilot first powers on the autopilot, it initializes in ROLL and Pitch modes. All other modes must be set by the pilot.
- ❑ Set the heading and altitude bugs before engaging other modes of the autopilot, otherwise, attempting to capture HDG and ALT, the autopilot may turn to a heading that is undesirable.
- ❑ Whenever the pilot is in a climb or decent, make sure the altitude is ARMED, verified by the autopilot mode window showing ALT in white. Otherwise, the autopilot will not recognize the desired altitude when it is reached.
- ❑ If the autopilot is navigating in VLOC mode on the HSI, switching the CDI key to another NAV source such as VLOC2 or GPS will knock the autopilot out of its NAV mode back to ROLL mode. If this happens, the pilot must push NAV again to rearm the autopilot back into NAV capture mode.

Chapter Debriefing:

We have now covered the G1000 system integration with an autopilot system. To fully appreciate the power of the system and to fully use its capabilities, the pilot must have a thorough working knowledge of the autopilot and how to use it to reduce the cockpit workload.

- ❑ Now that the pilot understands that the G1000 uses the autopilot as an integral part of the system, then they will understand that with an external autopilot such as the Bendix/King KAP 140, there are going to be some pieces of data that don't integrate very well.
- ❑ Now that the pilot understands that some autopilots integrated with the G1000 are analog units with a digital face, you will see that the autopilot must be a primary part of the scan flow to make sure that the autopilot is doing what it should be.
- ❑ Now that the pilot understands that the Garmin GFC/GMC autopilot completely integrates autopilot functions with the G1000, they should understand the importance of reviewing all supplement information with those autopilots to ensure a thorough working of its functions and indications as well as minimum operational altitude restrictions.

Now that the pilot understands these important areas and can correlate these into their everyday flying skills to operate the G1000 aircraft using the autopilot, they are ready to take the quiz and then to move to chapter thirteen!

Chapter Twelve Quiz: Autopilot Integration

The Chapter Quiz Scenario

This Chapter Quiz Scenario (CQS) is designed to depict a real-world flight situation and use the pilot's new knowledge of the G1000 autopilot system to answer some situational questions about how to safely operate their aircraft. They can then determine whether they "understand" and can even "correlate" the material covered with their existing aeronautical knowledge and are prepared to use this information in a way which will enhance their operational safety while using the G1000 equipped aircraft.

In this chapter quiz, the pilot will be asked to demonstrate their understanding of the autopilot system and some of its functions the pilot will use in this flight scenario between Spirit of St. Louis airport, Missouri (KSUS) and Will Rogers (KOKC) airport in Oklahoma City. Consider the following questions about this scenario:

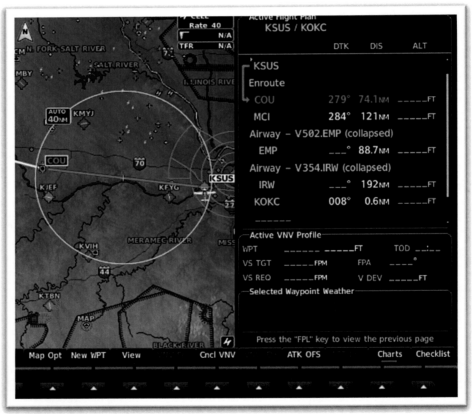

Figure 12.22 – Chapter Twelve Quiz scenario diagram

Question 1: On the above flight scenario, the pilot decides to engage the autopilot to use it to reduce cockpit workload. When the autopilot is first powered on, what modes are active?

     a) **HDG and ALT modes**
     b) **ROLL and Pitch modes**
     c) **NAV and GS modes**

Question 2: After takeoff and during the climb, the pilot engages the autopilot. When the autopilot is set into VS mode, what is the vertical speed that is selected by the system automatically?

   a) The vertical speed at the instant the VS key is pressed.
   b) 500 FPM
   c) Whatever vertical speed is selected by the pilot.

Question 3: The pilot receives a heading vector from approach control. When the autopilot is in heading mode, what controls the heading that the autopilot follows?

   a) The HDG knob.
   b) The Course knob on the PFD.
   c) The Course set in the flight plan window.

Question 4: When changing altitudes, what is the proper procedure if the autopilot is in ALT hold mode?

   a) Select the new ALT in the ALT selector window, press VS and select the vertical speed desired.
   b) Select the new ALT in the ALT selector window, press FLC and select the airspeed desired.
   c) Both A and B are correct.

Question 5: Which answer is true regarding the electric trim system of the G1000 equipped aircraft with a coupled autopilot?

   a) It has a separate on/off switch that must be engaged after takeoff.
   b) It is integrated with the autopilot system and must be functional.
   c) It can be used when the autopilot circuit breaker is pulled out.

Question 6: Which answer is NOT true regarding the G1000 autopilot?

   a) The autopilot will not try to capture a glideslope below the aircraft.
   b) The autopilot will automatically shut-off when the pilot starts to flare the aircraft for landing.
   c) The airplane should be stabilized in a landing configuration prior to finalizing the autopilot approach coupling.

Question 7: Where would the pilot find information regarding the minimum altitudes that the autopilot can be used on climb-out and approach?

   a) The approved POH supplement that covers the autopilot.
   b) A placard that is displayed on the instrument panel.
   c) Both a and b are correct.

Question 8: When the pilot is approaching their destination, they decide to couple the autopilot to the instrument approach. Which of the following is <u>NOT</u> correct regarding using an autopilot in coupled mode?

    a) The autopilot automatically captures the localizer course on an ILS when properly armed.

    b) The autopilot automatically captures the glideslope when it is below the aircraft.

    c) The autopilot will not proceed past the missed approach decision point without the pilot pressing SUSP to continue to the missed approach holding fix.

Question 9: When the pilot is climbing over extended altitudes, what statement is <u>true</u> regarding climb modes on the G1000 autopilot?

    a) The autopilot in VS mode will automatically adjust for density differences as altitude increases.

    b) The autopilot in flight level change mode will tend to lower the nose rather than increase the pitch as altitude increases.

    c) The autopilot should only be used in Vertical Speed modes in excess of 800 feet per minute.

Grading Criteria:

The pilot will know when they have completed this chapter when they get all the answers correct and demonstrate a solid understanding of the material. When the exam is complete, grade the answers with the answer key in the back of this handbook. Incorrect answers should be researched by going back to the appropriate reference area in the chapter or the Garmin Cockpit Guide that comes with the aircraft. Once all correct answers have been achieved, proceed on to the next chapter. Come back to items in this chapter at any time.

Chapter Thirteen: Instrument Procedures

Chapter Objectives:

The objective of this chapter is for the pilot to demonstrate understanding regarding the use of instrument procedures while flying the G1000 by reviewing the content of this chapter. The pilot will then take the chapter quiz at the end which will check their knowledge about the material covered.

Completion Standards:

When this chapter is complete, the pilot will be able to describe and explain loading, activating, and flying instrument procedures using the G1000. The pilot will know when they have met the completion standards of the chapter when they have correctly answered all the quiz questions at the end of this section. If any questions are scored as incorrect, go back to the appropriate reference area in the chapter or the Garmin Cockpit Guide that comes with the aircraft. When the pilot has correctly answered all the chapter quiz questions, then they may proceed to the next chapter.

Instrument Procedures

The integrated nature of the G1000 certainly revolutionized VFR pilots flying tasks and we have covered that extensively so far. Now let's consider how to use this system in the IFR environment. Even if the pilot using this handbook is not yet IFR rated, they will appreciate the process of how the G1000 adds the three types of instrument procedures (approaches, arrivals, and departures) into the flight plan so the autopilot can fly these procedures like it was explained in previous chapters. There are many features that the pilot will learn to appreciate. In general, the flight plan is laid out in the following order:

Figure 13.1 – Order and flow of a flight plan

The PROC Key

The pilot uses the PROC key to call up the Procedures selection box on either the PFD, MFD or GCU. The options presented will be the same, but the detail will be much greater on the MFD. The pilot should have an airport selected before they press the PROC key, so the system focuses the procedure on the correct airport. If they call up PROC before the airport is selected, they will be allowed to key one in using bump scroll twist or the GCU keyboard; it just takes longer this way.

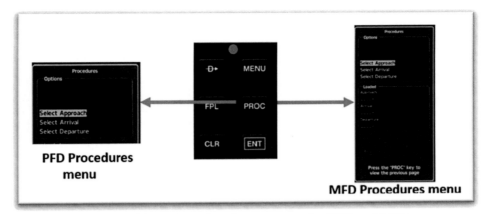

Figure 13.2A – Procedure key menus on the PFD and MFD

Since the G1000 flight plan system has the pilot specify an Origin airport, the system will offer Departure procedures for the Origin and the Destination airport will be the focus of Arrivals and Approaches. Interim airports where stops may be made along the way will have to be called up individually using the Direct To function and the D-> key.

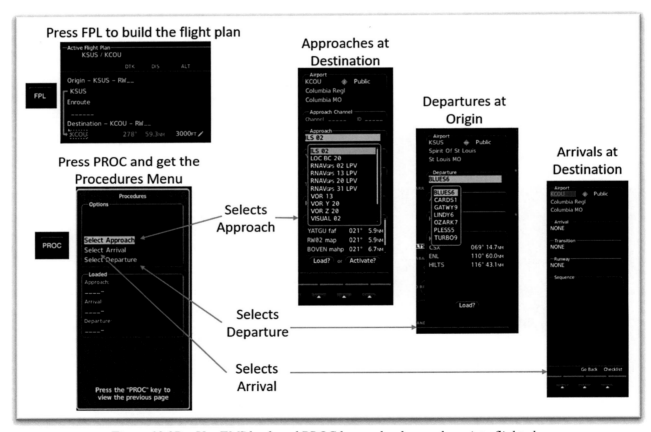

Figure 13.2B – Use FMS knob and PROC keys to load procedures into flight plan

Steps to Select and Load Procedures

1. Load Origin and Destination waypoints in the flight plan using FMS knob
2. On the MFD, PFD, or GCU, press the PROC softkey to display the Procedures Menu
3. Use FMS knob to select the desired procedure.
4. Press Enter to confirm its selection from dropdown and it is inserted into flight plan.

Note: The pilot should <u>never</u> delete any waypoints from a loaded procedure as it can confuse the autopilot. Instead, the pilot can use the "Activate Leg" option in the PROC MENU or the "Direct To" function to skip steps in the procedure when directed to do so by ATC.

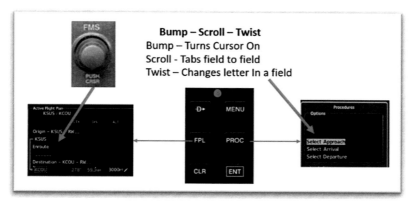

Figure 13.3 – Use FMS knob and PROC keys to load procedures

Departures Procedures

A Standard Instrument Departure (SID) or simply Departure procedures are formalized ATC instructions published in chart format to facilitate aircraft leaving busy terminal areas. They are designed to smooth the flow of traffic and simplify the process of getting an ATC clearance out of busy airspace in the general direction that aircraft is planning to travel. Not all airports have Departure procedures. When they are published, it is to the pilot's advantage to use them and if they do not want to use them, they must specify on their flight plan "No SID".

A Departure procedure is given a coded name for ATC purposes and since they tend to have multiple branches for flows to other metropolitan areas, they will have transitions.

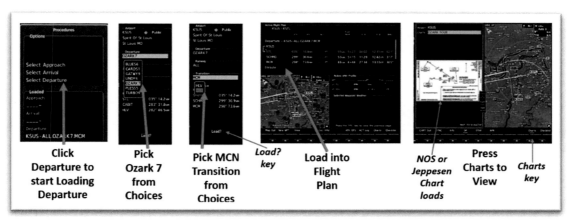

Figure 13.4 – Departure procedure loaded into flight plan with charts shown

Arrival Procedures

Like SID Departures, Standard Terminal Arrival Routes (STAR) or simply Arrival procedures are formalized ATC instructions published in chart format to facilitate aircraft arriving at busy terminal areas. They are designed to smooth the flow of traffic and simplify the process of getting an ATC clearance into busy airspace from the general direction that aircraft are traveling. Not all airports have Arrival procedures. When they are published, it is to the pilot's advantage to use them and if they do not want to use them, they must specify on their flight plan "No STAR".

An Arrival procedure is given a coded name for ATC purposes and since they tend to have multiple branches for flows from other metropolitan areas, they will have transitions.

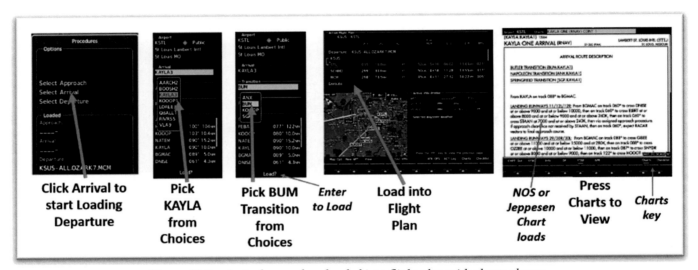

| Click Arrival to start Loading Departure | Pick KAYLA from Choices | Pick BUM Transition from Choices | *Enter to Load* | Load into Flight Plan | *NOS or Jeppesen Chart loads* | Press Charts to View | *Charts key* |

Figure 13.5 – Arrival procedure loaded into flight plan with charts shown

Approach Procedures

Instrument Approach Procedures (IAP), also known as Approaches, are published for many airports that a pilot may use in the national airspace system. These approach procedures are predefined and methodical procedures and accompanying charts that describe how to fly into an airport using ground or satellite navigational signals. Many airports have several approaches published by the FAA and the charts will describe the different ways the pilot could approach the airport depending upon traffic flow and winds. Some approaches are published based upon the use of ground-based navigation stations such as VORs and ILS installations and some approaches are published based upon GPS satellite signals such as RNAV/GPS approaches. The G1000 can distinguish the difference and provides guidance to the pilot and the autopilot to fly these procedures in the correct order. Even a VFR only pilot will appreciate the following description of how the G1000 flight plan system loads the steps of the instrument approach procedures and the autopilot follows them in an orderly fashion like it does with enroute flight plan procedures.

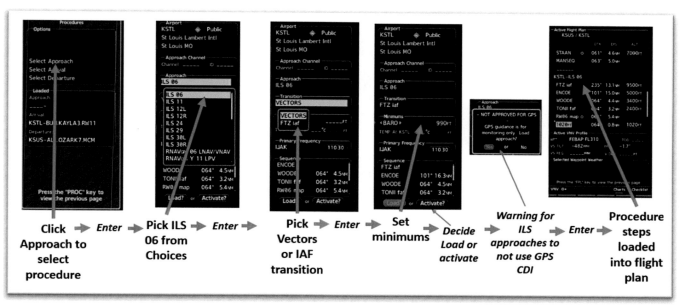

Figure 13.6 – Steps to load Approach procedure into flight plan with charts

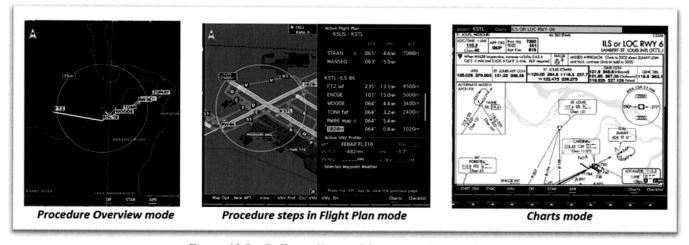

Figure 13.7 – Different Views of the Approach procedure

When the pilot selects the approach procedure and follows the process shown in Figure 13.6, they must make a choice whether to Load or Activate the Approach.

Selecting "Load" puts the procedure and any associated waypoints into the current flight plan after the destination waypoint. Selecting "Activate" both loads the waypoints and activates "Direct To" the first waypoint on the procedure. Procedures can be loaded and activated in the small PROC menu window on the PFD, as well. When using the PFD window, the plan view of the procedure will not be shown.

Use the following guidance:

➢ If still in the enroute phase of the flight plan, "Load" the procedure. This prepares the procedure for use at the correct time by using the Activate the Approach option in the Procedures menu.

➢ Any time ATC takes the pilot off a flight plan and gives the pilot vectors toward an approach course, then it is time to Activate the approach.

Figure 13.8 – Load or Activate choice for the procedure

Figure 13.9 – Procedure warning when loading an ILS approach

When loading an ILS approach procedure or any procedure where GPS overlay of that approach is not approved, the G1000 will give the pilot a warning message that they must acknowledge. This message advises the pilot that they must ensure the CDI is in the proper VLOC mode and not in GPS mode.

Activate vs Activate Vector-to-Final

When a pilot is flying an instrument approach, they typically fly directly to a fix within the approach procedure (typically referred to as an initial approach fix (IAF) and if using the autopilot, they are in the NAV or approach mode. Many times, they will receive ATC instructions to intercept that approach course at some point outside the final approach fix (FAF) using a heading vector. This is important as the pilot must change the operational mode of the autopilot to heading mode to adhere to the vector instructions given by ATC.

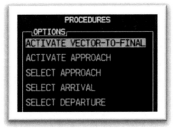

Figure 13.10 – Activate vs Activate vector-to-final

There are a few caveats to using the activate vector-to-final mode. Using this mode leaves some doubt in the pilot's mind as to where they are going to intercept the final course and how to identify interim step-down fixes along the way.

Once an approach is loaded, one can activate that approach at any time by again pressing the PROC key and selecting the choice for "Activate Approach", or "Activate Vector-to-final" (if VECTORS transition has been selected). To best adhere to ATC instructions while still maintaining situational awareness along the approach, it is recommended that the pilot simply activate the approach and use the menu key to "activate the leg" between the upcoming transition fixes they are being vectored to. Place the autopilot in the HDG mode to follow the heading vector issued by ATC. The pilot watches the stinger of the aircraft on the moving map to estimate when the aircraft is one minute from course intercept. The pilot now presses the approach key on the autopilot if they have been cleared for the approach. If ATC told the pilot to fly a vector and did not issue the "cleared for the approach" clearance, the pilot should not press the approach key on the autopilot just yet. To do so would cause the aircraft to turn inbound prior to receiving the approach clearance.

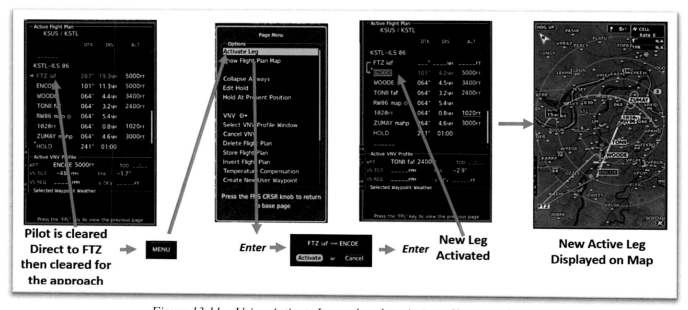

Figure 13.11 – Using Activate Leg rather than Activate Vector-to-final

There are times where "Activate Vectors-To-Final" are warranted but the pilot should prefer to always be flying toward a known activated leg of the procedure if possible.

Auto Sequencing of Flight Plan Waypoints

When loading and activating an instrument procedure into the flight plan, the GPS will automatically sequence to the next waypoint on an activated approach procedure. There are several notable exceptions to this rule. FAA regulations require GPS receivers to "suspend" auto-sequencing of waypoints within a flight plan at the missed approach point and while in holding patterns. In both of these situations, the pilot is required to make the final decision as to when to proceed to the next step in their procedure. In holding patterns, the GPS would have no way of knowing how many turns ATC would require to remain in that hold. At the missed approach point on the approach, only the pilot can make the decision as to whether they are going to land or not. In both cases, the G1000 will enter suspend mode and this will be highlighted on the PFD in place of the OBS key. The pilot must either press that Suspend key or press a "Go Around" button on the throttle, if one is provided. Once this condition is met, the G1000 is allowed to proceed with auto-sequencing to the next waypoint in the flight plan.

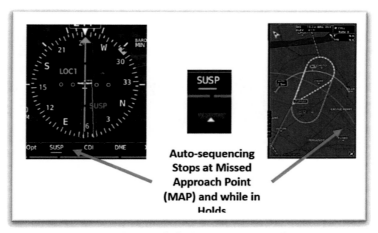

Figure 13.12 – Suspended auto-sequencing of waypoints

Missed Approach

As just discussed, the GPS will not auto-sequence past a missed approach point until the SUSP (suspend) softkey illuminated on the bottom of the PFD is pressed. In order to access this softkey, the pilot will have to press the OBS softkey and need to select the correct CDI mode to proceed to that fix. If a missed approach is desired after reaching the missed approach point, the SUSP softkey must be pressed in order to activate missed approach course guidance. At this point the GPS will plot a Direct To course to the missed approach holding fix.

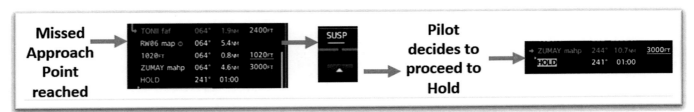

Figure 13.13 – Decision to proceed to missed approach fix

Holds

When entering a hold that is part of an instrument procedure the GPS will again go into suspend mode and the SUSP softkey will appear in the softkey on the PFD. The course guidance will be provided only for the inbound leg of the hold. The holding pattern will show on the map in magenta as the current flight plan leg. The pilot must fly the aircraft through the turns and the outbound leg of the hold unless the autopilot is engaged in NAV mode. Once it is desired to leave the hold, the SUSP key must be pressed to sequence to the next waypoint of the approach procedure loaded in the flight plan. It is possible that the hold is the last waypoint in the flight plan. In this case, the pilot may have to reload the Approach using the PROC key or may have to add a waypoint indicating an alternate has been selected if they are unable to land at the programmed destination.

Figure 13.14 – Direct entry holding pattern

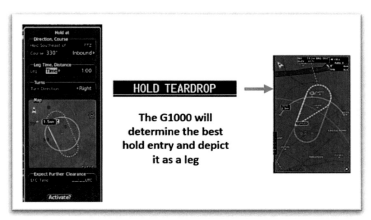

Figure 13.15 – Teardrop hold entry suggested

The recommended hold entry type will be displayed in the data bar at the top of the PFD as well as a turn suggestion shortly before reaching the holding fix.

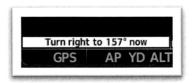

Figure 13.16 – Turn anticipation depicted

Conclusion

In this chapter, we looked at how to use the G1000 to load and activate instrument procedures into the flight plan. It is important that the pilot properly loads and activates the procedures, so they are in compliance with ATC instructions and clearances. The autopilot is prepared to fly the various components of those instrument procedures in an orderly and precise fashion but only if the pilot properly sequences the procedures and activates the legs when appropriate. By taking a methodical approach to instrument flying, the pilot can spend more time as the cockpit systems manager making sure the G1000 is doing its job. The same procedures can be used to enhance the safety of all IFR operations.

Chapter Debriefing:

We have now covered the area of the G1000 instrument approach procedures and how to properly load them into the flight plan and effectively incorporate them into their flight execution with the use of the autopilot.

❑ Now that the pilot understands that the G1000 uses the various databases to generate the electronic versions of the instrument procedure steps in the flight plan, they will understand why a thorough understanding of the autopilot and the coupling of that system to the Flight Plan can greatly enhance system safety.

❑ Now that the pilot understands how to effectively add, delete, and edit instrument approach procedures in the flight plan, they will also understand how to use the **D->** key and the MENU key to proceed to specific fixes within the procedure as directed by ATC.

❑ Now that the pilot understands that this system is a digital system incorporating multiple LRU functions together supplemented by software and computers, then they will realize the importance of keeping the aviation databases current and up to date and will never fly IFR without the most current information.

If the pilot understands these key points and can correlate them into their everyday flying and apply these skills to the operation of their G1000 aircraft, then it is time for them to take the chapter quiz and move on to chapter fourteen!

The Chapter Quiz Scenario

This Chapter Quiz Scenario (CQS) offers a real-world flight situation and use the pilot's new knowledge about G1000 instrument procedures to answer some situational questions about how to load and fly various instrument procedures. They can then determine whether they "understand" and can even "correlate" the material covered with their existing aeronautical knowledge and are prepared to use this information in a way which will enhance their operational safety while using the G1000 in the IFR system.

In this chapter quiz, the pilot will be asked to demonstrate their understanding of the instrument procedures on the G1000 and some of the things that they may have to perform while using its functions. This scenario is based upon a IFR flight scenario between Kansas City Downtown airport (KMKC) and Columbia, Missouri (KCOU), a tower-controlled airport.

Consider the following questions about this scenario:

Figure 13.17 – Chapter thirteen flight plan

Question 1: When the PROC key is first pushed, what choices are offered?

    a) **Approach, Vectors, Enroute.**
    b) **Approach, Arrival, Departure.**
    c) **Airport, Approach, Departure.**

Question 2: When an approach is loaded, how does the pilot activate the approach?

  a) **FPL key.**
  b) **Direct to key.**
  c) **PROC key.**

Question 3: If the pilot has been cleared for the approach, what must be done to fly the approach with the autopilot?

  a) **Activate Approach, select NAV on autopilot.**
  b) **Activate Vector, select heading in autopilot.**
  c) **Activate Approach, select Approach on autopilot.**

Question 4: When entering a hold for a missed approach what mode will the G1000 revert into?

  a) **HOLD**
  b) **DIRECT TO**
  c) **SUSPEND**

Question 5: In order to proceed beyond a hold what action must be taken by the pilot?

  a) **Activate the approach again.**

  b) **Press the SUSP softkey to take the GPS out of Suspend mode.**

  c) **Press the PROC key and select continue from the menu.**

Question 6: What statement is <u>not</u> true regarding flying approaches with the G1000?

  a) **The pilot can activate legs between step down waypoints on a approach.**

  b) **The pilot should delete waypoints on an approach procedure they don't need.**

  c) **Press the PROC key and select activate options from the menu.**

Grading Criteria:

The pilot will know when they have completed this chapter when they get all the answers correct and demonstrate a solid understanding of the material. When the exam is complete, grade the answers with the answer key in the back of this handbook. Incorrect answers should be researched by going back to the appropriate reference area in the chapter or the Garmin Cockpit Guide that comes with the aircraft. Once all correct answers have been achieved, proceed on to the next chapter. Come back to items in this chapter at any time.

Chapter Fourteen: Emergency Management

Chapter Objectives:

The objective of this chapter is for the pilot to demonstrate understanding of handling emergencies in the G1000 by reviewing the content of this chapter. The pilot will then take the chapter quiz at the end which will check their knowledge about the material covered.

Completion Standards:

When this chapter is complete, the pilot will be able to describe and explain emergency response and emergency management using the G1000. The pilot will know when they have met the completion standards of the chapter when they have correctly answered all the quiz questions at the end of this section. If any questions are scored as incorrect, go back to the appropriate reference area in the chapter or the Garmin Cockpit Guide that comes with the aircraft. When the pilot has correctly answered all the chapter quiz questions, then they may proceed to the next chapter.

Emergency Management

The G1000 system provides many sources of information to help the pilot identify and manage in-flight emergencies. The crew alerting system discussed in detail earlier in this handbook outlines every type of alert that is provided to a pilot. In this chapter we will discuss how the pilot can recognize and effectively manage different types of emergency situations. We will begin a discussion covering some of the system failures the pilot might encounter. In addition, this section will show how to recognize system failure by the indications given on the PFD and MFD, the appropriate pilot actions to take, and discuss other G1000 related emergencies.

> *Note: This section is a discussion in general on how to respond to emergencies and does not suggest the pilot use these procedures rather than what is in their aircraft's flight manual and/or checklist.*

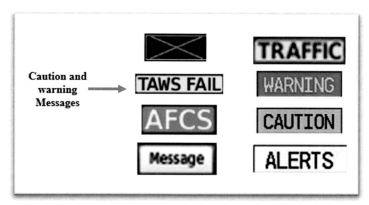

Figure 14.1 – G1000 caution and warning message symbols

The G1000 monitors all the onboard system's sensors and monitors its own LRU status and compares readings to what the manufacturer defined as normal operating ranges. When the system detects that a system is malfunctioning or offline, it will perform a system check and if no internal software reset corrects the deficiency, it will display a warning message to the pilot. If the system is a flight or engine instrument; the system will respond with a series of red or yellow Xs over the face of that display. A loss of ADAHRS data would result in a loss of altitude and airspeed and other critical flight parameters and those instruments would be covered with red Xs. A loss of engine sensors would result in certain engine gauges being covered with colored Xs depending upon the aircraft manufacturer. In the diagram below, some of the indications are red and some are yellow.

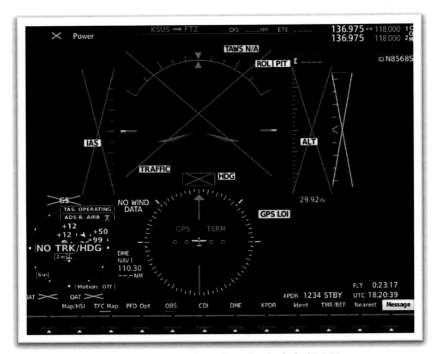

Figure 14.2 – PFD with multiple failed LRUs

Loss of PFD Flight Instruments

The loss of any LRU pertaining to the control of the aircraft flight parameters should be considered a serious situation for any day VFR flight but can be dire if such a failure occurs in IFR or night flight conditions. The pilot should immediately use the checklist to address the failure and should not hesitate to declare an emergency to get ATC assistance and even request vectors to a location where repairs can be made. The pilot should immediately cross check standby instrumentation to maintain situational awareness and should expect to hand fly the aircraft when cooperating LRUs render the autopilot useless. The pilot should remain calm and use aeronautical decision making to make rational decisions. Sometimes resetting a circuit breaker can bring LRUs back online. As painful as it sounds, a reset of the avionics master switch or even resetting the aircraft master switch are not out of the question once all other options are exhausted.

Electrical System failure

The G1000 system is electrically based and therefore it is very dependent upon electrical power and the engine driven alternator/generator to keep the system operating and the battery(s) charged. The alternator is an electro-mechanical device and is therefore susceptible to internal failures, external control failures such as control units, relays, and circuit breakers; and incidental failures such as broken belts, shorted wires, and broken mounts or pulleys. It is essential that the pilot do everything required on the preflight and during the engine run-up to make sure that the alternator is providing proper charging voltage, the battery is properly charged, and the engine is operated above the critical idle speed for that aircraft electrical load configuration. The pilot must ensure that flight is not initiated if any portion of that system is showing signs of failure or degradation. One common area that is overlooked by many pilots is the condition of the battery itself. The battery is a consumable item and degrades its ability to perform with time, number of charge/discharge cycles, and with temperature. A battery is rated in terms of "Amp Hour" capacity. That is how many amps a battery can produce for 1 hour before becoming exhausted. A battery is severely limited in its storage capacity in low temperatures. That is why a worn-out battery tends to fail or run down quickly during starting in cold temperatures.

Figure 14.3 – Don't neglect aircraft battery condition

The pilot should be very wary of jump-starting an aircraft with a dead battery. If there was no reason for the battery to fail (such as the master switch being left on), one should immediately have the system troubleshot and/or the battery replaced prior to attempting flight. Jumpstarting the battery for engine start can lead to operating the aircraft in a jeopardized condition. The best case is that the battery will again be dead for the next start, and the worst case could be electrical system failure in flight due to insufficient residual voltage left at low power settings to keep the alternator charged and primed with an "exciter" voltage.

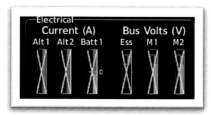

Figure 14.4 – Electrical system bus failure

If a "Low Voltage" caution or "Failed Alternator" warning appears during flight, the pilot must take immediate action to conserve power. We call this electrical load shedding.

*Definition: **Electrical Load Shedding** –The process of reducing system electrical appliance demand to extend the finite capacity remaining of an electrical power source after a system failure or degradation.*

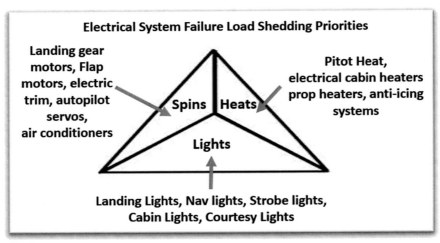

Figure 14.5 – Electrical system load shedding priorities

Just like the real-life story of Apollo 13 and its dramatic return to earth with catastrophic power system failures, the pilot must learn to systematically reduce the power consumption of the electrical systems based upon a prioritization of system or appliance need. The G1000 has some internal automatic load shedding that it performs, especially when system voltage drops below 22 volts. In this case, the pilot will see screens dim, and COM radio transmitter output wattage will be reduced. Be proactive. The highest power consumption appliances will be those that "Spin, Heat, and Light" in that order. This means that items such as landing gear and flap motors, pitot heat, autopilot servos, trim motors, and pumps will demand the most power followed by any non-LED lights such as landing and taxi lights and NAV lights. These high demand items must be considered for load shedding in order to extend the longevity of the time left on a battery after an alternator failure.

AHRS failure

If the AHRS or ADAHRS LRU fails, the pilot will see red "X's" over the Attitude Indicator and the HSI. Once the AHRS has failed, an ALERT will flash and when prompted will tell the pilot there is a HDG Fault and a Magnetometer fault.

The pilot at this point must use the standby attitude indicator and the magnetic compass for primary attitude and heading information. Depending upon what LRU has failed, the autopilot may still be used, but this will only work in ROLL mode and NAV mode. When experiencing an AHRS failure, The MFD screen will appear normal, and the pilot will continue to utilize most functions of the MFD.

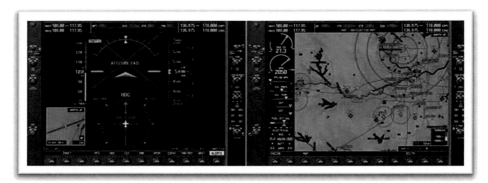

Figure 14.2 – GRS AHRS failure

ADC failure

If the ADC fails, the pilot will lose Airspeed and Altitude information indicated by red "Xs" in place of the Airspeed and Altitude tapes. In addition, the G1000 will no longer be able to compute and display VSI, Outside Air Temp, and TAS information indicated also by red "Xs" in their place. An ALERT will begin to flash telling the pilot the G1000 is not receiving Airspeed information. The Mode C operation of the Transponder will also be lost, as the ADC is where the Transponder gets its pressure altitude information.

The pilot will have to use the standby airspeed indicator and altimeter to control the aircraft. During an ADC failure, the MFD will continue to operate without losing any components. Also, while flying with an ADC failure, the pilot may continue to use the Autopilot. However, the Altitude hold function of the Autopilot will not be operational.

Figure 14.3 – ADC failure

Magnetometer failure

If the GMU magnetometer fails, the pilot will lose heading information from the system. A red X will be displayed over the letters HDG on the top of the HSI presentation. Heading functions from the autopilot will become inoperable. Component failures of this type are indicated to the pilot by the red X and the pilot will also receive an advisory for each system or component failure. This is the case for all engine instrumentation.

During a Magnetometer failure, the pilot will obtain heading information using the magnetic compass or the standby G5 display unit. The MFD is still operable, however the pilot will notice they will no longer be able to use the "Track Up" mode on the moving map.

Figure 14.4 – GMU 44 Magnetometer failure

PFD failure

If the Primary Flight Display fails, the pilot will lose PFD information displayed on the left of the two displays. The system may automatically switch into the reversionary back up mode. In this mode, the PFD information is transferred to the right-side display where the MFD information is normally displayed. When in the reversionary mode, the PFD information, coupled with the engine instrument indications are shown on the MFD display. The engine indications will be displayed on the left side of the screen as they normally appear on the MFD. With a PFD failure, the pilot will lose COM 1 and NAV 1 information (not pictured) and all moving map references. The pilot will receive ALERTS notifying there is a Crosstalk Error, the Audio Panel, EIS, Air Data, and the AHRS will all be using Back-up Paths to GIA 2.

If the system does not automatically switch into the reversionary mode, there may not have been a true PFD failure, but the screen itself is malfunctioning or has failed. The G1000 may not recognize a problem with the display screen so if there is any problem with the PFD display screen, the pilot should press the RED display backup key located on the bottom of the audio panel. This will manually turn the right-side display into PFD information. Sometimes this problem can be rectified using the PFD MENU key and adjusting the PFD brightness to Manual mode and turning the brightness up to 100%.

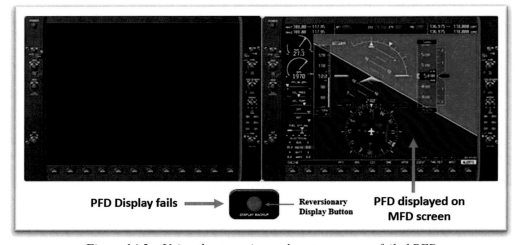

Figure 14.5 – Using the reversionary key to recover a failed PFD

MFD Failure

If the MFD fails, the pilot will lose all information on the right of the two display screens. In this case, the right screen will go blank, and the system will once again go into reversionary mode, but this time the engine information will automatically cycle over to the left side of the PFD display screen. The pilot will receive an ALERT that there is a "Crosstalk Error", and will lose some flight planning information, but will still be able to pull up the current flight plan information on the PFD. Another component that will fail with the MFD is COM 2 and NAV 2.

If the system does not automatically switch into the reversionary mode, there may not have been a true MFD failure, but the screen itself is malfunctioning or has failed. The G1000 may not recognize a problem with the display screen so if there is any problem with the MFD display screen, the pilot should press the RED display backup key located on the bottom of the audio panel. This will bring the engine information that was previously on the MFD side over to the left side of the PFD display screen.

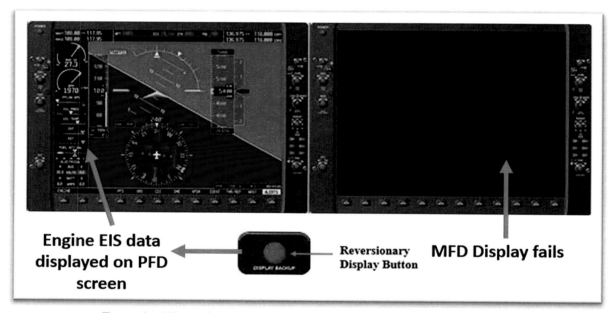

Figure 14.6 Using the reversionary backup key to recover from a failed MFD

Final Considerations

Each manufacturer has their own configuration including installing dual alternators and dual ship batteries and this can even vary from model year to model year. See the aircraft flight manual (AFM) for details on various aircraft model's electrical system and follow its recommendations on how to handle electrical and other emergencies.

Conclusion

In this chapter, we looked at the emergency operations aspects of the G1000 system. Because the system is so complex in terms of interoperating systems, it stands to reason that if something fails, there will be a cascading effect of that failure. The G1000 system has been designed with dependability in mind and the ways that system failures are detected are used to alert the pilot as soon as possible to give them the most amount of time to diagnose and plan for the proper response to that failure. The pilot should try to diagnose the failure using checklists and quick reference guides provided with each aircraft. Some failures can be remedied by a pull of a circuit breaker, others can't. The pilot needs to know what the messages mean when they come up on the crew alerting system (CAS) or when a red X appears over an instrument. The abnormal and emergency checklist for the aircraft have many of the procedures needed to deal with G1000 system failures.

Remember

- ❑ System and system component failures can be very distracting. Keep in mind that the pilot can sometimes use the autopilot to fly the aircraft while dealing with emergencies.
- ❑ During a PFD or MFD failure or anytime the reversionary backup screen mode is selected, the pilot will lose the large MFD map including the ability to display charts and graphical procedures.
- ❑ During an alternator failure, the pilot can extend the useful life of their battery by disabling certain items that "light, spin, or heat".

Chapter Debriefing:

We have now covered the G1000 system emergencies procedures and the pilot should now understand how the system detects, displays, and resolves emergencies. They must have a thorough working knowledge of this area in order to safely operate the G1000 aircraft.

- ❑ Now that the pilot understands that the G1000 monitors the status of all the LRUs so that it never displays invalid data, then the pilot will also understand that anytime data is not considered accurate or reliable by the system, it is covered with a red X.
- ❑ Now that the pilot understands why knowing how to deal with system outages and know how the system will produce various annunciations to help them make the correct response to each situation, then the pilot will also understand that the backup instruments are very important to cross checking the failed instruments to ensure a complete picture is obtained.
- ❑ Now that the pilot understands that electrical system malfunctions may require load shedding of high consumption appliances, they will realize that pitot heat, landing gear motors and flap motors are some of the heaviest electrical consumers.

Now that the pilot understands these key points and can correlate them into their everyday flying and apply these skills to the operation of their G1000 aircraft, then it is time for them to take the chapter quiz!

Chapter Fourteen Quiz: Emergencies and Emergency Management

The Chapter Quiz Scenario

This Chapter Quiz Scenario (CQS) suggests a real-world flight situation and allows the pilot to use their new knowledge of G1000 emergencies to answer some situational questions about how to safely operate their aircraft during an emergency failure. They can then determine whether they "understand" and can even "correlate" the material covered with their existing aeronautical knowledge and are prepared to use this information in a way that will enhance operational safety while using the G1000 equipped aircraft.

In this chapter quiz, the pilot will be asked to demonstrate their understanding of the G1000 emergency procedures and some of the chores that they may have to perform on this flight scenario between Lexington, Missouri and 3GV and Kansas City International airport (KMCI). Consider the following questions about this scenario:

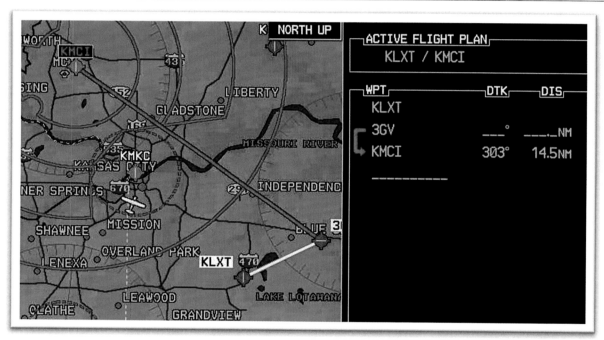

Figure 14.10 – Chapter fourteen quiz scenario diagram

Question 1: If the pilot experiences a loss of the PFD, what would the proper course of action be?

   a) **Push the Red Display Backup key if the system does not automatically switch to reversionary backup mode.**

   b) **Push the MENU key and seek the display options.**

   c) **Cycle the avionics master switch.**

Question 2: If the LOW VOLTS warning is displayed, what has happened?

    a) The standby battery has been activated.

    b) The system voltage is low, and the system needs to be restarted.

    c) The alternator may have failed or the idle is set below the critical idle speed and the pilot should raise the power setting if at idle or begin load shedding.

Question 3: In this scenario with a suspected failed alternator, what type of electrical items should the pilot load shed first as they start to diagnose the problem and respond?

    a) PFD and MFD.

    b) Lights, pitot heat, and fuel pumps.

    c) Everything except standby instruments.

Question 4: Can the autopilot still be of use when experiencing a Magnetometer failure?

    a) YES, but only in ROLL or NAV mode.

    b) Yes, all functions operate normally.

    c) NO.

Question 5: While flying this scenario in IFR conditions, the pilot encounters a red X on the face of the airspeed indicator, altimeter, and vertical speed indicator. What should be done first?

    a) Attempt troubleshooting and start load shedding.

    b) Ignore the red indications and attempt to fly the aircraft with the backup AHRS unit.

    c) Assume that they have had a LRU failure and immediately begin reference to the standby instruments.

Grading Criteria:

The pilot will know when they have completed this chapter when they get all the answers correct and demonstrate a solid understanding of the material. When the exam is complete, grade the answers with the answer key in the back of this handbook. Incorrect answers should be researched by going back to the appropriate reference area in the chapter or the Garmin Cockpit Guide that comes with the aircraft. Once all correct answers have been achieved, proceed on to the next chapter. Come back to items in this chapter at any time.

Glossary

Aircraft Automation Management - The ability to control and navigate an aircraft by means of the automated systems installed in the aircraft.

Automation Competence - The demonstrated ability to understand and operate the automated systems installed in the aircraft.

Automation Cross-filling A process where data entered on one display unit is simultaneously updated on the other unit to avoid conflicting data that could lead to errors in the system.

Autopilot -An integrated mechanical, electrical, or hydraulic system developed to control a vehicle with little or no intervention from a human controller,

Automated Navigation Leg - A flight conducted between two separate waypoints in which the aircraft is controlled primarily by the autopilot and the on-board navigation systems.

Automation Surprise - The characteristic of an automated system to provide different types and varieties of cues to pilots other than what they expected.

Automation Bias - The relative willingness of the pilot to trust and utilize automated systems in the cockpit.

Crew Resource Management(CRM) – A methodical process used in the cockpit piloted by coordinated actions of multiple crew members to ensure that all procedures are adhered to, vigilance is maintained, aeronautical decision making is optimized, and safety is enhanced.

Critical Idle Speed – The speed at which when the aircraft is idling with electrical equipment on, the alternator and the charging system provides a positive current charge as reflected by the Ammeter.

Critical Safety Tasks / Event - Those mission related tasks / events that, if not accomplished quickly and accurately, may result in injury or substantial aircraft damage.

Data-link Situational Awareness Systems - Systems that feed real-time information to the cockpit on weather, traffic, terrain and flight planning. This information may be displayed on the PFD, MFD or on other related cockpit displays.

Electrical Load Shedding –The process of reducing system electrical appliance demand to extend the finite capacity remaining of an electrical power source after a system failure or degradation.

Emergency Escape Maneuver - A maneuver (or series of maneuvers) performed manually or with the aid of the aircraft's automated systems that will allow the pilot to successfully escape from an inadvertent encounter with Instrument Meteorological Conditions (IMC) or other life-threatening situations.

FAA/Industry Training Standard (FITS) A training methodology and accompanying set of training standards which uses a student-centric, scenario-based approach to teach complex procedures to reduce the total number of general aviation accidents by integrating risk management, aeronautical decision making, situational awareness, and single pilot resource management into every flight operation.

- **Perceive** –at the completion of the chapter, the pilot will be able to describe the scenario activity and understand some underlying concepts, principles, and procedures that comprise the topic, but may not yet understand how these fit in the grand scheme. *Progression to the next scenario should not be attempted until the pilot can function at the Understand level.*

- **Understand**– at the completion of the chapter the pilot will be able to describe the classroom scenario topic in terms of definitions, basic usage, and applicability, and can start to demonstrate those topics in lab sessions or in a chapter exam. *Note: This is the minimum grading level that the pilot can be considered at in order to complete the chapter and move on to the next chapter.*

- **Correlate** – at the completion of the chapter, the pilot is able to thoroughly understand the topic without referring back to the back to the appropriate reference area in the chapter or the Garmin Cockpit Guide that comes with the aircraft and can correlate this topic with other topics and can properly integrate those topics with *risk management, aeronautical decision making, situational awareness, and single pilot resource management into the pilot's flight operations. Note: This grading level would be considered the desired level for the pilot to complete the chapter and move on to the next area.*

G1000-Equipped Aircraft *An aircraft which has an integrated glass cockpit model G1000 manufactured by Garmin Corporation of Olathe, Kansas installed in place of the traditional aircraft instruments and radios.*

IFR Automated Navigation A route segment flown on autopilot from departure until reaching the decision altitude (coupled ILS approach) or missed approach point (autopilot aided non-precision approach) on the instrument approach. If a missed approach is flown it will be flown using the autopilot and on-board navigation systems.

Line Replaceable Unit (LRU) A modular aircraft equipment design started in the late 1960s which consolidates parts of a common system or components of a system into a common aircraft location such as an equipment box, tray, or circuit board, facilitating ease of aircraft or system maintenance and troubleshooting.

Mission Related Tasks - Those tasks required for the safe and effective accomplishment of the mission(s) that the aircraft is capable of and required to conduct.

Multi-function Flight Display MFD - Any display that combines navigation, aircraft systems, and situational awareness information onto a single electronic display.

Primary Flight Display (PFD) - Any display that combines the primary six flight instruments, plus other related navigation and situational awareness information, into a single electronic display.

Proficiency - The ability to accurately perform a task within a reasonable amount of time. The outcome of the task is never seriously in doubt.

Scan Flow The order used by the pilot or crew of an aircraft when monitoring the various components of the flight deck, the systems, the electronics and radios, while at the same time maintaining situational awareness outside of the aircraft.

Scenario-based Training (SBT) - A training system that uses a highly structured script of real-world experiences to address flight training objectives in an operational environment. Such training can include initial training, transition training, upgrade training, recurrent training, and special training. The appropriate term should appear with the term "Scenario-based," (ex. "Scenario-based Transition Training") to reflect the specific application.

Simulation - Any use of representations of aircraft systems to simulate the flight environment. Pilot interaction with the simulation and task fidelity for the task to be performed are considered the requirements for effective simulation.

Single Pilot Resource Management (SRM) A methodical process used in the cockpit piloted by a single crew member to ensure that all procedures are adhered to, vigilance is maintained, aeronautical decision making is optimized, and safety is enhanced. This can also be considered the process of managing all the resources (both on-board the aircraft and from outside sources) available to a single-pilot (prior and during flight) to ensure the successful outcome of the flight is never in doubt.

TAA An aircraft which has a Primary Flight Display (PDF), a Multi-function Flight Display (MFD), an integrated GPS or like guidance system, an autopilot which can couple to that guidance system, and a Flight Management System (FMS) which provides for a way to enter information or retrieve information from a database and submit it to this integrated suite of aircraft systems.

VFR Automated Navigation A route segment flown from departure until entry to the 45-degree leg in the VFR pattern.

TAA Aircraft Study Guide

Cockpit Display Posters for various G1000 Aircraft

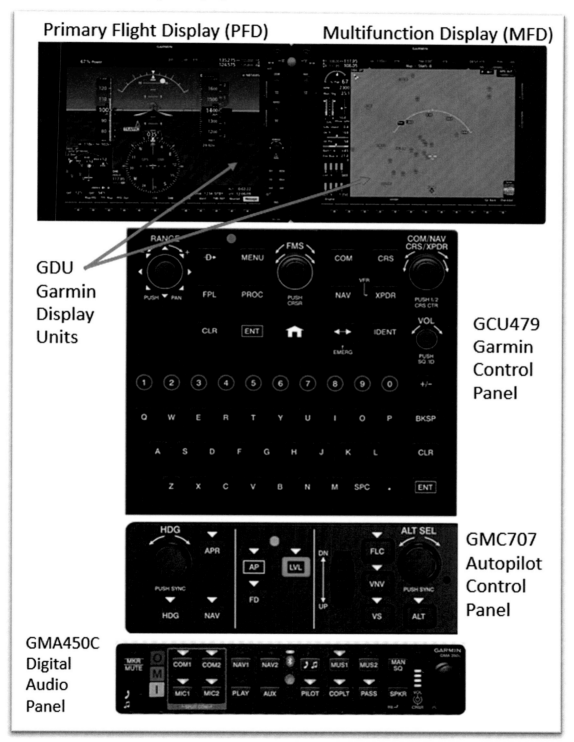

Cirrus Perspective Plus G1000 Cockpit (*Photo courtesy Cirrus Aircraft*)

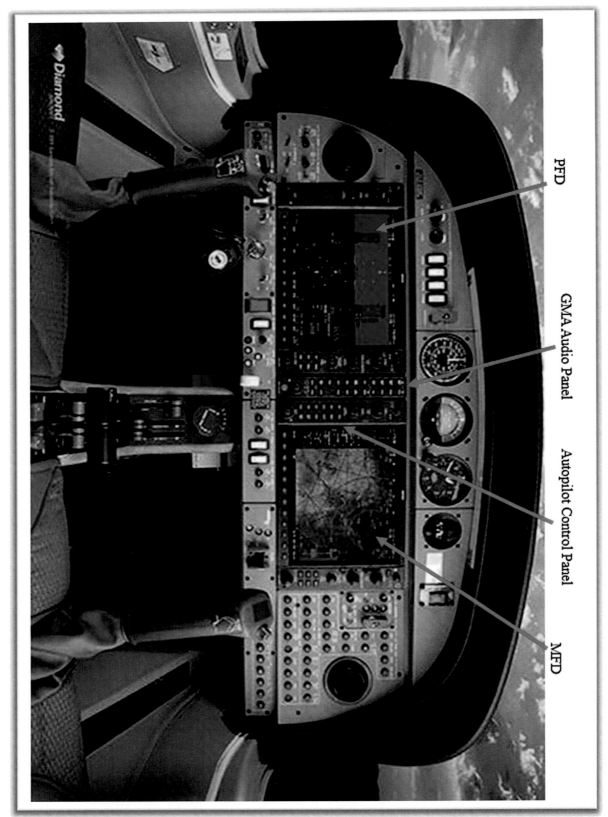

Diamond DA42 G1000 Cockpit (*Photo courtesy Diamond Aircraft Industries*)

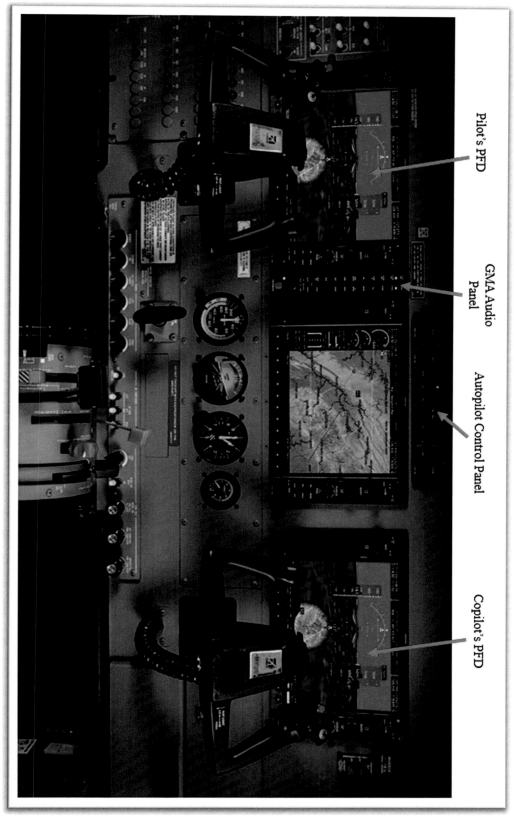

Cessna Caravan G1000 NXi (*Photo courtesy Textron Aviation*)

Cessna 182T G1000 (*Photo courtesy Textron Aviation*)

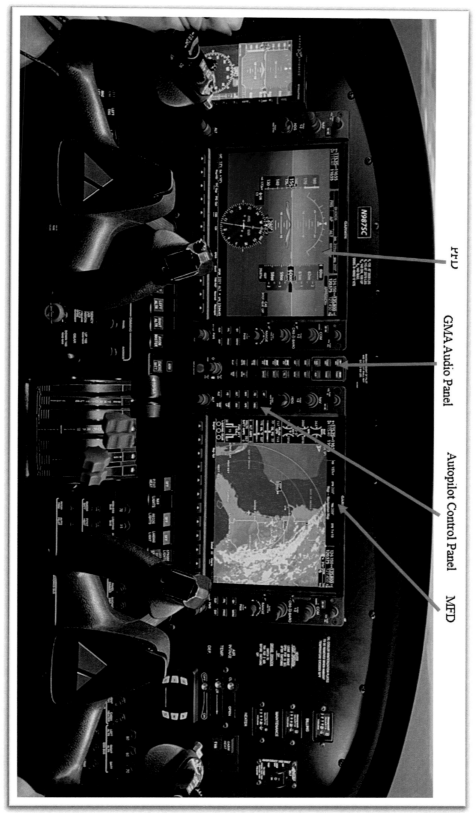

Piper PA44 Seminole G1000 NXi (*Photo courtesy of Piper Aircraft Corporation*)

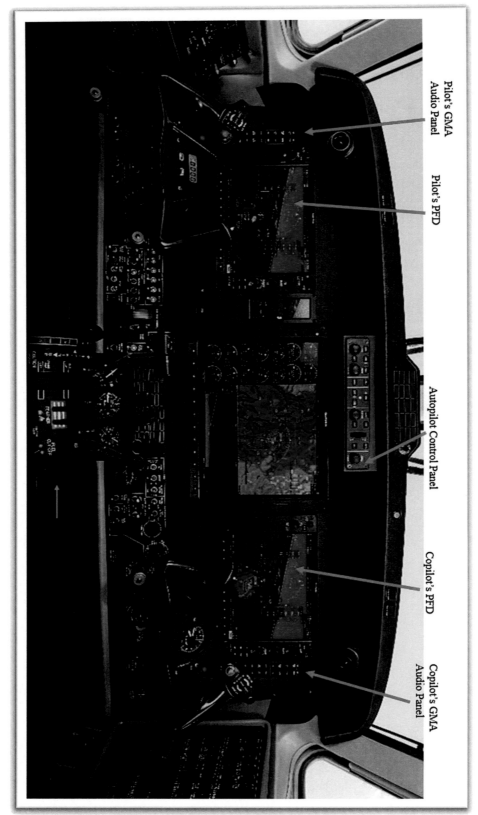

Textron Aviation King Air 350 G1000 NXi (*Courtesy Textron Aviation website*)

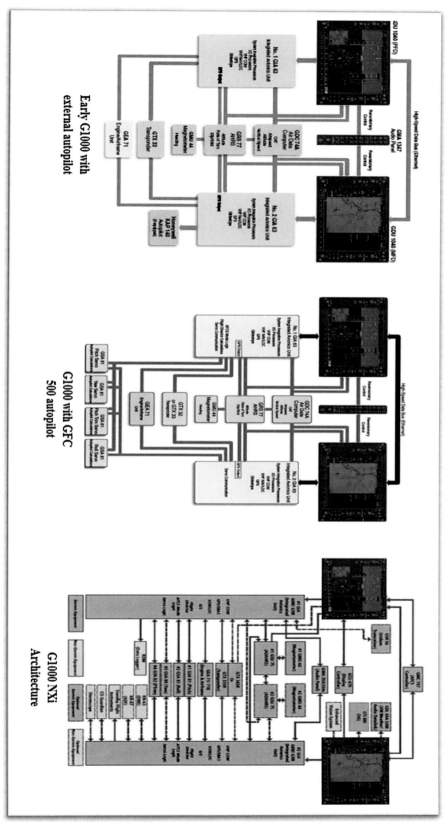

Various Garmin G1000 LRU architecture drawings (*Diagrams Courtesy Garmin International*)

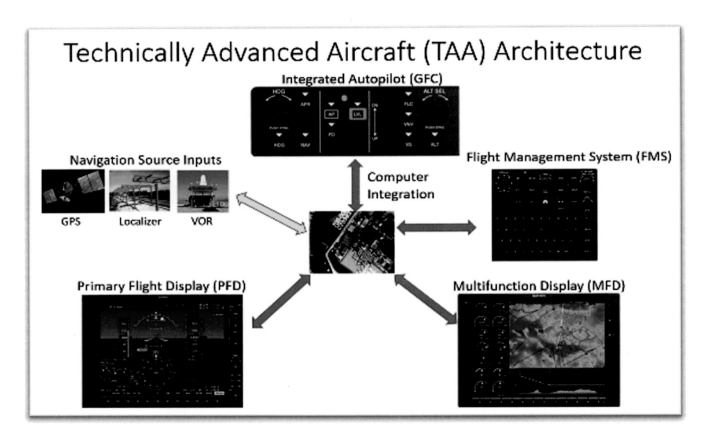

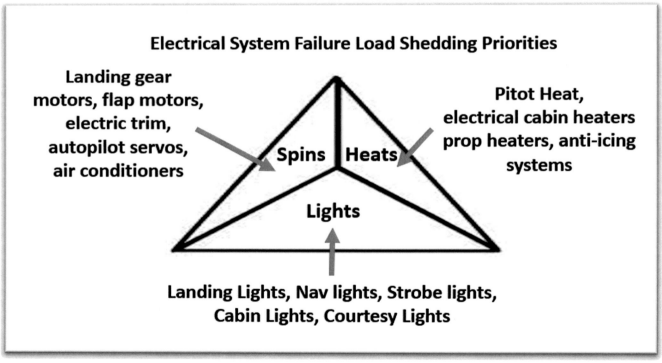